TURF
WARS

STEVE TONGUE

TURF WARS

A HISTORY OF LONDON FOOTBALL

First published by Pitch Publishing, 2016

Pitch Publishing
A2 Yeoman Gate
Yeoman Way
Worthing
Sussex
BN13 3QZ

www.pitchpublishing.co.uk
info@pitchpublishing.co.uk

ISBN 978-1-78531-191-8

Typesetting and origination by Pitch Publishing

Printed by Bell & Bain, Glasgow, Scotland

Contents

1. **Early days** (**1863-1899**)   **13**

FA founded in 1863 after Blackheath lead the breakaway from football to rugby, crying 'hacking is the true football game'; Wanderers, originally based at Snaresbrook, win first FA Cup at Kennington Oval; Football League begins in 1888 after professionalism is legalised, with no southern clubs until Woolwich Arsenal join Division Two five years later; early days of Millwall, Tottenham Hotspur, West Ham, Fulham, Brentford, QPR, Orient, Barnet and Wimbledon, under various names.

2. **Taking shape** (**1900-20**)   **37**

Tottenham win 1901 FA Cup as non-league team; Arsenal win promotion; Chelsea and Clapton Orient join expanded Second Division, followed by Fulham and Spurs; London stages first official Olympics in 1908; ambitious Fulham director Henry Norris proposes merging or ground-sharing with Woolwich Arsenal, then takes over Arsenal and moves them north of river despite objections from Orient and Spurs; North London rivalry takes bitter turn post-war as Norris persuades Football League officials that Arsenal should replace Spurs in top division; huge expansion of league with 22 new clubs, including Brentford, Millwall, Palace, QPR, joined by Charlton.

3. **Capital gains** (**1921-39**)   **69**

London clubs at last making an impact; Spurs are Cup winners and Division One runners-up; Arsenal dominate the early 30s with David Jack and Alex James after Herbert Chapman joins as manager from Huddersfield and Henry Norris is banned for life;

West Ham in the chaotic first Wembley cup final; Charlton go from Division Three to Division One runners-up in three seasons under Jimmy Seed after Fulham almost beat them to it; Brentford's best-ever period in top six, eclipsing Chelsea; QPR and Palace are stuck in Division Three but Millwall escape; Thames FC come and go in two seasons; Orient just survive.

Interlude I: War   115
War-time football with guest players; London League and London War Cup; 60,000 watch Arsenal in Wembley cup final despite Blitz; volunteers and casualties from clubs as in WWI.

4. Austerity (1946-60)   124
A return to normality and huge upsurge of interest and attendances; Charlton reach successive FA Cup finals but only Arsenal and Chelsea are with them in the top-flight until Spurs return and win the 1951 title at first attempt by pushing and running; Chelsea's first-ever title (1955) and European jaunt before West Ham and Johnny Haynes's Fulham join the top division; Palace and Millwall stuck in the new Division Four

5. Glory days (1961-70)   159
A new era as the maximum wage is abolished and Haynes becomes the first £100-week English footballer; Spurs become first club this century to complete league and cup double; European football grabs the imagination and brings trophies to swinging London; Moore, Hurst and Peters (plus Cohen) win the World Cup; even Leyton Orient make the top division while QPR win League Cup at Wembley; but hooliganism on the rise with London clubs to the fore.

Interlude II: Non-league football   193
Thriving non-league scene in London from the start despite competition from a dozen professional clubs; from Casuals in the first Amateur Cup Final (1894), London supplies almost 20 different winners; leading amateurs appear as late as 1955 in Chelsea's title-winning team; 100,000 watch Amateur Cup finals at

Wembley featuring teams such as local rivals Walthamstow Avenue and Leyton, Barnet and Enfield; after the FA abolish amateurism in 1974, Barnet and Wimbledon go on to achieve Football League status while mergers eventually propel Dagenham & Redbridge to the same level.

6. Transition (1971-90)   201

The mighty are fallen as old guard of managers depart (Greenwood, Nicholson, Sexton, Mee); Arsenal emulate Tottenham's double but Spurs, Chelsea, West Ham all relegated before Spurs revive as foreign influx begins; QPR peak; Palace make the top division; the 80s become a dire decade for football as crowds plummet everywhere; success in south London as Charlton, Millwall, Palace and Wimbledon all reach Division One; QPR try to merge with Fulham while Charlton have to leave home; eight London clubs in the top division before football changes forever

7. Greed is good (1991-2000)   240

The Premier League, pay-per-view television and all-seater eras begin, dominated just like the original Football League by the North and Midlands; five seasons until a London side even makes the top three, then Arsene Wenger, one of the first foreign managers, makes Arsenal a force again; Chelsea, under the controversial Ken Bates, rebuild Stamford Bridge and their fortunes; after Crystal Palace's greatest season, Barnet, founded in 1888, reach the league 103 years later; Wimbledon finish in the top six then begin a long slide; new ground for Millwall but Charlton get back to The Valley and reach the Premier League; Fulham flourish under colourful foreign ownership, overtaking QPR.

8. Plus ca change (2001-16)   267

Arsenal's run as top London club for nine seasons in a row is ended as Abramovich buys Chelsea and hires Mourinho; but it is under Roberto di Matteo that they become London's first European Cup winners after 56 years; Arsenal move grounds but struggle to win trophies; London stages Olympics again and Spurs and West Ham vie for the stadium; Barnet and Brentford plan new homes too; Dagenham & Redbridge reach the league, briefly, but Wimbledon disappear to Milton Keynes and are then reborn in Kingston; Arsenal, Chelsea and Tottenham the biggest three in the capital – just like 100 years ago.

Acknowledgements

MANY thanks to all who helped with numerous queries over the past months, especially those with impressively detailed knowledge of a particular club like Iain Cook (Arsenal), John Fennelly (Tottenham), Rick Glanvill (Chelsea) and the Moore, Hurst and Peters of West Ham United, Steve Marsh, John Northcutt and John Powles.

Also to David Barber, Dr Graham Curry, Norman Giller, Peter Goringe, Ian Nannestad of *Soccer History* magazine, Keir Radnedge, Andrew Riddoch, Phil Shaw, Dave Simpson and Nick Szczepanik. To Duncan Olner for the front cover and, above all, Paul and Jane Camillin and Derek Hammond at Pitch Publishing for making it all possible.

Introduction

F EW cities in the world have as many professional football clubs as London and it is fair to say that none have the history or variety of clubs and characters explored in these pages; from Wanderers to AFC Wimbledon; from Charles Alcock and Lord Kinnaird, through Herbert Chapman and Bill Nicholson to Jimmy Greaves and Bobby Moore, Mohamed Al-Fayed and Roman Abramovich.

The Football Association – the first of its kind anywhere – and with it the FA Cup were founded in the capital, and Wanderers, originally based at Snaresbrook, dominated the competition's early years.

In the transition to professionalism, the North and Midlands monopolised the first four decades of league football, before three clubs in particular began to challenge them. By 1910 Arsenal, Chelsea and Tottenham Hotspur were in the top division together and established as London's big three – just like 100 years later. That trio have all now won a major European trophy, along with West Ham United, forever blowing bubbles and hoping to make the big three into a quartet.

Although the hierarchy has changed surprisingly little, others have had their moments, often prolonged ones. As the Appendix shows, seven different clubs have finished a season as London's top team, including Brentford and Charlton Athletic. Fulham, Millwall and QPR have competed in

Europe. All of those, and even 'little' Leyton Orient, played in the top division, as, of course, did Wimbledon, only nine extraordinary years after joining the Football League.

The downside of this variety is the struggle to prosper or even survive in such a crowded field. Every London league club without exception has suffered serious financial problems at one time or another, often leading to the necessity to defend or expand their own territory.

So the turf wars began early. Chelsea were only founded because Fulham declined to move into the new Stamford Bridge stadium, the so-called Pensioners immediately upsetting other clubs like Tottenham by leaping straight into the Football League.

Most famously, Woolwich Arsenal, the capital's first professional club, decided the district on the south bank of the Thames bearing their name could no longer support them. Having failed to interest Fulham in a ground-share or merger, they upped sticks from south London to north, enabling Charlton to flourish in a manner they might not otherwise have done, but infuriating Tottenham and the perennially struggling Orient.

'You cannot "franchise" a football club,' wrote an aggrieved Arsenal follower in the local paper, unknowingly adopting a phrase that Wimbledon supporters would come to curse 90 years later.

Yet owners have always been open to considering new alliances. QPR proposed merging with Brentford (Chapter 5), then faced a hostile takeover-merger from Fulham (Chapter 6). Charlton and Wimbledon were forced to leave home, the latter permanently, only to spawn a new club progressing equally fast through the leagues.

Despite the pressures and problems that allowed only a short life for the ill-starred Thames FC (Chapter 3), most of the established professional clubs, and many in the local non-leagues, are now well into their second century.

This is their story, and that of many others great and small. After 40-odd years chronicling their daily deeds as a journalist, it has been a hugely enjoyable task to write it.

Steve Tongue
London SE7
2016

Note 1: For the purposes of the book, 'London' has been defined as the 33 Greater London boroughs. So Barnet, Brentford and Dagenham & Redbridge are all featured, despite having postal addresses in Hertfordshire, Middlesex and Essex respectively; whereas (apologies) Watford are not.

Note 2: Attendance figures, featured copiously and often quoted from the outstanding series of Breedon books (see Select Bibliography), were mostly estimates until the 1925/26 season. Where the two clubs disagree on a figure, I have used the home team's as being the more reliable.

Chapter 1

Early days (1863-1899)

FA founded in 1863 after Blackheath lead the breakaway from football to rugby, crying 'hacking is the true football game'; Wanderers, originally based at Snaresbrook, win first FA Cup at Kennington Oval; Football League begins in 1888 after professionalism is legalised, with no southern clubs until Woolwich Arsenal join Division Two five years later; early days of Millwall, Tottenham Hotspur, West Ham, Fulham, Brentford, QPR, Orient, Barnet and Wimbledon, under various names.

I F LONDON was central to the development of English football, in holding the meeting at which the Football Association was founded in 1863, its involvement in what modern educationalists would call key stage two – when the Football League began on a supposedly national basis – was surprisingly slow.

But first things first. Central London it was that staged that first meeting at the Freemason's Tavern in Great Queen Street, Holborn on 26 October 1863. A number of letters to publications like *Bell's Life, The Field, The Daily Telegraph* and *The Times* had suggested that the many different rules practised locally by the public schools in particular needed sorting out. Were handling and/or running with the ball to be allowed? And hacking at shins? Should the updated Cambridge (University) rules of 1863 be adopted? A letter published in *The Times* earlier that month, signed by an Old Etonian calling himself 'Etonensis' and calling a meeting, had the desired effect, although with a rather different cast list to the one he had expected.

The public schools and universities more or less ignored the invitation. Of the dozen or so men who turned up in Great Queen Street, almost all were from clubs and schools in the London area: Barnes, Blackheath, Crusaders, Forest (later to become Wanderers), NN (No Names) Club (Kilburn), the original Crystal Palace, War Office (later Civil Service), Kensington School, Surbiton and two other Blackheath schools Perceval House and Blackheath Proprietary School.

There were observers from Sheffield FC (acknowledged with their formation in 1857 to be the oldest club in the world, despite a counter-claim by Cambridge University), and from just one leading public school (Charterhouse, based at the time near Smithfield). The historic motion proposed by Ebenezer Morley of Barnes was passed: '...that it is advisable that a football association should be formed for the purpose of settling a code of rules for the regulation of the game of football'.

Arthur Pember of Kilburn was named president, Morley was secretary and the subscription was one guinea a head. Charterhouse declined to join in and so did Sheffield, who did not initially appear to fancy such a London-based project but joined at the fourth meeting in November.

The football historian Dr Graham Curry says: 'It was almost certainly because the FA was seen by them, and most others, as being an association of London clubs. For many years, reports in Sheffield newspapers referred to the FA as the London Football Association. As time went on, it became clear that the FA was or would be the national governing body.'

It soon became clear that ideas about 'football' still differed. The secretary of Sheffield FC wrote that the proposed rules allowing handling and hacking were 'directly opposed to football, the latter especially being more like wrestling. I cannot see any science in taking a run-kick at a player at the risk of laming him for life'.

At that fourth meeting, on 24 November, which followed a trial match at Cambridge four days earlier, delegates were still narrowly voting in favour of handling. But early in December, the Blackheath representative Francis Campbell found less support for his contention that 'hacking is the true football' and by the end of the year the three SE3 clubs had left in a huff. A Rugby Football Union would follow in 1871, with Blackheath to the fore, and claiming, like Sheffield FC, to be the oldest of their particular type in England.

With the rules clarified and Charles Alcock, an old Harrovian who had moved from the North East to Chingford at an early age, becoming a hugely influential figure as FA secretary from 1870, thoughts increasingly turned to competition. The following year, Alcock instigated a knockout tournament to be called the Football Association Challenge Cup Competition.

It was a chaotic start as clubs dropped in and out, but in the end London provided eight of the 12 contestants in Barnes, Civil Service, Clapham Rovers, Crystal Palace, Hitchin, Hampstead Heathens, Upton Park and Wanderers. Queen's Park, the bold adventurers from Glasgow, who had to scratch in the semi-final because they could not afford another trip to London, and Donington School from Spalding were the only entrants from outside the Home Counties.

The Wanderers, essentially composed of old Harrovians like Alcock, had emerged from the Forest club on the borders of Snaresbrook and Leytonstone (where Forest School remains). As the name implied, they tried to operate by avoiding the expense of a permanent ground but by the end of the 1860s were mostly to be found playing at Kennington Oval.

A successful season of friendly matches in 1870/71 set them up to become the first FA Cup winners, albeit after reaching the final with two walkovers, a draw against Crystal Palace – both teams going through to the semi-final – and a solitary victory by 3-1 against Clapham Rovers.

History was theirs, however, when the final was won 1-0 against Royal Engineers, the Sappers from Chatham (who still play under their original name). According to *The Sporting Life* report of the match, these were 'certainly the two most powerful organisations supporting Association Rules'. Alfred Stair from Upton Park refereed and a crowd of 2,000, each paying one shilling (5p), was present at the Oval. The scorer was one Morton Betts, playing under the pseudonym A.H. Chequer. (He was a member of Harrow Chequers, a team who had scratched in the first round, and possibly, therefore, the most famous ringer in the history of football).

The ubiquitous Alcock had a goal disallowed but captained the winning team on the ground they were conveniently familiar with, where he had even become secretary of Surrey County Cricket Club.

The word 'challenge' in the cup's title was important, the idea being that the holders should be guaranteed a place in the following year's final, where they would be challenged by whichever club emerged from the semi-final round. They were even given a choice of ground. Fortunately, this notion lasted no longer than the second season, in which the Wanderers won again, by 2-0, against Oxford University at Lillie Bridge in Chelsea, which Middlesex County Cricket Club had recently left. Sporting priorities of the time were demonstrated by the morning kick-off in order to avoid the Boat Race. Alcock was no longer in the side but the formidable Scot Lord Kinnaird was, scoring one of the goals in the first of his nine finals.

With Queen's Park scratching despite being given a bye to the semi-final, the second season was even more of a Home Counties competition and remained so until the late-1870s, by which time the main provincial strongholds of Sheffield and Nottingham were represented.

Nobody managed to challenge the success of what were still essentially southern-based old boys' teams, plus the armed forces and Oxbridge universities, as a list of the 20 finalists in the first ten seasons shows: Wanderers (five, all won), Royal Engineers (four), Old Etonians (four), Oxford University (four), Clapham Rovers (two), Old Carthusians (one).

The Clapham team, founded in 1869, were characteristic of the age in playing both football and rugby union, which they did on various south London commons. Apart from winning the 1880 final against Oxford, their two other claims to fame were having the scorer of the first-ever FA Cup goal (by Jarvis Kenrick against Upton Park in November 1871) and fielding the youngest player in a final, 17-year-old James Prinsep, who held that record until Millwall's Curtis Weston came on as a late substitute against Manchester United in 2004. The club were wound up during the First World War, although a modern version, wearing the same pick and grey shirts, still play in Mitcham.

Not until the 1880s would the balance of power move north – and dramatically so.

In the meantime international football arrived, conceived in London and born in Glasgow. Five unofficial matches at the Oval between English and Scottish players living in London were followed in November 1872 by the first official international in the world, a goalless draw in the Scottish capital on St Andrew's day.

Having played in all five of the unofficial games, Alcock was no doubt mortified to be injured when the big day came and had to content himself with having suggested the idea, proposed a venue (in the north of England, which was declined), insisted on 11-a-side ('more than eleven we do not care to play'), picked the England team and run the line as an 'umpire'.

Surprisingly, there was no-one in the side from The Wanderers; Oxford University being best represented with three players. Barnes, Crystal Palace and Harrow Chequers of the London clubs provided one each as well as the 1st Surrey Rifles, based at Brunswick Road, Camberwell, whose William Maynard started as one of the eight forwards and then swapped with goalkeeper Robert Barker. Alcock did play, and score, in the fourth match between the countries in 1875, one of two years in which he also refereed the cup final.

With the principles of the FA Cup and international football established – England also played Wales at the Oval in 1879 – the next highly significant developments concerned professionalism and the Football League.

* * * * *

The appearance of Blackburn Rovers in the 1882 cup final marked a move away from London as football's epicentre, even though they too were descended from the old boys team of a public school. John Lewis, the joint founder, was a sort of Lancastrian Alcock, who started the Lancashire FA, refereed cup finals and later served both the FA and Football League.

The northern upstarts lost their first final to Lord Kinnaird's Old Etonians, a result that *Bell's Life* snobbishly said would be 'well received in every part of the kingdom'. But Rovers' appearance showed the way the wind was blowing, as did their list of opponents: Bolton Wanderers, Darwen, Wednesbury and The Wednesday (a replayed semi-final in Huddersfield and Manchester) before coming to the Oval for the final.

The following year, local rivals Blackburn Olympic won the cup by defeating the holders 2-1 after extra time in an epoch-changing game. Only once more thereafter did any of the southern amateur sides even make the semi-final, when Old Carthusians (Charterhouse old boys) suffered an equally symbolic defeat in 1885, losing 5-0 to Blackburn Rovers at Derby. The crowd for the final had been a record 8,000, many of them down from Lancashire and described in the *Pall Mall Gazette* as 'a northern horde of uncouth garb and strong oaths'.

Olympic had caused eyebrows to be raised and questions asked when their team of factory workers and pub landlords underwent several days' special training at Blackpool. The FA had only agreed that same year that players in the semi-finals and final could even have their rail fares paid. How, it was being asked, could full-time workers be taking so much time off if they were not being illegally paid, or at least compensated?

The word 'shamateurism' may not have been coined for another ten years or so, but the situation was clearly similar to senior amateur football some 80 or 90 years later: everyone knew payments were made, but nobody would officially admit it.

Until the following January, that is, when somebody suddenly did in a wonderfully matter-of-fact way. That month, Preston North End came to London and drew an FA Cup fourth-round game 1-1 with Upton Park, after which the home club complained that their opponents were paying players. Preston's secretary-manager Major William Sudell, who had recruited a number of his team from Scotland, openly admitted the fact, claiming that it broke no rules. He was shocked when the FA disagreed and kicked Preston out of the competition. (Upton Park, no relation to West Ham United, lost in the next round to eventual winners Blackburn Rovers).

There was a similar complaint, with a different outcome, when Notts County, having lost the semi-final to Rovers, reported a Scottish international called John Inglis, who had joined from Glasgow Rangers. This time the FA decided that Inglis was earning a living as a mechanic in Glasgow, not as a footballer, and allowed him to play in a winning final against his fellow countrymen of Queen's Park.

But the tide could no longer be held back and Preston's determination in October to form a rival British Football Association with like-minded clubs prompted an FA sub-committee to investigate the whole subject. On 20 July 1885, they decided 'in the interests of Association Football, to legalise the employment of professional football players, but only under certain restrictions'. These were that players had to be born or to have lived for two years within six miles of their club's ground.

The ever-influential Alcock was all in favour, pointing out that 'professionals are a necessity to the growth of the game'. The London Football Association, founded in 1882, disagreed, which goes some way to explaining why for the first time the capital's football was lagging behind.

After Blackburn Olympic's success of 1883, their captain Albert Warburton said: 'The Cup is very welcome to Lancashire. It'll have a good home and it'll never go back to London.' It did so, of course, but not for another 18 years.

* * * * *

Football and its popularity were spreading fast. By 1888 a remarkable 149 clubs entered the FA Cup, necessitating regional qualifying groups. The only doubt about which region would provide the winner, however, was whether the Midlands could challenge the North's hegemony. West Bromwich Albion, finalists three years running from 1886-88, and Aston Villa (1887 winners) did so, backed up by Wolverhampton Wanderers, Small Heath Alliance (later Birmingham) and the Nottingham clubs, Forest and County.

Paying players – Blackburn Rovers' wage bill in 1885/86, the season of their third successive FA Cup win, was more than £600 – necessitated arranging more matches and, in March 1888, William McGregor, a Scottish draper who had moved from Perthshire to Birmingham and became another of the great pioneering administrators, suggested 'home and away fixtures each season' for '10 or 12 of the most prominent clubs in England'.

The name of Old Carthusians was put forward by the secretary of Bolton Wanderers but with no professional clubs yet in the South, the chosen dozen came either from the North (Accrington, Blackburn Rovers, Bolton, Burnley, Everton, Preston North End) or the Midlands (Aston Villa, Derby County, Notts County, Stoke, West Bromwich Albion and Wolverhampton Wanderers). By the turn of the century, the North was ahead of the Midlands by seven league titles to four, including the first five in a row (Preston and Sunderland two each, with one to Everton in between).

Even the FA Cup Final venue went north for a couple of years. In 1893, Surrey decided they did not want their cricket ground used any more so the next two finals were played at Fallowfield, Manchester, where 45,000 watched Wolves beat Everton, and then at Goodison Park, for Notts County's victory over Bolton (37,000). Those attendances were highly relevant. Half-day working on Saturday was increasingly prevalent, public transport was improving and newspapers had picked up on the growing appetite for the game.

By 1895 Charles Burgess Fry, well placed as an all-round sportsman to make a judgement, said football was replacing cricket as the national sport, so popular was it. Significantly for London, between 1881 and 1891, Leyton, Tottenham, West Ham and Willesden had the highest rates of population growth in England.

Clubs were springing up too all over the capital, where the London Playing Fields Association had been founded in 1891 to 'encourage the playing of cricket, football and other games by the clerks, working men and boys of London'. By that date too, the city had its first professional club, which would become and remain London's most famous of all.

In the meantime, southern pride was upheld to a degree by Corinthians, a unique band of brothers brought together by Pa Jackson, assistant FA secretary, who not only deplored professionalism but insisted on the highest standards of sportsmanship.

The late Bryon Butler's *The Official History of the Football Association* suggests they would have won the cup at least once had they deigned to take part in anything so vulgar (and been allowed to, since many of the players also represented other clubs). While it is dangerous to read too much into a single result, Corinthians, who could field a team full of internationals, had some outstanding ones over a span of 20-odd years: they beat 1884 Cup winners Blackburn Rovers 8-1 and Bury's 1903 FA Cup winners 10-3.

* * * * *

Fulham, Leyton Orient, Tottenham Hotspur, QPR and Millwall can all claim earlier origins, but the club known all around the world these days as **Arsenal** would be the capital's first to turn professional and reach the Football League.

Not for some time, of course, although ambition was discernible early in the history of a club born late in 1886. Woolwich Arsenal munitions workers in nearby Dial Square (where a plaque on the new Royal Arsenal development commemorates the founding) were so enthusiastic that only ten days later Dial Square played their first match, against Eastern Wanderers on a muddy Isle of Dogs pitch, claiming a 6-0 win.

On Christmas Day, back at the Royal Oak pub by Woolwich Arsenal station, they decided that Royal Arsenal would be a less parochial name and that red should be the team colour, a couple of players having appeared for the long-established Nottingham Forest (1865). One of them, goalkeeper Fred Beardsley, managed as a favour to obtain some redcurrant shirts from his old club, the colour that would be worn 120 years later for the final season at Highbury.

Plumstead Common, a mile or so south of the factory, was the first home venue on 8 January 1887, for a 6-1 win over Erith. There would be three other grounds, the Sportsman, the Manor and Invicta, before the turn of the century.

A large workforce helped interest as well as providing a constant stream of players, and the club made rapid progress as the best in the area (Charlton Athletic, literally just up the Woolwich Road, were not formed until 1905). In 1889, they reached the semi-final of the London Senior Cup, losing 2-0 to Clapton, and later that year entered the FA Cup for the first time, immediately beating Lyndhurst 11-0. Following a 2-2 draw after extra time away to Norwich Thorpe in the next round, the Norfolk side reluctantly decided they could not travel to south-east London for a replay, so Arsenal progressed to the third qualifying round.

The home tie with Crusaders was also 2-2 after 90 minutes, but this time Arsenal scored three times in the extra half-hour.

The cup run ended at the fourth hurdle, at home to the powerful Swifts, who fielded four internationals and won 5-1 in front of a crowd estimated at 6,000. Encouraged by this run, the team won both the Kent Senior Cup and London Charity Cup, as well as reaching the London Senior Cup Final.

In September 1890 came a move to the Invicta Ground in Plumstead High Street, which the *Kentish Independent* promised would be 'one of the finest football grounds in the south'. About 8,000 people turned up for the opening fixture against the 93rd Highlanders and the following Easter 12,000 were present for a visit from Scottish club Hearts.

The club were progressing. As the same local newspaper reported: 'For the first two or three seasons the "Reds" were always classed under the heading of "medium" strength ... but the club has now grown to be one of the most formidable of those playing under the dribbling code in the south of England.'

As professionalism took off elsewhere, the best players could nevertheless be lured away and, in May 1891, the momentous decision was taken to turn pro under the name of Woolwich Arsenal – the first club in the South to do so. Knowing they would incur the wrath of the London FA and Kent FA, they resigned from both, which meant being unable to compete in any of the two bodies' local cup competitions. The club's decision may, however, have swayed the voting at the London FA's special meeting a month later, when a motion to ban any team from playing against professional teams or players was defeated by 76-67. A typical wage paid by Arsenal was £3 in winter and £2 in summer – better money than skilled workers received.

Restricted to friendlies and the FA Cup, Arsenal found any hopes of leading London's assault on the Northern and Midlands strongholds to be premature. In successive seasons, they were beaten in the first round proper of the cup, 5-1 by Small Heath and 6-0 by Sunderland, just as they had been the previous season at home to Derby County (2-1) when making their first-round debut in a competition they would have rather more success in much later on.

It was soon clear that professionalism would be difficult to sustain on friendly matches and one cup-tie per season, not least because public transport in the area was poor. So, in February 1892, Arsenal called a meeting in Fleet Street with leading southern amateur clubs, including Ilford, Luton, Millwall, Reading, Swindon and West Herts (Watford), to discuss playing league football. Again, the London FA disapproved and 11 teams who had agreed to join a southern version of the Football League were cowed into submission.

A Southern Alliance competition had begun the previous year without completing the agreed fixtures among the seven clubs, who were Erith, Old St Stephen's, Polytechnic, Slough Town, Tottenham Hotspur, Upton Park and Windsor & Eton. Old St Stephen's, founded in Westminster but playing in Denmark Hill and Nunhead, were one of the two clubs to complete their 12 scheduled matches (Tottenham, placed third, were the other) and were declared champions, which earned them an invitation to the first Southern League campaign of 1893/94. (The Northern League, still going today, had started in 1887).

Millwall Athletic, forerunners of the present-day club, were among the prime movers of the new competition and competed in the First Division with Chatham, Clapton, Ilford, Luton Town, Reading, Royal Ordnance Factories (amateur players from the Royal Arsenal works), Southampton St Mary's and Swindon Town. In the Second Division, Old St Stephen's (who later became Shepherd's Bush, playing at Loftus Road until disbanding in 1915) were joined by Bromley, Chesham, Maidenhead, New Brompton (later Gillingham), Sheppey United and Uxbridge.

Some familiar names were therefore already emerging. **Millwall Rovers** (Millwall Athletic from 1889), like Arsenal, started as a works team, in their case in 1885 based at the Morton & Co jam factory and playing at Glengall Road (now renamed Tiller Road) on the Isle of Dogs. One of their earliest players, a right-back named Jack Graham, has been credited as the source of the expression 'keep it on the island' on account of his prodigious if not always accurate clearances.

With a strong Scottish influence – Morton's had begun in Aberdeen – the team had a successful playing record in a first season of friendlies. The East End Football Association began towards the end of 1886 and with it a Senior Cup in which Millwall reached the following year's final against the Holloway-based Scottish expats club London Caledonians. It was played at the Essex County Cricket Club ground in Leyton High Road, near Leyton Orient's present home, where Herbert Sutcliffe and Percy Holmes of Yorkshire would one day share a world-record partnership of 555.

The final was drawn 2-2, giving Millwall a share of their first trophy – for six months anyway. They kept it for longer by winning the competition for the following two years.

Equally as ambitious as Arsenal, they turned professional for the start of the Southern League in 1893 and proceeded to become the new competition's most successful side, winning it for the first two seasons and finishing second to Southampton St Mary's in the next one.

In that period Millwall lost only three games out of 54, starting with an unbeaten season of 12 wins and four draws to take the title by a comfortable six points from Luton Town. The team's dominance was reflected in the number of goals scored: 68 by the champions, at an average of more than four per game, while Luton, next best, managed only 36.

With New Brompton promoted, there were 18 games the following season, when Millwall once more topped the table by six points, with Luton and Southampton again second and third. This time, 75 goals were scored.

For the first time that season, they also progressed beyond the qualifying rounds of the FA Cup before going out 3-1 to Sheffield United.

The following season, another long cup trip ended in a first-round defeat by the Football League Second Division champions Liverpool, and back down south, the league title was finally surrendered in 1895/96 by four points to the unbeaten Southampton.

The most successful Southern League teams were by that time all professional, while the amateurs found the going harder: in the second season Ilford lost all 18 games and dropped out, and the following year Royal Ordnance, the amateurs from the Arsenal factories, folded after seven matches.

Ilford's replacements were **Tottenham Hotspur**, who grew out of the Hotspur cricket club based around two schools, St John's and Tottenham Grammar. Effectively a boys team when starting out on Tottenham Marshes in 1882 as Hotspur FC, they were assisted by the warden of Tottenham YMCA, who was elected president. The only recorded matches in the first season were defeats, by 2-0 to a team called Radicals on 30 August 1882 and by 8-1 against Latymer the following January.

Fuller records exist for the following seasons, during which new premises were found in Northumberland Park, apparently on condition that players attended church once a week. In 1884, the name Tottenham was added to the distinctive original, which stemmed from connections with local landowners the Percy family and Harry Hotspur, son of the first Earl of Northumberland.

After a trip to watch Blackburn Rovers win the 1885 FA Cup Final, the northerners' blue and white halved shirts were adopted and a move followed to the Red House in Tottenham High Road, which remains part of the club's headquarters. Blackburn's colours were therefore used for the first competitive game, in the London Association Cup of 1885/86, in which St Albans were beaten 5-2 before an 8-0 drubbing from Casuals (later one half of Corinthian Casuals).

The following season brought a heavy defeat in the same competition by Upton Park, 6-0, but also a run all the way to an eventful semi-final of the East End Cup against London Caledonians. Originally, it was more of a non-event, for when their opponents failed to turn up on the appointed day, Spurs kicked off, scored and claimed to have won the match 1-0. A proper game was, however, ordered, which the Caledonians won by the same score.

There was controversy too – why would there not be? – around the inaugural meeting with Royal Arsenal on 19 November 1887. With Tottenham 2-1 up against the team who would later become their greatest rivals, the game was abandoned 15 minutes from time because the light was deemed to be too bad to continue. The first completed match between the pair was therefore the one in Plumstead the following February, when Spurs managed to field only nine players and were drubbed 6-2.

Still playing on the marshes until 1888, they found a ground in Northumberland Park and at the end of the first season there, buoyed by a profit of £6, joined the Football Association.

A season of competitive league football in the 1892/93 Southern Alliance League added some meat to the diet of friendly matches and London Senior and Middlesex Senior Cup ties, in which they tended to be knocked out by stronger sides like Clapton and Millwall.

As we have seen in that one season of the seven-team Southern Alliance, Spurs were the only team other than the champions Old St Stephen's to complete their 12 fixtures. Playing in red shirts and blue shorts (swapped for chocolate and gold four years later), they started with a 2-1 success away to Polytechnic and finished with seven wins, two draws and three defeats for a respectable third place behind the champions and Erith.

Being snubbed when applying to join the first season of the Southern League meant it was back to four or five cup competitions plus friendly matches for the next three years. The new FA Amateur Cup was at least on the agenda, albeit with a controversial outcome.

After beating Vampires in the first round (11 November 1893), the club were found guilty of paying a financial inducement by handing over ten shillings (50p) for new boots to Ernie Payne, an outside-left from Fulham who turned up without any kit because his had mysteriously disappeared at his old club. Spurs were banned for two weeks and so had to forfeit their second-round match against Clapham Rovers. The unfortunate episode heightened the debate around professionalism, which the London FA was still set against. Tottenham, growing more ambitious, appointed a first professional trainer and entered the FA Cup for the first time as one of their four cup competitions, winning three qualifying rounds before succumbing to Luton Town in a replay.

In December 1895, a momentous meeting voted in favour of turning professional. In the close-season, they were disappointed to fail with an application to join the Football League but were welcomed this time into the Southern League. The vote of confidence was justified by results and a growing reputation as north London's strongest club: in successive seasons they finished fourth, third, seventh, then in 1899/1900 lost only four matches from 28 and took the title.

Southampton, before and after dropping their 'St Mary's' tag, had replaced Millwall as the dominant team in the league, winning it three times in a row from 1897-99, but they lost their crown to Spurs, whose best season yet included attracting a record gate of 18,000 against Gravesend.

It was the first campaign at the new ground that became known as White Hart Lane, although it was not in that road at all and never has been. The venue was on Tottenham High Road, behind the White Hart pub, but White Hart Lane was always further to the west, like the railway station of the same name.

Be that as it may, Spurs had arrived and were now in white shirts and navy shorts, this time as a tribute to Preston North End. A clear force in the South, they would soon make history and a national reputation, for southern sides were at last having some success in the FA Cup.

For nine years from 1889, when Chatham reached the quarter-final, not a single team south of Birmingham emulated them until Southampton did so. Spurs did it in 1899, losing 4-1 to Stoke and the next year there was at last a guarantee of a southern finalist when the Saints and **Millwall** were drawn together in the last four.

Millwall had arrived there after a stunning victory over the Football League champions to be, Aston Villa, their greatest result to date. The semi-final at Crystal Palace was a goalless draw notable mainly for its physicality – 'plenty of fouls, damages to the participants therein,' reported the *Daily Mail*.

Following the replay at Reading, deservedly won 3-0 by the Hampshire side, the same paper observed that it was just as well there were not many matches each season as 'otherwise the mortality among footballers might be greater'.

Southampton went on to lose the final to Bury but the South's day, and Tottenham's, would soon come (see Chapter 2).

* * * * *

Woolwich Arsenal had little joy in the Cup, suffering a dispiriting run of six successive and mostly heavy first-round defeats from 1891-96. Left stranded when the London FA continued to oppose professionalism, they found salvation in the Football League's decision to expand its Second Division from 12 clubs to 15 for the 1893/94 season. With Accrington and Bootle dropping out, Arsenal were elected along with Liverpool, Middlesbrough Ironopolis, Newcastle United and Rotherham Town (later United).

Those names alone indicate the fearsome amount of travelling that would be involved in this great new venture. The nearest of the 14 away trips were to Burton, Lincoln, Burslem (Port Vale) and Walsall. For home games, they went back to the Manor Ground after the Invicta's owner, thinking he was on to a good thing, demanded a hefty rent increase.

So the first Football League game played by any London club came on 2 September 1893 and was also the first contested by Newcastle, who made the long journey home satisfied with a 2-2 draw after they had been 2-0 down. Walter Shaw and Arthur Elliott were the home team's goalscorers in front of a healthy attendance of 10,000.

The Arsenal team, in 2-3-5 formation, was: Williams; Powell, Jeffrey; Devine, Buist, Howat; Gemmell, Henderson, Shaw, Elliott, Booth.

After defeat the following Saturday at Notts County, less than half of that home crowd were present for a midweek fixture that brought a first win in the third game, 4-0 against Walsall Town Swifts, in which new centre-forward Joseph Heath from Wolves claimed a hat-trick.

The first of more than 200 meetings to this day with Liverpool ended in a 5-0 home defeat, the visitors showing the sort of form that would make them unbeaten Second Division champions that season as they scored five times before the interval.

A fortnight earlier, however, a record was established that remains to this day, when Ashford United from Kent were thrashed 12-0 in a first qualifying round of the FA Cup. It is still Arsenal's biggest win in the competition, as opposed to the 11-0 drubbing of Darwen in 1932 usually quoted.

Clapton were beaten 6-2 in the next round, bringing a South London derby against Millwall billed as 'the championship of the south'. Arsenal won it 2-0 and then knocked out the 2nd Scots Guards to earn a home tie in the first round proper against First Division club The Wednesday, which would end in a controversial 2-1 defeat.

The crowd could not understand why their team had been given only a free kick instead of a penalty when a Wednesday player handled in the area. Newspaper reports said the referee was pursued to the railway station by supporters who 'made their displeasure known'. So did the club, with a formal protest, all in vain. (Protests at one game the following year were more irate, when after a 1-1 draw against Burton the referee was knocked out by a spectator. The ground was closed for six weeks).

That first season finished with Arsenal ninth of the 15 teams, averaging a point a game after winning 12 and losing the same number, with four drawn. Progress for the rest of the decade was steady rather than spectacular, as the final league positions illustrate: ninth, eighth, seventh, tenth, fifth, seventh, eighth. In the best of those seasons, 1897/98, they were still eight points off promotion. Thomas Mitchell had taken over as secretary-manager for that season and may have been the first to hold that position, although Sam Hollis and Bill Parr appear to have had similar roles earlier in the decade. William Elcoat (not George, as he has often been called) took over from Mitchell for one season and was succeeded by Harry Bradshaw, who lasted rather longer.

One small bonus was the arrival in 1897 of Luton Town as the second southern club, but after three years they disappeared back whence they came, to be replaced by another faraway team in Blackpool. In 1900, Arsenal reported a loss of £3,400 – not all of it, presumably, in train fares.

There was serious talk about whether to go back to the Southern League, but Bradshaw insisted the club had sufficient potential to make it to the First Division. He won the day and would soon be proved right.

* * * * *

By the turn of the century two more of London's current league clubs had made it as far as the Southern League First Division and one of the capital's fiercest derbies was established. As their name implies, **Thames Ironworks**, later to become West Ham United, were a works team that grew quickly under a paternalistic employer who happened to have been a former FA Cup finalist with Oxford University.

Based in Canning Town, the firm was one of London's last remaining shipbuilders. A foreman named Dave Taylor is credited with supplying the first impetus in 1895 to the chairman Arnold Hills, who saw a football team as a way of bringing management and workers closer together following a damaging strike that year.

A friendly match, the first of more than 40 in that inaugural season, on 7 September was drawn 1-1 (not 0-0 as some sources have it) against fellow factory workers of the Royal Ordnance. Within a month, the new club were competing in the FA Cup, albeit in a 5-0 defeat by Chatham.

They even staged matches against Woolwich Arsenal (3-5) and West Bromwich (2-4) under artificial lights that year at Hermit Road, the rudimentary ground taken over in the summer of 1895 from Old Castle Swifts, who as the works team of the Castle shipping line paying extra wages to players claimed to be the first professional club in Essex.

Hills and secretary Francis Payne became influential figures in forming a London League the following year, the Ironworks joining the First Division. Eviction from Hermit Road meant no home games could be played for several months, as the owners of a new ground in Beckton denied that permission for improvements had been given and took the club to court.

The first league match at Hermit Road on 19 September 1896 brought a 3-0 win over Vampires, which set the tone for a good first season, with the Ironworks finishing as runners-up to the 3rd Grenadier Guards. There was a good run in the London Senior Cup, though not the FA Cup – exited in an 8-0 defeat away to Sheppey United.

After one year at Browning Road in East Ham, Arthur Hills decided to finance the new Memorial Grounds in Holland Road, West Ham as a major sporting venue. West Ham historian John Powles, who specialises in Thames Ironworks and uncovered details of the court case, believes claims of a 100,000 capacity to be wildly exaggerated, with a more modest 17,000 against Tottenham in 1901 likely to have been the record football crowd there.

Hills could not be faulted for ambition and was rewarded if not with huge crowds then with results and a first championship as the team pipped Brentford to the London League title by a point, losing only one game out of 16 and even winning a couple of FA Cup ties for the first time before going out to St Albans.

Hills next agreed, a little reluctantly, to embrace professionalism and with it a place in both the higher standard Southern League and the Thames & Medway Combination for the 1898/99 season.

The Irons promptly finished top of the Southern League Second Division with a 100 per cent home record and only two away defeats early on, remaining unbeaten thereafter with 17 wins and a draw. A play-off was still necessary, against Cowes IOW in the hardly equidistant venue of Millwall: the Irons won 3-1 and a further promotion/relegation test match against Sheppey (1-1) became irrelevant when the First Division was expanded to accommodate both for the following season, as well as Cowes.

There was an unfortunate start to the new campaign when the club were banned by the FA for a fortnight because of financial irregularities by an agent involved in recruiting new players. The side was nevertheless strengthened, notably with three players from Tottenham and Syd King, a full-back signed from New Brompton, who would become West Ham's first and longest-serving manager. One of the many benefits of reaching the top division was that regular derbies against Millwall, previous opponents only in friendlies, were therefore established, bringing record crowds of 13,000 and 12,000 to the Memorial Grounds for first an FA Cup tie and then a league game, both won by the visitors.

The league defeat came during a run of only one win in 15 games for the Irons, but they took some revenge in the final league game of the season, winning away 1-0 in front of 8,000. Finishing 14th out of 17 meant a test match to avoid relegation, as two other clubs had resigned, but Fulham from the Second Division were duly beaten 5-1 at the home of the champions Tottenham. Centre-forward Bill Joyce, who had just scored a hat-trick in beating the FA Cup finalists Southampton, became the hero by bagging another one. He could not have known that it would be the last match ever played by Thames Ironworks.

* * * * *

Football was flourishing in the west of the capital as well as the north, east and south, with Brentford, Fulham and QPR all joining the Southern League towards the end of the 1890s.

Fulham were the first of them to be established and claim to be the oldest of the current league clubs in London with their foundation in either 1879 or 1880, one or two years before Orient, albeit, in both cases, as a cricket club. A plaque commemorating

Fulham's birth can be found in St Andrew's Church, Greyhound Road W14, near the Queen's tennis club, for it was as Fulham St Andrew's Church Sunday School FC that they began. The first football captain was Jack Howland, an assistant supervisor of the Sunday School who organised weekly Temperance Society concerts to keep people out of the local pubs.

Playing in red and white halves, they won the West London Amateur Cup in 1887, then adopted the name of Fulham in 1888 and won the first West London League five years later.

Having played at half a dozen local grounds, they moved as early as 1896 to Craven Cottage – which therefore beats White Hart Lane (1899) as the oldest existing ground among the current league clubs – and changed from black and white stripes to red. In 1898, they turned professional in the London section of the Southern League Second Division, and after finishing tenth of the 12 clubs were runners-up to Watford the following season, leading to the unsuccessful play-off against Thames Ironworks.

Brentford joined the Southern League at exactly the same time, establishing another enduring local derby. They had been founded in 1889 at the Oxford and Cambridge pub by Kew Bridge when the Brentford rowing club voted narrowly in favour of adding football rather than rugby to their sporting repertoire.

Kew FC provided the first opposition in a 1-1 draw on 23 November 1889 and the West London Alliance (1893) and West Middlesex Senior Cup (1895) were the first major trophies. Adding the Middlesex Senior Cup and London Senior Amateur Cup brought an invitation to the Southern League for the 1898/99 season, although what was unusual was that Brentford remained amateurs for that first campaign. They finished it a commendable fourth, comfortably ahead of Shepherd's Bush and Fulham. The same year, however, Brentford were found guilty by the FA of paying their players, which as the club's website suggests was 'an act common with most leading amateur clubs in London but illegal'. Going legit by turning professional immediately followed. The ground by that time was at the Cross Roads, south Ealing and early kits were a colourful selection based on claret and blue hoops or stripes.

Not far away, **QPR** followed a similar sort of timeline, albeit with an earlier conversion to professionalism. Christchurch Rangers (founded 1882) amalgamated with St Jude's Institute (1884) and in 1887 changed the name to the present one. Like most other small clubs of the time, Rangers had a variety of grounds, mostly around Queens Park, Brondesbury and Kensal Rise.

In 1892, they changed colours from an Oxbridge-like light and dark blue halves to green and white hoops, and joined the West London League with Fulham, whom they beat in the final of the West London Observer Cup, retained for the following two seasons. Winning the London Cup and competing in the FA Cup for the first time in 1895 were further significant steps, followed by turning professional in 1898 and soon joining the Southern League.

Although it was a year after Brentford and Fulham, Rangers managed to be elected straight into the top division, where eighth place, a point behind Millwall, who knocked them out of the FA Cup, was a fair start. The first professional league match was a 1-0 defeat away to eventual champions Tottenham on 9 September 1899, followed a week later by victory over New Brompton.

Also very much in existence by that time were the club with the distinctive name of **Orient**, who claim 1881 as their foundation date, soon after Fulham, although they did not begin playing football formally until five or six years later. Homerton Theological College was the home of the founding fathers, who started a cricket team called Glyn (after Glyn Road, Clapton), later changed to Eagle.

Jack Dearing, a player and committee member who worked for the Orient Steam Navigation Company (later P & O), suggested Clapton Orient as a name, but the prefix was dropped in order to avoid any confusion with the established local club Clapton. To this exotic title was added a distinctive capital O on the back of their shirts (numbers being unheard of until the late 1920s). The team won the Clapton & District League in their second season, 1894/95, and moved into the London League Third Division two years later. Promotion quickly followed at the Whittles Athletic ground in Millfields Road, Clapton, where two railway carriages served as dressing rooms.

In June 1898, election to the top division of the London League was marked by a change of name, Clapton being incorporated after all 'with Clapton now being considered a good district socially', according to Dearing. The league by that time was being won by the reserve teams of stronger clubs like Tottenham and Millwall, whose first XIs were competing in the Southern League.

The Os would have to wait a while for their big step up. In the meantime, their first-ever London League opponents, in September 1898, were the original Barnet club, founded in 1888, although set to be disbanded and taken over only a couple of years into the new century.

Barnet, like Wimbledon (founded 1889), would remain amateurs for the first 75 years of their existence. Most of the clubs who eventually went into the making of Dagenham & Redbridge, namely Walthamstow Avenue (1900), Leytonstone (1886) and Ilford (1881), also came into existence early, as did others like Leyton (1868), Clapton (1878), Bromley (1892), Dulwich Hamlet (1893), Enfield (1893) and Hendon (1908) , all of whom would contribute to London's fine record in the 81 years (1893-1974) of the FA Amateur Cup. For more on all of them, plus Cray Wanderers, who claim to be Greater London's oldest surviving club, see Interlude II. By 1900, however, it was clear that professionalism was the way forward for the most ambitious of clubs.

Chapter 2

Taking shape (1901-1920)

Tottenham win 1901 FA Cup as non-league team; Arsenal win promotion; Chelsea and Clapton Orient join expanded Second Division, followed by Fulham and Spurs; London stages first official Olympics 1908; ambitious Fulham director Henry Norris proposes merging or ground-sharing with Woolwich Arsenal, then takes over Arsenal and moves them north of river despite objections from Orient and Spurs; North London rivalry takes bitter turn post-war as Norris persuades Football League officials that Arsenal should replace Spurs in top division; huge expansion of League with 22 new clubs, including Brentford, Millwall, Palace, QPR, joined by Charlton.

HUMILIATED when applying to join the Southern League in 1893 by receiving only one vote, **Tottenham Hotspur** brought huge prestige to the competition within eight years by winning the FA Cup as Southern League champions. Remarkably, it would take them another seven years to be allowed into the Football League.

As we have seen, Spurs quickly became one of the most successful sides in a league that was clearly of a high standard, at least at its top end, where all the leading teams were professionals and paid their players well.

They had reached the FA Cup quarter-final for the first time in 1899, losing to First Division Stoke City, then taken the Southern League title the following year under young player-manager John Cameron, a Scottish inside-forward. The 1900/01 campaign was an oddity in leaving them only fifth in the league table, yet bringing London's first major trophy of the professional era.

The Southern League title was effectively surrendered by the start of December, but form picked up just in time for the start of the FA Cup. It began against a famous club. Preston North End, the 'Invincibles' as Double winners a dozen years earlier, were struggling in the First Division but had knocked Spurs out of the cup 1-0 in the first round the previous season. The chance of revenge seemed to have gone when the visitors held out for a 1-1 draw in London but centre-forward Sandy Brown, scorer of the Spurs goal, came up with a hat-trick in the replay for a 4-2 win.

Proud Preston would go on to be relegated. Their fellow Lancastrians, Bury, were stronger opponents in the next round, a top-six side and the FA Cup holders, but a record White Hart Lane crowd of 20,250 saw them beaten 2-1 despite taking an early lead, with two more goals for Brown. Signed from Portsmouth the previous summer, he was becoming a crucial figure in the cup run and would remain so.

With Woolwich Arsenal beaten by West Bromwich Albion in that second round, Cameron's troops found themselves drawn in the quarter-finals away to the South's only other representatives, regular Southern League opponents Reading.

Beaten 3-1 in the league at Elm Park in November, Spurs could hardly have complained had they been on the end of a similar scoreline on 23 March. Reading deservedly took the lead and although John Kirwan equalised, the Londoners were desperately lucky just before the finish when defender Alexander

Tait somehow got away with punching the ball off the line. The replay five days later was more straightforward. Knowing that West Bromwich Albion, who were to be relegated with Preston, awaited the winners, Spurs cruised through 3-0, with Brown inevitably scoring a couple.

Forced to play a Southern League game two days before the semi-final, they decided on an early example of squad rotation by resting eight outfield players (and still beating Bristol City). Brown was one of those excused the Bristol game and on Easter Monday he became the dominant figure, stunning the Midlands majority in a 46,000-strong Villa Park crowd by scoring all his team's goals in a 4-0 win after a goalless first half.

The other semi-final was contested by two more teams involved in the First Division relegation struggle, Sheffield United and Aston Villa. When the former came through after a replay for their second final in three years, Tottenham, non-leaguers or not, had no need of any inferiority complex.

The cup final had returned to London, with Crystal Palace the regular venue, and interest in whether the trophy itself would do so was huge. On 20 April 1901 a staggering crowd turned up, comprising the first six-figure attendance recorded for a match in England – and almost certainly anywhere in the world. Perhaps the sheer numbers involved caused some confusion as at least two different figures are regularly quoted – 114,815 and 110,820. The FA's former historian, David Barber, confirms the latter figure as the official one. They saw 'a good game and a draw', according to the headline in the *Daily Graphic*, whose front-page cartoons featured United's heavyweight goalkeeper Willie Foulke, 'marvellously agile for his twenty stone'.

Agile or not, he was beaten twice after Fred Priest had put United in front. Brown – who else? – equalised with a header before half-time but after his second goal in the 51st minute, the Blades immediately equalised through Walter Bennett in controversial fashion. Spurs goalkeeper George Clawley fumbled a shot and as Bennett homed in on him, players variously appealed for a goal kick or corner. To widespread astonishment the referee awarded a goal, although pictures – it was the first final ever filmed – proved the ball had not crossed the line.

An aggrieved Tottenham side spent the following week at Southport nursing their sense of injustice and preparing for the replay at Burnden Park, Bolton. The attendance there was a disappointing 20,470, kept down it was felt by bad weather and the reconstruction of the local railway station. Once again United scored first, recovering from a poor start before Priest gave them the lead shortly before half-time.

Player-manager Cameron equalised seven minutes into the second half and, according to the next day's *Sunday Times* report, 'the Sheffielders had rather the better of matters' for a while. It was the Londoners who scored next, however, through Tom Smith and just before the end Sandy Brown completed his extraordinary cup campaign with a 15th goal in eight ties, including at least two in every round. Spurs had won the trophy, the only non-league side to do so, as well as ending 18 years of domination by the North (ten wins) and the Midlands (eight).

What has rarely been pointed out about their success is that the team contained only three Englishmen (none of them from the South), plus five Scots, two Welshmen (skipper Jack Jones and centre-half Ted Hughes) and an Irishman, Kirwan. The line-up for both games was: Clawley; Erentz, Tait; Morris, Hughes, Jones; Smith, Cameron, Brown, Copeland, Kirwan.

The defence of the cup lasted only one round. Brought up against old rivals Southampton in 1901/02, Spurs drew at home and away then lost the second replay at Reading 2-1. Tottenham's main task, however, was to achieve Football League status. Two more London clubs would beat them to it.

* * * * *

Like all the best birth announcements, news of **Chelsea** FC's arrival into the world was carried in the columns of *The Times*. The date was 11 March 1905 and the ambition evident in every sentence was not merely achieved but superseded with almost indecent haste.

Never mind a professional football club that planned to play at Stamford Bridge and apply to the First Division of the Southern League. Within two months, Chelsea (not even resident in the fashionable borough of that name) had talked their way straight into the Football League, and four months later were playing in a fine stadium with its main stand designed by the greatest football architect of the day and perhaps any other.

The ground had been used for some years by the London Athletic Club who, like Sheffield FC and Blackheath Rugby Club, claim to be the oldest surviving independent organisation in their particular sport. It was actually on the Fulham Road and in West Brompton rather than the more upmarket neighbouring borough of Chelsea, but the latter name struck the sort of chord that appealed to the new club's founders once they rejected Kensington FC.

Like Soames Forsyte, who would appear a year later in John Galsworthy's novel, 'Gus' Mears and his brother Joseph were both men of property, albeit 'as fond of sport as they are wealthy'. Indeed, Joseph had earlier built Fulham's ground at Craven Cottage and after the siblings bought the land at Stamford Bridge, their initial intention was to move Fulham there.

Being unable to agree rental terms with the Southern League club, however, they were on the verge of selling to the Great Western Railway, ignoring suggestions from London Athletic Club official Frederick Parker to start a rival club of their own. Parker's extraordinary version of events is that during discussions one Sunday morning about the way forward, he was badly bitten by 'Gus' Mears' dog but took it so well that the apologetic owner decided he was a fine fellow and agreed that a new football club was a capital idea. Hence the announcement in *The Times* as Chelsea, fathered by what would become one of London's great football dynasties, were born.

Scottish architect Archibald Leitch, designer of Fulham's Stevenage Road stand, was employed and the athletics ground upgraded within six months, by which time, to the chagrin of Fulham, Tottenham and other wannabes, Parker's persuasive tongue during canvassing visits to many northern clubs, and then at the Football League's annual general meeting, had talked the club into membership of the extended Second Division.

Liverpool supporters who a century later would sing 'Chelsea's got no history' presumably did not know it was their club who inaugurated Stamford Bridge as a football ground with a friendly match on 4 September 1905.

Finding suitable players by that date cannot have been easy. 'No club has rushed into fame with such sensational suddenness as Chelsea,' wrote John Tait Robertson, a 28-year-old assigned what he called the 'engrossing and intensely difficult task' of recruitment after being appointed secretary-player-manager in April. A Scottish international wing-half, he had appeared for Everton, Southampton and most recently Rangers, winning three successive Scottish League titles in Glasgow.

Robertson began cleverly by acquiring one of the football celebrities of the age, Willy 'Fatty' Foulke, already encountered here as Sheffield United's goalkeeper in their FA Cup Final against Tottenham. Foulke had played more than 350 games for United, appearing in all three of their FA Cup finals and winning a championship medal with them in 1898.

From 20 stone at the time of the Spurs final, he had clearly not been dieting and now weighed in at 22 stone 3lbs, only fractionally less than his two full-backs put together. Robertson, echoing that earlier cup final report, called him 'agile as a kitten'. The goalkeeper was quickly reunited with two of his Tottenham conquerors, John Kirwan and inside-forward David Copeland, one of several fellow Scots Robertson brought in to good effect.

His recruitment, well backed financially by the owners, we can be assured, was rewarded with excellent results, in which he continued to play his own part on the pitch. He went down as the scorer of Chelsea's first goal in league football in the 1-0 victory at Blackpool on 9 September, which followed an opening-day loss at Stockport a week earlier.

Joining the Second Division at the same time were not only Leeds City and Stockport County but **Clapton Orient,** who had been prompted into the bold step of turning professional two years earlier when the Middlesex FA banned them for infringing their amateur status – one of the heinous crimes being to pay a player for re-turfing the pitch in the close-season. Pleased to be accepted into the Southern League for 1904/05, and finishing eighth out of 12, the Os formed a limited company and after failing to be elected to the top division of the Southern League (Spurs apparently objecting on geographical grounds), they found greater support from Chelsea, who successfully lobbied for a second London team to join the Football League.

If Chelsea's ascent was achieved with 'sensational suddenness', Orient's rise from amateur football to the Football League in under two years was not far behind.

Perhaps it was *too* quick. A squad largely recruited in the summer by new manager Sam Ormerod began with defeats away to Leicester Fosse and at home to Hull City and had only two wins, over Glossop and Lincoln City, in ten games before Saturday, 11 November 1905, the day of the first-ever London derby in the Football League.

The next day's *News of the World* devoted a full page of closely condensed type to football and a report of good length to the derby, beginning with the observation: 'The first meeting of London's two Second Leaguers drew the largest crowd of the season at Millfields Road yesterday. Eight thousand spectators in such miserable weather is strong proof of the new interest in Metropolitan football.'

Orient apparently seemed more likely to score early on but just before half-time Chelsea's Frank Pearson, a centre-forward signed from Manchester City, put the visitors in front. After 'a hot attack' leading to a shot 'which struck Foulke's huge form', Kirwan and Copeland conjured up a second goal and before the finish Pearson scored his second. So 'Chelsea retired easy winners' by 3-0.

The success put them in fourth place, having lost just one of their 11 games, while Orient had only Gainsborough Trinity beneath them. The teams for this historic contest, listed in 2-3-5 formation, were:

Clapton Orient: Redding; J.Lamberton, Boyle; Proudfoot, Boden, Codling; Kingaby, G.Lamberton, Leigh, Evenson, Bourne.

Chelsea: Foulke; McEwan, Key; Mackie, Watson, McRoberts; Moran, McDermott, Pearson, Copeland, Kirwan.

By the time of the return game on 17 March, the clubs had continued to go in different directions and a 6-1 win at Stamford Bridge left Chelsea second in the table behind Bristol City while Orient had sunk to the bottom, six points adrift.

The shock on the day was that the Clapton side should take the lead, through Walter Leigh. 'A good-sized crowd turned up to witness the struggle,' the *News of the World* reported, most of them no doubt disappointed to see the home side, for whom Foulke was this time absent, fall behind. Soon, however, Pearson and Charles Donaghy had the Pensioners in front and by half-time it was 4-1. In the second half, Jimmy Windridge matched Pearson in scoring twice. After that, alas, 'an element of roughness became apparent and the referee had to display great tact in keeping the men in order'. It would hardly be the last time in a London derby.

At the end of the season six weeks later, however, Chelsea had missed out on promotion by one place to Manchester United, a remarkable ground-record crowd of 67,000 having watched a 1-1 draw between the clubs on Good Friday in their first-ever London meeting.

Orient duly finished their first campaign bottom with seven wins in 38 games, Ormerod having resigned and the club already undergoing the first of the many financial crises that would become familiar to supporters down the generations. Now they were faced with the prospect of applying for re-election after a single season.

It took a stirring speech to save them at the Football League AGM by Captain Henry Wells-Holland, who had been placed in charge of the club's perilous financial affairs. With a mixture of good sense, emotion and wild optimism, he spoke about Orient being 'first offenders' who would perform far better in future with their huge local population and a ground at Millfields that could 'easily be made capable of holding upwards of 60,000'.

Oldham Athletic were the strongest of the outsiders wanting to become the North West's latest league club, but it might have been that a general preference towards improving the geographical spread counted against them and in favour of the Londoners, who scraped home in the crucial vote by the closest of margins: 21 to 20.

The following season's London derby at Millfields was memorable for both clubs. Coming on the final weekend of the season, it saw Chelsea already celebrating promotion from the Second Division, just behind Nottingham Forest, although player-manager Robertson had resigned in November after having his duties slowly watered down.

A good number of their supporters helped swell the crowd to Orient's best yet of more than 21,000. A 1-0 away win, completing a Chelsea double, did no great damage, leaving the Os with three teams below them, and Fulham and Tottenham to be elected in successive years and swell London interest.

Once William Martin, a centre-forward converted from half-back, left Clapton for Stockport in 1908, a prolific goalscorer was lacking until the arrival of Scotsman Richard McFadden, who helped them to reach fourth place for a second successive season in 1912, followed by another top-six place two years later. It was an impressive period for a club destined to remain one of London's least successful. Sadly, McFadden would be one of those who did not return from the Great War.

Chelsea, meanwhile, had the highest average attendance in the country for five out of seven seasons from 1907/08 to 1913/14, peaking at 37,105. Their next derbies would mark be the start of a long rivalry with Arsenal before both were joined by Spurs, confirming that trio as the capital's big three for the next 100 years and more. Of course, there were ups and downs for all three, even in the few years before the war.

* * * * *

We left **Woolwich Arsenal** (Chapter 1) as London's Football League pioneers, who spent their first seven seasons there from 1894-1900 in the middle of the Second Division, still lacking any local matches but determined that reverting to the Southern League would be a regressive step and that the First Division was within reach.

Manager Harry Bradshaw was eventually proved right when the Gunners were finally promoted in 1904 – only for Bradshaw to up sticks for Fulham, with whom Arsenal's fortunes were to become closely intertwined.

If there was one benefit of the club's geographical isolation among Second Division clubs, it was demonstrated in a generally excellent home record. That helped a first serious promotion push in 1901/02, when finishing fourth, and again the following season, when third, only three points behind promoted Small Heath.

The progression continued and 12 months later the final step was taken, with a runners-up spot behind Preston in a tight finish: Preston 50 points, Arsenal 49, Manchester United 48. The Gunners' total of 91 goals in 34 games was almost 20 more than any other team, Irish international Tommy Shanks claiming 25 of them before being sold back to Brentford. No fewer than 67 goals were scored and only five conceded at the fortress that Plumstead had become, with 15 of the 17 home games won and the last two drawn 0-0.

Only 22 goals were conceded in total thanks largely to goalkeeper Jimmy Ashcroft, who was to become the club's first England international.

After Bradshaw's unexpected departure and with Phil Kelso from Hibernian in charge, First Division football came to London at last on 10 September 1904. After losing the opening game of the season 3-0 away to Newcastle (the eventual champions) a week earlier, Arsenal played a goalless draw at home to Preston, watched by around 25,000. A first victory came in the fourth game, 2-0 at home to Wolves with goals by Charlie Satterthwaite and Tim Coleman.

Ashcroft and his defenders again did a sterling job and it was the defence rather than the attack that ensured a respectable tenth place. Conceding only 40 goals was the sixth best record in the division, but scoring 36 was the joint worst.

Bizarrely, Arsenal were not far off equalling that total in a single game when a Parisian XI visited the Manor Ground in December for a rare international friendly and were beaten 26-1.

Hopes that finishing seventh in 1907 and in the top six for the first time two years later, as well as reaching successive FA Cup semi-finals (0-2 v Newcastle and 1-3 v The Wednesday), would lead to greater things proved unfounded. By the end of the 1907/08 campaign, Arsenal were not even top dogs in London, with newly promoted Chelsea standing just above them, albeit on goal average and with both teams only three points clear of relegation.

A week before the first-ever London derby in the top division, newspapers were already predicting an attendance higher than any game other than the cup final for what one of them called 'the baby First Leaguers of the West End against the pioneers of London football'.

Sure enough, the following Sunday's *News of the World* was able to confirm 'a record crowd that is not likely to be beaten for a long time'. The estimate was 65,000 and after a 2-1 victory, the paper reported, 'rejoicings were great in the Chelsea district last night', the home side having won 'on their merits, in spite of the gloomy forecasts of the experts'.

The teams for this historic occasion were:

Chelsea Whiting; Cameron, Miller; Key, Stark, Birnie; Moran, Rouse, Hilsdon, Windridge, Fairgray.

Arsenal Ashcroft; Gray, Sharp; Dick, Sands, MacEachrane; Garbutt, Coleman, Kyle, Satterthwaite, Neave.

George 'Gatling Gun' Hilsdon, shortly to become Chelsea's first England international, was the hero of the day, scoring both goals before his former West Ham club-mate Charlie Satterthwaite retrieved one for the visitors. Hilsdon finished the season with 32 goals all told to add to 27 a year earlier.

The goalless draw in the return game four months later was watched by 30,000, comfortably Arsenal's highest gate of the season.

The following season, the Woolwich club's single-point advantage over their new rivals (having won 2-1 at Stamford Bridge) meant finishing sixth, five places above them, in another tightly contested competition. From then until the war, however, there was no threat whatever to the still-dominant North and Midlands, even when a third London side appeared in the top flight.

* * * * *

Two significant events for sport in the capital occurred in 1908: the Olympic Games came to town and **Tottenham** were finally elected to the Football League. There was a connection between them, for the man who led Great Britain to a gold medal in the football tournament was a Spurs player, and indeed, director.

Vivian Woodward was an architect who joined Spurs as a centre-forward in 1901 but made only three appearances in each of his first two seasons because of business commitments. Once becoming more regular, he attracted the attention of the England selectors and scored goals for them at an astonishing rate of 29 in 23 games.

For five years, he was playing for England amateurs as well, scoring just as prolifically. Being close to his peak in 1908, he was an obvious choice for the Olympics, in which the English amateur team represented Great Britain *en bloc*.

If the Games as a whole were regarded as a success, London having replaced Rome at two years' notice when Mount Vesuvius erupted and the Italians pulled out, the football nevertheless remained low key. In the Paris Games of 1900, Upton Park had represented Britain and taken the gold medal by virtue of winning their only game, 4-0 against a French XI. In 1904 there were again only three entrants, two of them American and one Canadian.

Four years later, London did at least stage a recognisable international competition. All games were at the new White City stadium in Shepherd's Bush, where attendances for the six matches averaged a little over 3,000.

Of the eight teams, Hungary and Bohemia withdrew before the start and France fielded two sides, each beaten embarrassingly heavily by the accomplished Denmark, 9-0 and 17-1. Great Britain romped past Sweden 12-1 and then beat the Netherlands 4-0 in the semi-final, Harry Stapley of Glossop scoring all the goals to set up the expected final against the Danes.

Among the talented Danish squad were three brothers, one of them the captain Kristian Middleboe, and another Nils, a national athletics champion who five years later would return to London as Chelsea's first foreign player, while working in a bank.

Team-mate Sophus Nilsson set a record by scoring ten times in the win over France 'A' but in the final, watched by an estimated 8,000, he drew a blank while Woodward and Fred Chapman of South Notts scored the goals that gave Britain a 2-0 win and the gold medal. Woodward was the successful captain again four years later in Stockholm, when the Danes were once more the beaten finalists, this time by 4-2.

In between the two Games, he had moved from Tottenham to Chelsea, despite Spurs having finally reached the Football League, in fraught circumstances. Tiring of the Southern League in 1908, they rashly resigned from it, but then finished only fifth in the re-election voting for three Football League Second Division places. Stoke's resignation offered another opportunity but this time Spurs tied in the voting with Lincoln, twice, and only scraped home on a final ballot of the management committee.

Despite neither having won the Southern League nor had any sort of Cup run since the famous success of 1901, they immediately justified their new status. Winning a first Football League match 3-0 against the FA Cup holders Wolves set the tone for what would be a thrilling campaign. After taking only one point from lowly neighbours Clapton Orient in two games over Easter, a 1-1 draw at Derby on the final day meant edging out West Bromwich Albion from the promotion race. But the oddities of the goal average system meant that had they drawn 2-2, Albion would have gone up instead.

The revered Archibald Leitch designed a new main stand in time for the opening First Division game at home to Manchester United (a 2-2 draw in front of 32,275) and a copper cockerel perched on top of it.

Woodward, leading scorer in the promotion season, suddenly resigned following promotion and then turned up at Chelsea as three London clubs contested a First Division campaign for the first time. Although the 1909/10 season was therefore historic, it turned out ingloriously for the capital's representatives, every one of whom found themselves struggling to preserve their status.

By mid-December, the eight-page programme for the Chelsea-Spurs game showed the teams locked together in the bottom three, with Woolwich only a point better off.

The programme notes, for some reason entitled 'Daisy Cutters', bemoaned how 'somebody or other must have bewitched the Chelsea Club', since the team had not been at full strength since the first day of the season and had lost four international players for the previous week's game at Bury. A 4-2 defeat had resulted, even though a northern reporter was quoted as saying of Chelsea: 'They gave a clever exhibition of football, which would probably have led to a better result on a dry day.'

Woodward, the notes pointed out, would not be playing against his former club, but the writer was confident of beating Tottenham as 'on foreign soil they have obtained but one point out of a possible sixteen'.

The optimism proved justified for that feeble away form continued, Spurs suffering an eighth defeat in their nine away games, albeit only by 2-1. Indeed, the feature of the derby games that season was how close they were, with none decided by more than a single goal:

25 September: Arsenal 3 Chelsea 2 (15,000);
4 December: Arsenal 1 Spurs 0; (18,000);

18 December: Chelsea 2 Spurs 1 (40,000);
28 March: Chelsea 0 Arsenal 1 (40,000);
16 April: Spurs 1 Arsenal 1 (39,800);
30 April: Spurs 2 Chelsea 1 (35,000).

Every one of those results was crucial, for by the end of the campaign Chelsea were the fall guys, dropping back down to the Second Division with only 29 points from their 38 games. Arsenal survived despite falling from sixth the previous season to one place and two points above them and newly promoted Tottenham could claim to be kings of the capital, albeit with only a point more than the Gunners.

It was hardly a challenge to inspire fear elsewhere in the land, where Aston Villa won the league ahead of Liverpool, Blackburn and the FA Cup winners Newcastle.

Chelsea did not stay down long, returning two seasons later, then facing a relegation struggle twice in the years before the Football League ceased for rather more important matters.

* * * * *

It was **Arsenal** who made the drop next, in 1912/13, winning only three games to finish bottom of the 20-team division, with Spurs (17th) and Chelsea (18th) not far off joining them. One notable player who proved unable to save the Woolwich club was Alf Common, the man who had caused a sensation in 1905 by becoming football's first £1,000 player. Middlesbrough, faced with relegation, paid Sunderland that extraordinary sum for him and he kept them up, but despite enjoying one good season for the London club after joining them in 1910 at the age of 30, he failed to score in the first half of the relegation season and was sold to Preston for what he had cost, a more modest £250.

By that time, Arsenal were responding to their straitened circumstances by embarking on London's most dramatic and enduring turf war: moving from south London to north of the Thames.

As with so many football clubs before and after them, their problems at the time were a vicious circle in which small crowds led to a lack of money, which meant the best players being sold, results declining and so on and on.

A specific problem was that during the Boer War, from 1899 to 1902, munitions workers had less time for football and five-figure attendances, always rare, virtually disappeared. As we have seen, there was talk of returning to the Southern League, which manager Bradshaw resisted, only to move there himself with Fulham despite having taken Arsenal into the elite division of English football for the first time.

Bradshaw's successor, Phil Kelso, also found Fulham more attractive and new manager George Morrell, a Glaswegian who took over in 1908, also had to sell players. A minor row over expenses cost him the services of local teenager Charlie Buchan, who left for Northfleet and ended up as record scorer for Sunderland and an England international before eventually returning 15 years later.

By the end of the decade, the financial position was critical and Arsenal ended up being saved by a man who had lured away two of their managers to Fulham and was becoming a key figure in London football.

* * * * *

Henry Norris, born in Kennington in 1865, was another man of property who became one of the original directors when **Fulham** were formed into a limited company in 1903. It was also the year they finally gained promotion to the First Division of the Southern League after failing three times in four years via the play-off test matches.

In 1900, they were beaten heavily by Thames Ironworks and the following year finished well behind champions Brentford. In 1902, the test match was lost to Swindon and in 1903 to Brentford, only for chairman J.F. Hitchcock to persuade the league that his club deserved a rise.

So the 1903/04 season, playing in white shirts and black shorts for the first time, brought a host of London derbies with Spurs, QPR, Millwall, the newly christened West Ham United and Brentford among others. Fulham finished above the latter pair in 11th place, despite winning only one of the ten derbies (at home to Millwall). Hitchcock had strengthened the team as promised with players like goalkeeper Jack Fryer, a veteran of three FA Cup finals with Derby County, who later became captain.

Crowds could be impressive, with 14,000 turning up to see a goalless draw with Tottenham, who would go on to become runners-up to Southampton. In a long FA Cup run, Fulham beat QPR and West Ham in coming through no fewer than seven qualifying rounds and two replays before losing 1-0 to Arsenal.

Fortunes were becoming entwined with the Woolwich club. For the next season, 1904/05, manager Bradshaw was recruited and immediately helped his new club move up to sixth, with only Spurs of the London sides above them. A notable result was the 12-0 home win over bottom-of-the-table Wellingborough (inside-left Alex Fraser from Newcastle scored five) and a crowd of 20,000 was reported for more than one home game. Excused until the sixth qualifying round of the FA Cup, Bradshaw's men needed three games each time before knocking out Manchester United and Reading, then lost 5-0 away to eventual winners Aston Villa in front of 47,000 as Fryer's saves kept the score down.

This was a club on the up, their confidence demonstrated when, as we have seen, an approach from 'Gus' Mears to move into Stamford Bridge was turned down, thereby establishing an early turf war and changing the future face of west London football.

Norris, chairman by now, preferred much-needed improvements to Craven Cottage, which the London County Council wanted closed down for safety reasons. Fulham kept up with the neighbours by adding an Archibald Leitch stand of their own (now Grade II listed and named the Johnny Haynes Stand).

Although peeved to see Chelsea elected straight into the Football League, they were handsomely compensated with the

1906 Southern League championship. Losing only three games out of 34, they were not high scorers (44) but had much the best defence, pierced only 15 times, and finished five points clear of the ever-dangerous Southampton.

Retaining the title the following season proved the gateway to the Football League. An early 5-1 loss to Spurs was one of five defeats and the final margin was tighter – two points clear of Portsmouth, against whom a crowd of 30,000 was reported for a key game at the Cottage in February, won 2-0.

Thanks to Norris's energetic campaigning and despite Chelsea's un-neighbourly objections, league status was achieved along with Oldham Athletic when Burslem Port Vale and Burton United both dropped out.

The first season in the Football League began disappointingly with a 1-0 defeat at home to Hull City on a Tuesday afternoon in September 1907, but it finished in fourth place, only three points behind promoted runners-up Leicester Fosse. Fulham scored an impressive 82 goals (the second highest), five of them without reply in the two derbies with Orient, who nevertheless finished 14th, their highest position yet, despite 40 goals being the lowest in the division.

With Chelsea promoted a year before, Orient were the only opposition from anywhere in the south of England, which did at least mean that the name and reputation of Fulham were spread far and wide. So did a remarkable run to the FA Cup semi-final, starting and finishing with scoring records of opposite kinds.

Luton were beaten 8-3 in a club record FA Cup score still current, as were Norwich and then both Manchester clubs. United were destined to be First Division champions that season, with their local rivals in third place, yet both were seen off at Craven Cottage amid wild enthusiasm from crowds of 38,000 and 41,000 respectively.

In the semi-final at Anfield, alas, 50,000 saw Newcastle, another of the country's top four teams, go 2-0 up at half-time and win 6-0. Goalkeeper Leslie Skene, a Scottish international, was hurt early on in what remains the heaviest semi-final defeat suffered by any club in the competition. A 'painfully effete' Fulham said one report, 'were really outclassed'.

None of this did any harm to the politically ambitious Norris, who in 1909 was elected Mayor of Fulham. The team had peaked, however. Harry Bradshaw decided to take up a position as secretary of the Southern League and although Phil Kelso replaced him and would stay until 1924 as the club's longest serving manager, he oversaw nothing more than a series of mid-table finishes.

The first Football League derbies with Chelsea, against whom Fulham would go on to have one of the worst records of any side against their nearest and dearest, took place following the Pensioners' relegation in 1910.

Fulham won 1-0 in December with a goal by outside-right James Smith (Bob Whittingham missed a twice-taken penalty for Chelsea), but lost the return 2-0 at Stamford Bridge in April. Crowds of 30,000 and 40,000 testified to local interest. Chelsea finished third, then second the following year, when beating Fulham twice on successive days at Christmas, with the aggregate attendance rising to 77,000.

When Fulham met **Arsenal** in 1913/14 after the latter's relegation, the Cottagers won a strange game 6-1, all seven goals coming in the last half-hour. The Arsenal, as they were officially known at that point, finished above Fulham and Orient in third place but the greater significance was that the former south London club now lived on the other side of the river.

The new home might have been Battersea, Harringay or even Fulham itself. In 1910 Arsenal's debts prompted Norris, often ahead of his time, to issue a cheeky invitation to them to amalgamate with his club at Craven Cottage, and when that was ruled out, he suggested a ground-share, which was also turned down.

He appeared to believe that Arsenal had the better prospects and soon became their majority shareholder and then chairman, still remaining a director at Fulham, while his friend William Hall did the opposite: director of Arsenal, chairman of Fulham. Little wonder the links between the clubs were so close.

Norris, however, would begin to sever them. Faced with the prospect of Second Division football as Arsenal's calamitous 1912/13 season drew on, he decided on equally drastic measures. 'Supposing there was a place only ten minutes from Piccadilly where one could go and see a first-rate football match?' he asked. In Islington, close to what was then known as Gillespie Road underground station, which had been opened in 1906, he found such a site, owned by the Ecclesiastical Commissioners (later the Church Commissioners).

Many Arsenal supporters who did not relish crossing London to watch their team were horrified. One of them, writing to the *Kentish Gazette,* used a phrase that would recur many years later in relation to another London club, who wanted to move much further afield: 'You cannot "franchise" a football club,' he insisted, 'Woolwich Arsenal must stay near Woolwich.'

Tottenham and Clapton Orient, already within three miles of each other and fighting for local support, were naturally just as appalled by the prospect, but lost the turf battle, if not the war: a Football League meeting in March 1913 decided nothing in the existing rules could block it.

Norris triumphantly agreed a 21-year lease on the land, agreeing out of respect for the owners not to play on Good Friday or Christmas Day (a stipulation which stayed in place until Arsenal bought the freehold in 1925). The last game in south-east London was a 1-1 draw with Middlesbrough on 26 April 1913, watched by only 3,000. The first at the new home, back down in Division Two, was on 6 September, when a crowd more than six times larger saw Leicester Fosse beaten 2-1 in a stadium not quite finished. Dressing rooms were an important missing element.

One more point secured during the 38 games – from a 2-2 draw at home to Orient in April, for instance, watched by 35,000 – would have made it the most successful of campaigns, resulting in instant promotion. Crucially, however, Morrell's team finished behind Bradford Park Avenue on goal average, thanks to the old failing of not scoring enough goals. That would lead indirectly to one of the great controversies of London football history.

* * * * *

Although war on Imperial Germany was declared in August 1914, football surprisingly continued until the end of the season, amid some controversy about whether such frivolous pursuits should be allowed among healthy young men whose contemporaries might be dying for their country.

The following month, an anti-sports campaigner was ejected by Fulham officials when he attempted to address the crowd at a game against Orient. Football was, however, ready to play its part. In December, 34 players from 11 clubs signed up at Fulham Town Hall, a venue 'specially lent by the Mayor H.G. Norris', with Orient's Capt Henry Wells-Holland – the man whose impassioned speech had saved his club from re-election after one season in the league – among those on the platform.

According to contemporary reports, 'Orient and Croydon Common responded particularly well', with the former's captain Fred Parker the first to come forward. After beating Leicester Fosse in a final Second Division match in April 1915, Orient's players were given a send-off in a military parade and that weekend the so-called Footballers' Battalion, the 17th Battalion of the Middlesex Regiment, moved to a training camp in Surrey.

The team had finished ninth in the table, which was one of the more respectable positions among London's league clubs. Chelsea (despite reaching the FA Cup Final) had only Spurs below them at the foot of the First Division and in Division Two Arsenal were no better than fifth and Fulham 12th.

The Football League and Southern League then suspended their competitions for the duration of the war, although a London Combination competition ran for the next four seasons. Chelsea, West Ham, Chelsea again and then Brentford won it, the latter two after a truncated version with ten clubs playing each other four times.

For 1915/16, no midweek games were allowed and the duration of all matches was soon reduced to 80 minutes. Only expenses were payable. The programme for Arsenal's derby against Spurs at the start of that season pointed out that all the players were now appearing 'as amateurs, for the love of the game' and listed the whereabouts of many of the first-team squad as 'practically every man doing something in his country's welfare ... for the complete subjection of the thrice-accursed Hun'.

Clubs fielded whoever was available or happened to be in London at the time, with many guests. In 1918/19, West Ham used 62 players.

Grounds were often needed for more important matters than games-playing: White Hart Lane was taken over for the manufacture of gas masks, Spurs playing at Clapton Orient's Millfields and even Highbury. The Army took over QPR's Park Royal ground, which was turned into allotments.

Orient finished bottom of the Combination twice but their sacrifice in the war was greatest of all, according to no less a figure than King George V. Three of their leading current players never returned from the conflict: top scorer Richard McFadden died along with William Jonas and George Scott. 'Good luck to Clapton Orient FC, no football club had paid a greater price to patriotism,' said the King.

Of course, they were not alone in suffering. Many other footballers and ex-players died, including Walter Tull, formerly of Tottenham and one of the first black officers in the British Army, who had been mentioned in dispatches; Ed Lightfoot, Jim Fleming and Findlay Weir of Spurs; Arsenal's eccentric Welsh international goalkeeper Leigh 'Dick' Roose; former West Ham men Bill Jones, Bill Kennedy and Arthur Stallard; Phil Smith of Chelsea; Frank Cannon, who had played for four London clubs, most recently Brentford; Brentford's Patrick Hagan and Henry Purver; Fulham's Bob Suart, Ernie Thompson and William Maughan; George Lake of Chelsea; Charles Green and George Porter of Millwall; John Williams, who had played for Millwall and Crystal Palace; Palace's John Bowler, Ernie York and former captain Harry Hanger. QPR's first England international Evelyn Lintott, a players' union chairman who had moved to Bradford City, died on the first day of the battle of the Somme; former

Rangers' men also lost were Ben Butler, Henry Pennifer and Harry Thornton.

Tull, brought up in a Bethnal Green orphanage, had joined Spurs from Clapton, with whom he won the FA Amateur Cup in 1909, the first mixed-race player to win a medal in English senior football. A victim of racial abuse, he played only ten times in two years before signing for Northampton Town's Herbert Chapman – of whom much more later.

At last, the Armistice was declared on 11 November 1918. The Football League would soon undergo huge expansion and cause an equal measure of controversy in north London.

* * * * *

By 1918 Henry Norris, a recruiting officer at the War Office during hostilities, had been knighted and become a Tory MP. Among his many friends in high places were the Archbishop of Canterbury, who personally signed Arsenal's lease for Highbury, and the Football League president and Liverpool owner John McKenna, who would crucially help him and Arsenal at the 1919 league AGM, when the First Division was to be extended from 20 to 22 clubs.

For previous expansions – for example in 1898 and 1905 – the bottom club(s) had simply stayed up and two others were promoted. This time, Derby County and Preston duly moved up from the Second Division and Chelsea, bottom but one in the First Division, were immediately reprieved on something of a sympathy vote, clubs having remembered that Manchester United only finished above them by beating Liverpool in a match-fixing scandal that resulted in seven players being banned for life.

That left one place to be filled, which Tottenham felt should be theirs, despite having been bottom dogs in 1915. Instead, McKenna talked up Arsenal's credentials as loyal 25-year members of the league and ordered a vote of all nominated clubs. To Norris's delight and Tottenham's dismay, it resulted: Arsenal 18, Spurs 8, Barnsley 5, Wolves 4, Nottingham Forest 3, Birmingham 2, Hull 1.

So Tottenham found themselves replaced in the top division by their new, unwanted local rivals, who had been no higher than fifth in the last season before suspension, with Barnsley and Wolves above them in the table. Spurs would have to begin the post-war era back in the Second Division along with Fulham, Clapton Orient and one new London member.

* * * * *

Thames Ironworks had effectively been replaced by **West Ham United** in June 1900, shortly after Bill Joyce's hat-trick had prevented relegation from the First Division of the Southern League. The next most significant development was a move in 1904 from the unsuitable Memorial Grounds to land owned by a Roman Catholic school on Green Street, where the 16th century Green Street House, just along from the Boleyn Tavern, had associations with Anne Boleyn.

Attendances improved at what became known as the Boleyn Ground – and only later as Upton Park – especially for derbies against Millwall and Spurs, although it took a long while to average five figures.

Millwall and Tottenham's visits apart, a big FA Cup tie was required to bring out the crowds, above all when 27,000 turned up to see Manchester United beaten in the last minute of a third-round tie in 1911 before a quarter-final defeat by Blackburn Rovers.

In the league, however, the Irons, as loyalists continued to know them, were knocking down few trees. Fifteen seasons until the war were mostly spent in mid-table, with only one relegation fight, in 1909, and one real title challenge – third place in 1913.

That was the season that saw the departure of local boy and leading goalscorer Danny Shea, who had 121 goals in six seasons to his name. He was sold to First Division Blackburn midway through the 1912/13 season but thanks to back-up from Londoner George Hilsdon, returning from a prolific period with Chelsea, the best Southern League finish under the new name was achieved.

If war-time football was something of a lottery, results did West Ham no harm and a Football League meeting in March 1919 admitted them to the Second Division, which like the First was being expanded to 22 clubs. Arsenal, Chelsea and Tottenham, London's big three, were therefore joined by a club who would attempt from that day until this to make it a big four.

* * * * *

In 1910, three years before Arsenal moved to north London, **Millwall** had moved in the opposite direction. As any crows flew, the distance from their second Isle of Dogs ground to 'the more populus' New Cross was barely a mile and a half by way of the Greenwich Foot Tunnel (opened 1902), albeit a little longer via either Blackwall Tunnel (1897) or the even newer Rotherhithe Tunnel (1908).

Vying with Southampton and Tottenham as the most successful Southern League team towards the turn of the century, they almost folded altogether in the summer of 1901 after being evicted from the East Ferry Road ground. With little apparent likelihood of finding funds for a new one and virtually every player having moved on, it took the enthusiasm, publicity and finance generated by a public meeting at Poplar Town Hall to offer new hope. By the following September, a new home known as North Greenwich (confusingly, since it was still on the island and not in the district of the O2 known by that name today) was ready. So was a new team.

Sixth place was commendable in the circumstances, although they would only once more be higher before the war, finishing third in 1908 after Fulham (twice) and QPR had both won the title.

The style of the team and the dockers who supported them was not altered by the move south. 'Sensitive players, often with better skills, are too easily scared by their robust play,' wrote a Chelsea player who did not enjoy the experience of visiting The Den for a supposed 'friendly', adding that the crowd were in the habit of 'jeering at the away team'.

With old rivals West Ham having made the Football League for the 1919/20 campaign, Millwall initially denied any intention of applying for election but did not know of the league's exciting plans. At the AGM in 1920, the management committee announced that the Southern League Division One would be invited *en masse* to form a new League Division Three.

It was a sensible promotion for Millwall, Brentford, Crystal Palace and QPR, who with one exception – bizarrely, Grimsby Town were put in with them for one season – would avoid any away trips further than the four they were already familiar with to south Wales (Cardiff City, Merthyr Town, Newport County and Swansea Town).

* * * * *

For **QPR**, the new century had brought seven seasons of mid-to-lower-table Southern League finishes amid financial problems reflected in never staying for long at one ground (no senior club in the country has moved as often). In 1901, the lease was terminated at the Kensal Rise Athletic Ground and a new home found at nearby Latimer Road, Notting Hill, the teams changing in a nearby pub. Local residents were unhappy and the owner gave them notice at end of the season.

For 1902/03, it was back to Kensal Rise, owned by All Saints College, and by 1904/05 there was another move, to Park Royal, as well as a more permanent change from blue and white stripes to hoops. The 1907/08 season brought a newer ground in the same area, boasting a much larger capacity, the team responding with an exciting season under a first official manager in former Scottish international James Cowan.

The previous season, they had been 18th but with champions Fulham promoted to the Football League and replaced (another geographical oddity) by Bradford Park Avenue, the new campaign quickly turned into a genuine championship challenge.

On Christmas Day, a crowd of almost 30,000 saw a goalless draw with Plymouth, their main rivals for the title. In the return game in Devon on Good Friday, a 1-1 draw kept the Rs top and after clinching the title by beating West Ham 4-0, they were able to afford two heavy defeats at the end of the season, losing 5-2 at Southampton and 8-3 at Swindon. Those scorelines reflected the generous nature of the football at both ends of the pitch, Rangers scoring far more goals (82) than anyone else and conceding more than most.

To round off a fine season, half-back Evelyn Lintott became the club's first England international and as Southern League champions, Rangers took part in the first FA Charity Shield match, successor to the Sheriff of London Charity Shield game between a leading amateur and professional club.

Rangers held the Football League champions Manchester United 2-2 at Stamford Bridge in April, although when it was replayed for the only time in what became the traditional pre-season date in August, United won 4-0.

That was an unsettling pre-season altogether as Rangers made an unsuccessful application to join the Football League, finding to their displeasure that Spurs, who had finished only eighth in the Southern League , were elected instead.

QPR made a poor defence of the title, ending up in 15th place, before proposing that summer that 18 Southern League teams should form a new Football League Third Division. They were ten years ahead of their time: Football League clubs voted 27-13 against.

In 1912 came the compensation of another Southern League title, once again pipping Plymouth, and earning another Charity Shield fixture, lost 2-1 to league champions Blackburn. Two matches that season were played at White City because of a rail strike, attracting bumper crowds of 26,000 and 20,000, more than twice the Park Royal average.

It was an experiment that would be repeated more than once in future.

* * * * *

Elsewhere in west London, **Brentford** won the Southern League Second Division in their first season as a professional club, 1900/01, but struggled for a while after being promoted. Bottom but one and then bottom in a strong league, they survived relegation both times, the first after drawing a test match with Grays, who refused to play extra time and so forfeited the game.

The second season at the higher level brought 27 defeats in 30 games, but showed the difference in class of the top divisions, when neighbours Fulham were beaten 7-2 in the test match to earn a reprieve.

Fulham were promoted anyway and drew a crowd of 12,000 to Brentford's Boston Park ground in York Road, which would be the last year there. For the 1904/05 season, an orchard once owned by local brewers was transformed into Griffin Park, where West Ham were the visitors for a first Southern League game (0-0) on 4 September.

It proved to be a fourth successive season in the bottom six before rising to mid-table security at last for a couple of years. Fulham, champions for two seasons running, continued to prove popular visitors, with 15,000 watching the 1905/06 derby.

In 1908, Fred Halliday started an 18-year association with the club as secretary-manager, having finished the previous season with a 2-1 win at Griffin Park in charge of the Southern League's northern intruders Bradford Park Avenue.

In his first season, Brentford were bottom but again survived when the league was extended from 21 to 22 clubs. Relegation, long postponed, finally happened in 1913, Halliday standing down as manager to concentrate on his secretarial duties. Several thousand pounds in debt, and condemned to play in a Second Division dominated by small Welsh clubs, Brentford were expected to be wound up but resolved to fight on.

The players responded by winning their first nine games, crowds picked up and the team came third behind Croydon Common and Luton, finishing with some big wins over opposition like Ton Pentre (7-0), Treharris (7-0), Aberdare (6-3) and Caerphilly (5-1).

Coming out of the war years as London Combination champions ahead of Arsenal enabled them to look ahead to the new peacetime era with optimism.

* * * * *

By moving from the Isle of Dogs to New Cross in 1910, Millwall immediately offered a challenge to **Crystal Palace** as south London's biggest club – neither Charlton Athletic nor Wimbledon being of much significance at that stage.

The original Crystal Palace club were featured early in Chapter 1 as founder members of the Football Association, reaching the first FA Cup semi-final but not apparently lasting much longer. For ten years from 1895, the name was therefore more significant as the venue of the FA Cup Final in the grounds of the Great Exhibition building of 1851.

As crowds for the final grew and grew, reaching six figures for Tottenham's triumph in 1901, so did the notion of having an anchor club there and The Glaziers – a name reflecting the glass structure of the edifice – were founded in September 1905 with the help of Edmund Goodman, seconded from Aston Villa (hence the claret and blue colours), who appointed the first manager and within two years took over the position himself.

Like Chelsea, founded the same year, Palace immediately applied to the Football League but unlike Chelsea were turned down and joined the Southern League instead, where they quickly established themselves.

In the first season, they lost only one game – at home to Southampton Reserves by 4-3 after leading 3-0 – winning the Second Division from fellow newcomers Leyton and being promoted with them. There was even an unexpected record that stands to this day, thanks to a quirk in the fixture list, when Chelsea were required to play their Football League match at home to Burnley on the same day as their FA Cup third qualifying round trip to Palace. Prioritising the league game, the west London club sent their reserves to take on Palace and were hammered 7-1. That result is still the record defeat by a Football League club against a non-league side in the FA Cup.

From finishing bottom but one the following year at the higher level, Palace shot up to fourth under Goodman in 1907/08 and until the war were frequently in the top six, finishing as runners-up to Swindon in 1914 and denied the title only on a goal average of 1.98 to 1.88. The London Challenge Cup was won for the second season running and Horace Colclough, a full-back, became the club's first England international.

The highlight before that was a run to the FA Cup quarter-finals of 1907, which began with a stunning 1-0 first-round victory away to Football League champions-elect Newcastle United, achieved with top scorer Horace Astley's goal. Closer to home, Fulham and then Brentford were both beaten 1-0 in replays and in the fourth round Everton, another First Division club and the eventual runners-up, were held 1-1 before losing the replay 4-0 at Goodison Park.

Turfed out of their original home by the Admiralty in 1915, Palace moved to the Herne Hill cycle stadium and three years later took over The Nest, near Selhurst railway station, from **Croydon Common.**

For a long time, the Commoners were the only other south London club of repute. A team of that name, based around St Luke's Mission Church, Croydon had been founded in 1897, although the club that emerged as professionals ten years later were effectively a new entity, and would have been named Croydon Town if the local amateurs Croydon FC had not objected.

A strong team of new recruits from Arsenal, Tottenham, Southampton, West Ham, Orient and others immediately finished third in the Southern League Second Division and won it the following year, despite the main stand being burnt down.

That prompted a move to a new home, the Nest, but the club lasted only one season in the higher division in 1909/10, when they played two very local derbies with the more successful Crystal Palace, the home game watched by a crowd of 10,000.

Promotion back up was achieved again in 1913/14, but once more they finished in the bottom two and amid financial difficulties the club was wound up in 1917. Their full story can be found at www.croydoncommon.com.

* * * * *

The amateurs Wimbledon won various local competitions, folded in 1910 under the weight of debt, then revived as Wimbledon Borough, quickly dropping the appendage and moving into Plough Lane in 1912. At that point, northern clubs were still dominating the FA Amateur Cup, challenged mainly by Clapton and Bromley but not by **Charlton Athletic**, who although founded in the same year as Chelsea and Palace (1905), merely knocked around local leagues and did not even join the Southern League until after the war.

As the first Charlton team photograph shows, the club began as a boys' side, started by teenagers around West Street (now Westmoor Street), not far from the present Thames Barrier. Perhaps those boys were even inspired by Woolwich Arsenal, only a couple of miles to the east and enjoying their first season as a First Division side.

Charlton's first ground was at Siemens Meadow, named after the important local electrical engineering firm, followed by Woolwich Common, where the archery and shooting events were held at the 2012 London Olympics. Next came Pound Park, close to The Valley, and Horn Lane.

Successful in a range of local competitions, the club decided to spread their wings following Arsenal's departure for north London and in 1913 entered the London League, competing for the first time the following season in the FA Cup but ceding home advantage to Dartford after being guaranteed £4 (!) in gate money.

It soon ran out and in 1915 Charlton effectively shut down before being revived by a small group of enthusiasts, who found a potential ground in a chalk pit near the railway station. Turned down by the Isthmian League, the main amateur league around

London, they joined the Kent League for the 1919/20 season instead and by finishing fourth were inspired to turn professional and join the Southern League, just as most other London clubs were about to move upwards to the new League Division Three.

Initially left behind, they would soon catch up, to complete a body of Football League clubs in the capital that, apart from one brief interlude, would remain unchanged until Wimbledon joined them more than 50 years later.

Chapter 3

Capital gains (1921-39)

London clubs at last making an impact; Spurs are Cup winners and Division 1 runners-up; Arsenal dominate the early 30s with David Jack and Alex James after Herbert Chapman joins as manager from Huddersfield and Henry Norris is banned for life; West Ham in the chaotic first Wembley cup final; Charlton go from Division 3 to Division 1 runners-up in three seasons under Jimmy Seed after Fulham almost beat them to it; Brentford's best-ever period in top six, eclipsing Chelsea; QPR and Palace are stuck in Division 3 but Millwall escape; Thames FC come and go in two seasons; Orient just survive.

C HAPTERS of this book starting in the first full season of a new decade tend to feature **Tottenham Hotspur** and the FA Cup. Twenty years on from 1901 they were at it again, this time under the tactically astute Scot Peter McWilliam, appointed manager in December 1913 after winning three league titles with Newcastle.

Furious after being demoted while fifth-placed Arsenal replaced them, Spurs made their point emphatically in a run of three outstanding seasons.

In the first post-war campaign of 1919/20, they proved to be clearly the outstanding team in the Second Division, dropping only one point in the first dozen games – which included a double over Clapton Orient – and winning the title by six points from Huddersfield Town with 102 goals scored.

Bert Bliss, a little inside-left with an unexpectedly powerful shot, scored 31 of them and caused havoc in a left-sided triangle also featuring wing-half Arthur Grimsdell and winger Jimmy Dimmock, all three of whom already were, or later became, England internationals.

So did Fanny Walden, a diminutive outside-right, and Jimmy Seed, an inside-right released by Sunderland after the war when still suffering from a gas attack and rescued from Mid Rhondda by McWilliam, who joined late that season and will play a notable part as a manager later in this chapter.

It was exciting football and naturally the crowds loved it; 44,268 came to see the Orient game (and nearly 33,000 the away match) and 52,179 were at White Hart Lane for a narrow defeat by Aston Villa in the FA Cup quarter-final, when full-back Tommy Clay scored a decisive own goal. Villa went on to win the cup but 12 months later it would be Spurs' turn.

League matches at that time were played against the same opponents in successive weeks and, after a difficult start back in the top division, Spurs hit their stride with a double over Chelsea, winning 5-0 and 4-0, the combined attendance for which was 123,000.

The eagerly awaited Arsenal matches came in January, bringing a 2-1 win at the Lane and a 3-2 defeat at Highbury a week later.

By that time the FA Cup was under way, favourable draws pitting Tottenham against Bristol Rovers (6-2), Bradford City (4-0, with a hat-trick by Seed) and Southend United (4-1). The quarter-final brought Villa back for a repeat of the previous season's tie and this time the result was reversed. Dimmock crossed for John Banks, a right-winger replacing the injured Walden, to score the only goal.

Semi-final opponents were Preston and with two Second Division sides, Cardiff City and Wolves, contesting the other semi-final, whoever won would be favourites to take the trophy. Just as in 1901, Preston were in the lower half of the division and once again found the Londoners too good for them. The venue was Hillsborough, where two goals by Bliss earned a 2-1 victory and a place in the final.

Wolves turned out to be the opposition after a semi-final replay, which Spurs were quite content with, since the Wanderers were a side from the lower half of the Second Division, finishing 20 points behind Cardiff. Stamford Bridge, where Tottenham had played in front of such a huge crowd for their league game six months earlier, suited the Londoners too and naturally they had huge support among another attendance in excess of 72,000 despite so much of the stadium being open to the bad weather.

Tottenham's line-up was: Hunter; Clay, McDonald; Smith, Walters, Grimsdell; Banks, Seed, Cantrell, Bliss, Dimmock.

King George V was introduced to the teams in pouring rain without the benefit of so much as an umbrella and was doubtless pleased to return to the one covered stand to watch a game in which a heavy pitch failed to prove the traditional leveller for the lower-division side.

As the *Western Times* put it two days later: 'The heavy rain-storm just as the King entered the field of play quickly had the turf under water in places. The first half was, in consequence, of a hard, scrambling nature. Tottenham played with the greater skill.'

That skill was rewarded eight minutes after half-time, when 20-year-old Jimmy Dimmock regained possession after losing it to a defender and scored with a low shot just inside the far post.

'Dimmock's goal was beautifully obtained and his shot just afterwards that struck the crossbar deserved another goal,' the newspaper continued. 'Tottenham were undoubtedly the better team. Their forwards were much superior, both in combination and in their shooting in front of goal. Dimmock and Seed performed splendidly.'

Thus McWilliam, a winner with Newcastle in 1910 after three losing finals, became the first person to win the cup as player and manager on separate occasions (player-manager John Cameron having done it for Spurs in 1901).

Five league games still remained, the first of them only two days after the final, and not surprisingly perhaps only one of them was won, but sixth place was a perfectly acceptable return to the higher division. The season finished on a high note with the FA Charity Shield match in which league champions Burnley were beaten 2-0.

With Arsenal three places below them, McWilliam's side could claim to be top dogs in the capital, which they confirmed the following season. Once again, it was victory over Chelsea that sparked the best run, albeit not until Christmas Eve.

From then on only four games were lost, carrying Spurs to second place behind Liverpool – the first time that a London side had finished so high. In another long FA Cup run, they looked capable of retaining the trophy. Brentford, Watford, Manchester City and Cardiff were beaten before a semi-final against old foes Preston, who they had beaten 5-0 and 2-1 in the league. At Hillsborough, Seed gave Tottenham a half-time lead, Preston equalised through Archie Rawlings and Bliss was annoyed to have a goal disallowed because the referee had blown for treatment to an injured player. But Tommy Roberts scored the winner for Preston, who went on to lose the final to a Huddersfield Town penalty.

Tottenham had peaked and the only reason London supremacy was maintained for a couple more seasons was that Chelsea and Arsenal were performing so poorly and newly promoted West Ham had only just established themselves.

In 1927, manager McWilliam left when Middlesbrough virtually doubled his £850 salary – then found himself being relegated the following year along with Spurs in one of the most extraordinary seasons in league history.

It was surely the closest ever. After a long unbeaten run in the autumn, Spurs were looking upwards and even towards the end of

March were still seventh. But the table was so tightly compacted that more than half the clubs were not safe from relegation.

Selling Seed to struggling Sheffield Wednesday after he refused a new contract, with wages reduced from £8 to £7, proved costly. The Yorkshire side beat Tottenham twice in April and he scored in each game. Beating Arsenal 2-0 in between times was Spurs' only win in the last eight games. When the maths were done after the final Saturday, Spurs – who had finished a week earlier and gone on tour to Holland – were down.

Bottom-placed Middlesbrough had 37 points, Tottenham 38 and no fewer than seven teams, including West Ham, had 39. The difference between 22nd and fourth was just seven points. Fifteen wins and eight draws had not been sufficient to keep Spurs up: a modern equivalent would be about 48 points in a 38-game Premier League season.

It took Spurs five years to regain First Division status under manager Percy Smith from Bury, with all the 1920s heroes now departed and George Hunt from Chesterfield emerging as a prolific goalscorer and another England international. In successive seasons, he scored 24, 33 and 32, contributing to one near-miss (third place in Division Two), then promotion a point behind Stoke City and even a third-place in the top division, making an immediate impact as Spurs have so often done after going back up.

But the fall from grace this time was spectacularly quick: from third place in 1933/34, they sank to the very bottom the following season, the campaign's humiliations including defeats of 5-1 and a record 6-0 – at home – by champions Arsenal. The balance of power had moved to Highbury, not just from White Hart Lane but from everywhere else as well.

* * * * *

From the start of the 1930s, **Arsenal** were the dominant club in the land. Once Henry Norris's politicking had manouevred them back into the top division straight after the war, they would retain that status for longer than could ever have been imagined and become one of the most famous sporting names anywhere.

Initially, it was all unspectacular: second fiddle to Chelsea, who shot up to third place in the first post-war season and then, as we have seen, to new neighbours Tottenham as well. In 1924 (when Chelsea went down) and 1925, Arsenal finished in the bottom four.

The dominant side and champions in those two seasons were Huddersfield Town, managed by Herbert Chapman, whom we came across briefly in Chapter 2 when he spent three seasons as an inside-forward at Tottenham before becoming player-manager of fellow Southern League club Northampton Town.

If Spurs gave him a taste for London life, it turned out to be a bad day's work for them.

Having revived moribund Northampton but failed to get them to follow Tottenham into the Football League, he moved on to Leeds City just before the war, resigning and then finding himself briefly banned when the club were caught up in an illegal payments scandal and disbanded.

Chapman was out of football until approached by Huddersfield early in 1921. After lifting them clear of any relegation concerns, he won the FA Cup the following season (the year Spurs lost to Preston in the semi-final) and then achieved third place to continue a run that established the Terriers as a breed apart, the finest in the land.

His tactics, first developed at Northampton, revolved around sucking the opposition in and counter-attacking, while encouraging his defenders to be more constructive in their use of the ball. With a better class of player at Huddersfield the success was spectacular, bringing three successive league titles from 1924–26. It was the first time such a thing had ever been achieved.

But by the time of the third triumph, Chapman was back in north London.

Arsenal had sacked the unimpressive Leslie Knighton, manager for six years since the end of the war, for going behind the back of Sir Henry Norris, who had imposed a transfer limit of £1,000 on him, and offering Sunderland seven times as much for inside-forward Charlie Buchan.

Norris's advertisement in the sporting press for a successor was careful to point out that 'gentlemen whose sole ability to build up a good side depends on the payment of heavy and exhorbitant (sic) transfer fees need not apply.'

In successive meetings, Huddersfield had beaten Arsenal 4-0, 3-1, 6-1, 4-0 and 5-0. Never mind league titles – Sir Henry and his fellow directors had seen with their own eyes what a Chapman team could do, and they must have been thrilled when word came via a journalistic contact that he was willing to leave the champions. Crowds of up to 50,000 at Highbury, where the club had just bought the stadium outright, were said to be a factor (Huddersfield's average was 18,000). A handsome salary of £2,000 – twice what he was earning in his native Yorkshire – did no harm either, and Arsenal had their man.

After dramatically lifting them to second place behind his old club in 1926 (on the back of a record 34 goals from former miner Jimmy Brain), success was for a while confined to the FA Cup: two quarter-finals, a semi-final and two finals in five successive years.

Despite what the job specification had stated, heavy recruitment was required – and granted. Chapman signed Buchan from Sunderland, as Knighton had failed to do, for £2,000 plus £100 a goal in his first season, in which Buchan scored 21. Even more costly was giving the England international a 'bung' of £125, one of the illegal payments that caused Norris to be banned from football two years later. Buchan made his debut in the first game of the 1925/26 season, a 1-0 defeat at home to Spurs, who had a good record at Highbury before their relegation in 1928.

Norris's departure therefore became the start of the Hill-Wood dynasty, Chapman getting on much better with Sir Samuel, who would be followed as chairman by his son Denis and grandson Peter before the boardroom upheavals of the early 21st century.

Football changed in 1925 with a crucial amendment to the offside law. Previously, three defenders had to be between a player and the goal for him to be onside, and teams like Newcastle United, marshalled by Northern Ireland international Bill McCracken, had their offside trap down to a fine, frustrating art. The story is told of a visiting player arriving at Newcastle station, hearing a guard's whistle as he stepped off the train and saying: 'Blimey, offside already!'

Now only two defenders – normally one and the goalkeeper – needed to be goal-side and the results were spectacular. From 1,192 goals in the top division in 1924/25 (an average of 54 per team), the total shot up to 1,703 (average 77). Chapman's Huddersfield, champions both seasons, improved from 69 to 92; Manchester City scored 89 times and were relegated, while Burnley conceded 108 but stayed up.

Teams still took a while to adjust. If Arsenal thought they would have an easier time of it at St James' Park after the change, they were horribly wrong, suffering a 7-0 beating in October, which was only their second loss of the season after the equally unwanted home defeat by Tottenham on the opening day. Buchan insisted tactics must change and helped persuade Chapman to convert the No 5, previously (as the name suggested) a centre half-back, into a third back.

In readjusting his midfield, Chapman effectively employed a 3-3-4 for the rest of a season, which was Arsenal's best to date, though still not quite good enough to win the league. Their defensive record, even with that bad day at Newcastle, was the joint second best behind champions Huddersfield, but an apparently impressive total of 87 goals (up from 46 in Knighton's dismal final season) was only the sixth best, even with Brain's 34.

Being runners-up proved something of a false dawn. Successive seasons next produced finishes of 11th, tenth, ninth and 14th, during which the formation slowly became a 3-2-2-3, the so-called WM formation: three at the back, two wing-halves (numbers 4 and 6) marking the opposing inside-forwards, two creative inside-forwards (wearing 8 and 10) and three at the front, wingers 7 and 11 plus the centre-forward, the fabled No 9.

Chapman did not like the close-passing style of earlier years, preferring to open up the opposition with a single well-judged longer ball. He insisted that inside-forwards and wingers should track back and wanted 'eight defenders when our goal is challenged'.

But Chapman also believed strongly of his teams that 'some of their best scoring chances have come when they have been driven back and then have broken away to strike suddenly and quickly'.

With only two trophies to aim at in those days, Arsenal's FA Cup Final defeat of 1927 was a particularly bitter blow, even if the passage there was stormy. Four of the five victories to get to Wembley, the recently established venue for the final, had been by a single goal and lowly Port Vale forced a fourth-round replay by drawing 2-2 at Highbury. Even the semi-final was a struggle past another Second Division side, Southampton, on a slippery Stamford Bridge pitch.

The cup was certainly something of a distraction as league form collapsed in the spring with a run of six successive defeats, including heavy losses of 7-0 (to West Ham), 6-1 (Newcastle again) and 5-1 (Sunderland).

For the final, Arsenal were only slight favourites against Cardiff City, also a mid-table side, having beaten them 3-2 in London but lost 2-0 in Wales over Christmas and the new year.

The Welsh club had been league runners-up to Chapman's Huddersfield three years earlier and lost the cup final to Sheffield United the season after, so Chapman knew the abilities of a team familiar with Wembley.

Ever since the war, the cup final had been a low-scoring affair and once again a single goal decided the destination of the trophy. The irony this time was that, as the *South Wales Football Echo* headline gleefully recorded that night, 'Welsh player's costly mistake gives the Bluebirds victory'.

Goalkeeper Dan Lewis was a Welsh international signed three years earlier from Clapton Orient (without ever having played for them) who had not yet become the automatic No 1. Come the final, he was, however, the man in possession of the jersey, an item of kit he would blame for his calamitous moment.

In the 75th minute, Cardiff's Hughie Ferguson hit a low shot from just inside the penalty area that Lewis seemed to have held, only for the ball to squirm away from him – off his shiny new jersey, he claimed – and then off his elbow into the net as Cardiff's Len Davies followed up with intent. It was enough to take the cup to Wales for the first time. Arsenal had been poor. One of the lessons learnt was that they should never use a brand new goalkeeper's jersey. Another, which would take longer to resolve, was that Chapman needed a top-class 'keeper.

As ever, there were still league games to play after the final so his team were able to finish with some local pride restored by beating Spurs 4-0 to end up 11th, two places above them.

A distraught Lewis recovered sufficiently to become first-choice in the following three seasons, although when Arsenal reached the cup final again in 1930 – against Chapman's former club Huddersfield – he was injured and missed out. He had played every game bar one of a run that included wins over Chelsea (2-0) and West Ham (3-0) and an unexpectedly troublesome semi-final against a physical Hull City, who led 2-0 late in the first game and then had a man sent off for a wild kick in the replay, when a goal by David Jack gave Arsenal victory.

It was the season that Jack Lambert, once a Yorkshire miner, made his name after a couple of unconvincing years. He finished it with 23 goals in 28 games. As Chapman continued his expensive recruitment drive, James arrived from Preston for £8,750, his own terms sweetened by a job demonstrating sports equipment at Selfridges and a newspaper column. He would prove perhaps the most important player of all in Arsenal's system, sweeping passes to the wings for Joe Hulme and new youngster Cliff 'Boy' Bastin, who would either supply Lambert with crosses or cut in to shoot themselves.

Other key signings and members of the cup final team included left-back Eddie Hapgood from Kettering, who would go on to captain England, and Jack from Bolton, who replaced Charlie Buchan for a world-record fee of £10,890 and was described by Chapman as 'the best bargain of my life'.

On Easter Monday, five days before the cup final, Arsenal were involved a record-breaking 6-6 draw away to Leicester, goalkeeper Lewis's knee injury contributing to the scoreline and forcing him out of the final. Charlie Preedy, a practical joker born in India and signed from Wigan Borough, wore the jersey and was spared Lewis's embarrassment of three years earlier, although only just.

Arsenal: Preedy; Parker, Hapgood; Baker, Seddon, John; Hulme, Jack, Lambert, James, Bastin.

The *Daily Herald* reported that Preedy's 'unsteadiness in goal might have proved fatal'. In front of him, the Arsenal defence was lacking a key player in injured stopper Herbie Roberts but they led from the 16th minute, when in a pre-planned move James took a quick free kick to Bastin and ran forward to score from the winger's pass.

Chapman's team were then able to play the counter-attacking football in which they specialised and, despite Preedy's 'unsteadiness', they not only held out but scored a classic late second goal on the break through Lambert.

Forty-six years after their foundation in Dial Square, Arsenal had a major trophy at last, which would prove the first of seven in nine seasons. Five of them were to be the championship itself, starting the very next year.

In 1930/31, they were irresistible in winning the league with a record 66 points, which would not be equalled until Tottenham's Double season 30 years later. There were 127 goals in the league, Lambert scoring 38 of them in 34 games, Jack 31 and wingers Bastin and Hulme 42 between them (remarkably, runners-up Aston Villa went one better with 128, five of them at home to Arsenal in a rare setback).

'Spectators want a fast-moving spectacle,' Chapman had claimed, and he provided it for them. London derbies drew the biggest crowds. Up to 54,000 saw West Ham force a 1-1 draw and Chelsea beaten 2-1, and as ever there was a huge attendance for the visit to Stamford Bridge as 74,667 watched Arsenal win 5-1 in November, with a hat-trick by Jack in the last half-hour.

Yet at home, inconvenient dates or bad weather could result in some low gates too. Regulars missing a midweek game at home to Grimsby in January immediately after going out of the FA Cup to Chelsea must have cursed when they heard the result: 9-1. It is still Arsenal's record win in the top division, with Jack scoring four times and Lambert three, but only 15,751 watched it.

The most regular team in that first championship season, listed with conventional numbering, was: Harper; Parker, Hapgood; Jones, Roberts, John; Hulme, James, Lambert, Jack, Bastin.

London's first league title was finally secured in April when rivals Villa were beaten by Liverpool. After 42 years, the North and Midlands had lost their monopoly.

Merseyside wrested it back the following season when Everton finished two points above Arsenal despite losing to them twice, and Chapman's frustration was compounded with a controversial defeat in the FA Cup Final.

It could have been the first so-called Cockney Cup Final, long before Spurs against Chelsea in 1967, but as Arsenal were beating Manchester City 1-0 in one semi-final, Chelsea lost the other to Newcastle 2-1. At Wembley, newsreel pictures showed that the ball was out of play before Jack Allen equalised for the Tynesiders. Arsenal, lacking the injured James, had still taken the lead through Bob John but the consensus, sportingly agreed by Chapman, was that Newcastle deserved to win through Allen's second goal. Arsenal had achieved the poor man's Double, as runners-up in both major competitions.

The following season, 1932/33, they suffered one of the most infamous defeats in the club's history before regaining the league title. For the FA Cup third-round tie away to Walsall of the Third Division North, Chapman gave a first-team debut to three players – none of whom would ever appear again following the 2-0 defeat. He was particularly incensed by one of them, the unfortunate Tommy Black, who conceded a penalty for the second goal and was sold to Plymouth Argyle within a week.

From a lapse of only one win in eight matches, Arsenal won a crucial game 5-0 at home to eventual runners-up Villa, finishing four points ahead of them. The total of 118 league goals was 26 more than any other team, calling into question the tag of 'lucky Arsenal' that attached itself to them as a result of soaking up the pressure and hitting teams on the break.

Opponents found themselves hit hard and often that season as Bastin and Hulme scored 53 between them from the wings, while new signing Tim Coleman from Grimsby chipped in up front, as well as the ageing Lambert.

In March, Chapman, ever the innovator and later described by Arsene Wenger as 'the greatest visionary the English game has ever seen', came up with the idea of white sleeves for the red shirts for easier identification, followed by blue-and-white socks. Some of his other ideas included the renaming of Gillespie Road underground station as Arsenal (Highbury Hill); planning a 45-minute clock behind the goal; taking over Clapton Orient as a nursery club (both rejected) and championing continental football, floodlights, goal-judges and numbers on shirts.

His reputation had spread as far and wide as Arsenal's and it was all the more stunning for the football world when he died halfway through the following season.

A rare goalless draw at Birmingham just after Christmas 1933 would prove to be his last match in charge. The point meant Arsenal ended the year in a strong position to retain their title, with only three defeats from 23 games.

Planning ahead as always, Chapman undertook two scouting trips up north, then ignored the club doctor's advice and attended a third-team game at Guildford despite suffering from a heavy cold. Returning home to Hendon, he was diagnosed with pneumonia, and on the first Saturday in January, spectators all over the country setting out for matches were shocked to see newspaper billboards reading 'Herbert Chapman dead'. He was only 55 and, according to trainer Tom Whittaker, 'had worked himself to a standstill'.

The home game that day against Sheffield Wednesday, a 1-1 draw, went ahead amid an understandably muted atmosphere, although one of the biggest crowds of the season had turned out to pay their respects. Arsenal players were in tears in the dressing-room.

An English Heritage blue plaque now marks Chapman's house at 6 Haslemere Avenue, Hendon, close to the North Circular Road. A bronze bust by Sir Jacob Epstein sat in the entrance hall at Highbury for many years and remained there after the conversion into flats, while a replica was installed at the directors' entrance to the Emirates Stadium, where a statue also stands outside.

Chapman would no doubt have felt that the best tribute would be to continue the run of success he had begun, and Arsenal did so almost up until the Second World War. For the rest of the 1933/34 season, Joe Shaw became caretaker manager with a general manager in the rotund form of George Allison, who then took the reins for the following season.

Allison was a board member, journalist and broadcaster, who must have struggled to remain neutral while describing the 1927 FA Cup Final defeat by Cardiff for BBC radio. He was regarded as personable enough, although players inclined to compare him to his predecessor naturally felt he came up short, and clearly Whittaker did much of the tactical work. The pair had inherited a wonderful squad, although one drawing to the end of its natural cycle.

Following the mournful Sheffield Wednesday match, there were three successive defeats, including newly promoted Tottenham's 3-1 win at Highbury in front of a 68,828 crowd, before the team rallied. Losing only two more matches from 16, they finished three points ahead of Huddersfield, with Spurs third.

The number of goals declined to 75 but shot up again as a title hat-trick was completed the following season. In March 1934, two months after Chapman's death, powerful centre-forward Ted Drake had arrived from his local club Southampton for what turned out to be the bargain price of £6,500. Scoring seven times in ten games at the end of the season indicated his potential, fully realised in the next campaign.

His 42 in 41 games during 1934/35 remains the club record, as does scoring all seven on an astonishing December afternoon at Villa Park the following season (one other effort hit the bar).

In the meantime, in November 1934, the future Chelsea manager was one of seven Arsenal players who took part in the infamous Battle of Highbury, in which England beat the world champions Italy 3-2. Drake infuriated the Italians early on with a challenge that led to them playing with ten men for most of the game and club-mate Hapgood was one of those who suffered in retaliation, having his nose broken by a carefully aimed elbow.

It was the fourth time Highbury had staged an England game, and the stadium was about to be further improved with a new East Stand and cover for the North Bank. When Spurs visited one month before the Italy game, 70,544 were present and for once Tottenham were sent back down the Seven Sisters Road with tails between legs, beaten 5-1 and on their way to relegation in their dramatic collapse from third place to 22nd.

A new high was then set, never to be broken at Highbury, when 73,295 were present in March to see what turned out to be a goalless draw against principal championship rivals Sunderland.

The Wearsiders, finishing four points behind at the top of the table, had their revenge as champions the following year. Arsenal, despite Drake's 24 goals in 26 games, dropped to sixth in the league but won the FA Cup again, when he scored the only goal of another low-scoring final, against Sheffield United.

In 1936/37 they finished third, five points behind champions Manchester City, before claiming one more title the following year – only just, when rivals Wolves lost their final match.

Naturally, the first-team had evolved in five years since Chapman's death. Grown too: 29 players were used in the 1938 title success. By the end of that campaign, Yorkshireman George Swindin – later to become manager – was the most regular of three goalkeepers and although the back three of Male, Roberts and Hapgood remained, James (retired the previous season), Jack (retired to manage Southend in 1934) and Lambert (sold to Fulham in 1933) had gone. Of the wingers, Hulme played only a handful of games but the younger Bastin was still prominent.

Wilf Copping, a terrifying Yorkshireman who played his part in the Battle of Highbury, and 'Gentleman' Jack Crayston were the complementary first-choice wing-halves for the best part of five years from 1934. Other well-known names included the Compton brothers, full-back Leslie and winger Denis, and centre-half Bernard Joy, Great Britain captain at the 1936 Olympics, the last amateur international to win a full England cap and a future football correspondent of London's *Evening Standard*.

For the 1938/39 season, Allison created a sensation by adding to the club's rapidly rising debt in paying a world-record £14,000 for Wolves' Welsh inside-forward Bryn Jones, who at Molineux had just been denied a championship medal by his new club. Players like Hapgood and Bastin felt Jones was more of what these days would be called a second striker than the playmaker needed to replace James and his first season was not a great success, Arsenal's 55 goals being their lowest since 1925 as they dropped to fifth place.

It had been a glorious decade for the club, brought to a premature end in the first days of September when after Drake scored four goals in the 5-2 win over Sunderland, Prime Minister Neville Chamberlain went on the radio to announce that following the German invasion of Poland there would not, after all, be 'peace in our time'.

* * * * *

Arsenal, Chelsea and Tottenham may have established themselves as London's big three early on, but by the time of the Second World War, three other clubs had reached the top division – two of whom, Brentford and Charlton, would finish the Thirties with the best league results in their history.

West Ham were the other Londoners to ascend to Division One, a rise which took them only three seasons. Joining the Football League in the first post-war season of 1919/20 gave them derbies against Tottenham, Fulham and Orient. Spurs, the champions-elect, were beaten 2-1 with a double by Syd Puddefoot in March, watched by 30,000 – the Boleyn Ground's best crowd yet. That followed two defeats in a week by Clapton Orient, after winning and then losing against Fulham.

From the inauspicious beginnings of a 1-1 draw at home to Lincoln City on 30 August and a 7-0 defeat at Barnsley two days later, the campaign quickly improved, finishing in seventh place, one behind Fulham. Local lad Puddefoot carried on where he had left off before the war, and indeed during it, scoring five against Arsenal on Boxing Day 1915 and seven in the 11-0 win over Crystal Palace (April 1918) in war-time London Combination matches.

In the first league campaign, he was comfortably top scorer with 21 and scored another five in FA Cup wins over Southampton and Bury before Spurs ended the run with a 3-0 win at White Hart Lane.

As goals from other players were in short supply over the first three seasons, Puddefoot was the key figure and it was just as well the club had turned down Sunderland's offer for him in the last season before the war. From seventh place in 1919/20, they improved in successive seasons to fifth, fourth and then second behind Notts County.

It was ironic that promotion came in the season 1922/23, after Puddefoot departed, leaving supporters bewildered by both the sale and his choice of club: Falkirk. (He would return briefly, almost ten years later). Fortunately, an obvious replacement had emerged in Vic Watson, a Cambridgeshire man who became the club's greatest goalscorer.

A dozen of his 298 league goals came in Puddefoot's last season, whereupon he took over as principal striker in the momentous campaign that finished with promotion and the first Wembley FA Cup Final.

Oddly, a poor start was made with only two wins before the middle of October. Doing the double over Clapton Orient in successive weeks was the start of a tremendous league run, in which a Boxing Day defeat at home to Manchester United (after winning at Old Trafford the day before) was the only loss until mid-April.

In the FA Cup, meanwhile, Watson and his little inside-left Billy Moore saw off Hull City in the first round and Third

Division Brighton (after a replay), before Plymouth were beaten 2-0. The quarter-final against Second Division rivals Southampton proved a protracted affair, with 1-1 draws away and then at home, followed by a 1-0 win at neutral Villa Park.

There were only five days left before the semi-final against Derby County, happily to be played in London at Stamford Bridge and once again avoiding First Division opposition. Derby had had the better of the league games early in the season, and had just knocked out Spurs at White Hart Lane, but the Hammers were much improved and overwhelmed them from the start, building on two quick goals to win 5-2, with inside-forwards Moore and Billy Brown each scoring twice. The East Enders were in the cup final against Bolton Wanderers and, for the first time, that meant Wembley.

The organisers of the hugely ambitious British Empire Exhibition planned for 1923/24 knew they would have a problem familiar these days to the bodies charged with running modern sporting events in handsome new stadia: what to do with them afterwards. This one was solved in part by contacting the Football Association, who had for some time been pondering the idea of a new home for the cup final.

Remote from the growing traffic problems of central London and on the right side of the capital for visitors from the North, Midlands and West, suburban Wembley had an obvious appeal.

The FA, to its credit, resolved to act and in the spring of 1921 signed a 21-year lease to stage the FA Cup Final on a site known as 'Watkin's Folly' after the man who wanted to build London's equivalent to the Eiffel Tower there but belatedly discovered that the foundations would simply not support it.

The nation proved rather keener to support a national sports stadium, which with its iconic twin towers and capacity of 127,000 was finished in an impressive 300 days, at a cost of £750,000, just in time for the 1923 final.

'At last we have a ground for everyone who wants to see the cup final,' declared FA secretary Frederick Wall, which proved a catastrophic underestimate – like the decision not to make the game all-ticket.

Had two provincial clubs reached the final, as was normally the case, perhaps the FA would have got away with it. As it was, West Ham's participation in the biggest game of their 28-year history and the enormous interest in the new venue led to chaos.

It has been estimated that anything from 200-300,000 people turned up but, of course, nobody could count them. The official number, adding ticket holders to those who paid before the turnstiles were broken down, was 126,047 – almost 1,000 below capacity.

With the gates theoretically shut 75 minutes before scheduled kick-off, tens of thousands continued to pour in, under or over gates, turnstiles and walls. The Bolton team, having long abandoned their transport, reportedly came across two West Ham fans with a shovel, tunnelling in.

As crowds pressed from behind in the standing areas, all that those at the front could do was spill on to the pitch. When King George V arrived, a shocked secretary Wall told him: 'I fear, Sir, that the match may not be played.' But somewhere out in the middle, the band of the Grenadier and Irish Guards played on and when they struck up the national anthem a first semblance of order was restored.

Wall's version of events was that thousands of what he called 'trespassers' on the pitch then surged towards the Royal Box for a close-up of the King and were directed down the tunnel to the exhibition grounds.

The popular version is that the game only came to be played because of one man and his horse. PC George Scorey had dropped in at Rochester Row police station and been told to get to Wembley as fast as Billy – or Billie – would carry him.

That was not fast at all once he saw the crowds, but after finally making it on to the pitch, he said in a BBC radio interview years later: 'All I could see was a sea of heads. It looked an impossible task but, with His Majesty looking down, I knew the game had to go ahead somehow... I'm positive that any credit I received was due to Billy. He seemed to understand exactly what was wanted of him. The other factor was the general good temper of the crowd.'

In the same interview, PC Scorey is quoted as saying that Billy/ Billie may have received more attention 'because he was white', yet years later, in 1957, he dismissed the whole myth of the 'white horse final', telling an acquaintance in Chislehurst that the horse was a grey and that film had been overexposed in the newsreels and photographs to make him stand out.

Whoever deserves the credit and whatever the colour of the horse, the game kicked off at last, almost an hour late and with spectators milling round the touchlines.

West Ham: Hufton; Henderson, Young; Bishop, Kay, Tresadern; Richards, Brown, Watson, Moore, Ruffel.

When the Irons fell behind after only two minutes, the identity of the scorer was hardly unexpected: David Jack, later of Arsenal, had been the marksman in all three 1-0 victories that had taken Bolton past Huddersfield, Charlton and Sheffield United to get them to Wembley. Now he beat Ted Hufton in the West Ham goal.

Barely ten minutes later the crowd pressed forward, spilling on to the pitch and causing play to be suspended for several minutes. At half-time, there seemed so little chance of getting the players as far as the dressing rooms that the referee merely kept them on the pitch for five minutes and restarted.

The London side's fortunes did not improve, Watson missing their few chances, and they protested in vain that Bolton's second goal had been assisted by a spectator and not actually crossed the line.

Even without the hindsight of later disasters at Bolton, Ibrox, Hillsborough and elsewhere, it is obvious that the outcome in 1923 could have been far more serious than it was. There were no fatalities despite several hundred injuries being reported and 22 people needing hospital treatment. 'The corridors and tunnel leading from the dressing rooms to the pitch were like ARP casualty stations,' one Bolton player recalled later.

'Cup Final Chaos That Was Nearly a Disaster' the *Sunday Pictorial* headlined, while by Monday the papers were demanding to know who should bear responsibility. They variously decided upon the supporters *(Daily Express),* police, stewards and the FA *(Daily Mirror)* and police planning *(Daily Herald).*

Sir Frank Swettenham, a 73-year-old colonial official given space for a letter in *The Times,* was not over-critical of the hoi-polloi and pointed out that 'I was never asked for my entrance or seat tickets and have them still'.

The football authorities were able to blame the British Empire Exhibition organisers, claiming that ticketing, police and crowd control were all down to them. The FA did, however, agree that future finals should be all-ticket, although staging them at Wembley was soon called into question. Needing far more events to support it, the stadium came to be declared unviable and was placed into administration before entrepreneur Arthur Elvin bought it and then sold it back to the owners in exchange for shares. He became chairman of the company, later improving the financial prospects by introducing greyhound racing and speedway there.

For West Ham, the final had quickly to be forgotten. Having fallen behind with their league fixtures, Syd King's team had to play nine of them in 23 days before the final, knowing there would still be two more afterwards.

By using his strongest side right up to the final, he ensured the Hammers kept in contention for promotion, and winning 2-0 at Fulham only two days after the final was the key result. Finishing runners-up to Notts County, they pipped Leicester City on goal average, entirely through having won 6-0 away to them in February with a hat-trick by Moore, who finished with 15 goals to Watson's 22.

The first season in the top division was a struggle mainly because of injury to Watson, who played no more than 11 games. The team managed only 40 goals in 42 matches, yet still finished as London's highest placed club for the first time, in 13th place, with Tottenham, Arsenal and relegated Chelsea all beneath them.

So London's four-pronged attack on the First Division lasted only one season, and apart from Arsenal's second place in 1925/26, the three survivors found it difficult for a while even to get anyone into the top ten. West Ham were top dogs the following season, finishing sixth and then again three years later in seventh, but at other times they were uncomfortably close to relegation, finally going down in 1932.

Even with Watson still knocking in the goals – 50 in 44 league and cup games was his best in 1929/30, when he was rightly recalled to the England team – the Hammers perished after taking only one point from the final ten games.

There was no prospect of a return to Wembley, although Tottenham's visit for a third-round tie in 1927 brought a Watson hat-trick, a new gate record of 44,417 and revenge for the previous season's 5-0 exit at White Hart Lane. (The club have continued to insist on 42,322 against the same opposition in 1970 as Upton Park's highest crowd, but Hammers historians have verified the earlier figure.)

Chelsea, twice, and Arsenal ended any cup hopes in successive seasons from 1930–32 and ironically the best run came in the first season back in the Second Division, 1932/33, at the same time as the possibility of going straight through the trapdoor into the Third Division South. Bottom on Good Friday, they began a revival the following day, continued it on Easter Monday and were seen to safety by four successive wins, one of them at home to Spurs.

In the cup Corinthians, West Bromwich, Brighton and Birmingham were all beaten before a semi-final against reigning First Division champions Everton at Molineux, lost 2-1 despite the inevitable goal by Watson. The season was soured by the sacking in November of Syd King, who two months later committed suicide in St Mary's Hospital, Plaistow 'while of unsound mind'.

After relegation, new manager Charlie Paynter oversaw an improvement until the war without quite managing a return to the higher division. Third behind champions Brentford and Bolton in 1935 was the best effort, losing out on goal average as Watson left for one season at Southampton before retiring with a West Ham record of 326 in 505 games.

The next season, 1935/36, the Hammers were fourth as Charlton Athletic, like Brentford before them, went up, boosting London's representation in the First Division to four once more.

* * * * *

Although profiting from Woolwich Arsenal's departure to north London, **Charlton** had been left behind amid the great expansion of 1920/21. Immediately after the war, they joined the Kent League for a single season before becoming professional and appointing as manager Walter Rayner from Tottenham, the club that had designs on them as a nursery club (but later opted for Northfleet further down the Thames instead).

The Southern League, having lost 22 clubs to the new Football League Third Division in 1920, was happy to welcome ambitious Charlton, who found themselves in a hotch-potch 14-team division with nine reserve teams plus Aberdare Athletic, Boscombe, Chatham Town and Thornycrofts.

Winning, drawing and losing eight of their 24 games, they finished in eighth place, suggesting they were not yet ready for the Football League, but when the opportunity arose at the end of the season they grasped it, being voted in ahead of Bath City (who never ever made the jump). Thus the Addicks – a nickname ascribed to a local fishmonger's habit of supplying the players with haddock after games – ascended to a new level for the third successive year to begin league derbies against QPR, Brentford and Millwall.

Was it too much too soon? Probably so. The Valley needed thousands of pounds spending on it and, within a year of the opening Football League game, won 1-0 at home to Exeter City, the secretary was handing in his resignation, complaining that he could 'hardly ever' persuade the chairman to pay outstanding bills.

With the team regularly in the lower half of the table, crowds soon dropped off from an encouraging 15,000 at that first match, although they came back briefly for the uplifting FA Cup run of 1922/23. After home wins in the qualifying rounds over Northampton and Darlington, Charlton were given no chance in the first round proper away to Manchester City, one of the country's top ten clubs.

'Charlton make history up north' reported the *Kentish Independent* after a remarkable 2-1 win. The winning goal came from the bandaged head of centre-half Arthur Whalley, one of the players banned for match-fixing following the Manchester United-Liverpool scandal of 1915, but allowed to return after the war.

The second round brought a home tie against Preston, the previous season's beaten finalists, and a record 22,490 saw them beaten 2-0 with goals by Steve Smith and Bert Goodman after the visitors had missed a penalty. Next up were West Bromwich, another First Division club with a crop of internationals, destined to finish seventh that season. Goodman scored the only goal in front of a delirious crowd of more than 31,000 and Charlton were in the quarter-finals after knocking out three top-division clubs in succession.

Three other London teams also made the last eight – West Ham, QPR and Tottenham – but all four were kept apart in the draw, which gave Charlton home advantage again, this time against Bolton Wanderers.

For the third time in little over a month, The Valley's attendance record was broken, as 42,023 packed in, which would have serious consequences.

In the second half, by which time David Jack had scored for the visitors, fences and railings gave way and spectators spilled on to the pitch, leaving children among those unconscious. A number of people were taken to hospital but fortunately there were no serious casualties. There was no further scoring and, as we have seen, Bolton went on to Wembley, where they would encounter even more chaotic scenes.

The brief boost to Charlton's finances had no lasting effect and for the following season the bizarre decision was taken to move four miles away to Catford, which would prove even worse than the exodus to Selhurst Park 63 years later. The club shared The Mount with local amateurs Catford South End, even adopting their colours of light and dark blue stripes, but in a bad winter crowds were so poor that they were soon back at The Valley, where the reserves had continued to play.

Alex 'Sandy' MacFarlane came in as the latest in a long line of former Scottish internationals recruited by London clubs as manager, but in his first season the Addicks were bottom but one of the division and had to apply for re-election with QPR. MacFarlane left for a year to manage Dundee, then returned to oversee an unexpected change in fortunes and promotion in 1928/29, winning the division on goal average from neighbouring Crystal Palace, to replace Clapton Orient. For all the upheaval, financial and geographical, the club had progressed in ten years from the Kent League to the Football League Second Division.

Fred Whitlow, a Bristolian centre-forward who had moved to Dundee with MacFarlane, returned to score 23 goals and Wilson Lennox's 18 included all five in the 5-2 victory at Exeter. Whitlow then hit another 27 in the Second Division, which began with 25,000 watching the win over Cardiff City, and finished sandwiched between Tottenham and Millwall (promoted the season before) in 13th place. After no wins against their closest neighbours in the last 12 meetings in the lower division, there was also the satisfaction of two draws at The Valley and The Den.

For the next two seasons, Millwall finished one place above them until, in 1932/33, Charlton slumped to the bottom and were relegated with Chesterfield. Changing the official nickname to the Robins – hence the uninspiring 'Red Red Robin' theme tune that still greets the team today – was supposed to herald a change of luck, but the appointment of Jimmy Seed as manager proved rather more significant.

Having retired as a Sheffield Wednesday player, the former Tottenham FA Cup winner returned to London as manager of Orient and was lured south of the river by what he rightly perceived as greater potential after two difficult seasons in Clapton.

Seed benefited from some useful patronage. First he was installed at Orient for £12 a week thanks to Herbert Chapman, who called him the finest captain of the time at Sheffield Wednesday and was audaciously planning to make Orient into Arsenal's nursery club. When the football authorities rejected that proposal, Seed stayed on and got to know Albert Gliksten and his brother Stanley, a pair of timber merchants who were on the advisory committee put in place at Orient by the official receiver.

Later in 1931, the Glikstens began another London football dynasty by buying a controlling interest in Charlton, where MacFarlane resigned as manager during the relegation season of 1932/33. At Arsenal's championship banquet that summer, an alphabetical coincidence had the representatives of Charlton and Clapton Orient next to each other and Seed suggested himself to Albert Gliksten as MacFarlane's successor.

Thus his first campaign at The Valley in 1933/34 included two matches against his former club, one of them won and the other drawn, as Charlton finished fifth. Over the next three seasons, the club came close to pulling off one of the great feats of football history.

Winning 70 games out of 126 in that time took them from the Third Division South against the likes of Aldershot and Newport County to finish runners-up in the top division, only three points shy of champions Manchester City.

The Glikstens, having initially lavished £25,000 on new players, and far more on badly needed ground improvements, were no longer inclined to speculate in order to accumulate, a policy the family more or less pursued for the next 50 years.

Seed's first two signings cost £450 between them. He succeeded in similarly cost-effective recruitment and by developing an excellent scouting network, above all in his native North East. A key signing, Ralph Allen, the brother of Newcastle's 1932 FA Cup Final hero Jack, cost only £650 from Brentford and in 1934/35 scored 32 goals in 28 games from the team's record total of 103.

Top of the Third Division South table going into the new year, Charlton were briefly threatened by Coventry City, but held them in an exciting 3-3 draw at The Valley, watched by 25,000, and finished eight points clear of Reading as Coventry faded.

Seed promised to give the same players a chance back in the Second Division, which must have pleased the owners, who nevertheless allowed £3,250 to be spent on a future captain and England wing-half, Don Welsh from Torquay United.

Another significant arrival, out of tragedy, was that of someone who would go on to become the club's greatest player. Early in that first promotion season, football was stunned by the death of Scottish goalkeeper Alex Wright in a swimming accident the morning after Charlton had won away to Welsh's Torquay.

Harry Wright (no relation) took over first-team duty, and manager Seed followed up his brother's recommendation to try out a big Durham man called Sam Bartram, who had finally accepted he was a goalkeeper after failing a trial with Reading as a wing-half, the position he played for Sunderland Schools.

The initial four-week trial in London was inglorious, beginning as it did with the concession of ten goals in two reserve games. Seed told him there was much work to be done, which a grateful Bartram threw himself into, and from January 1935 he kept the first-team jersey for most of the next 20 years.

His style was ahead of his time. Using the confidence gained from playing in outfield positions, he would come out of the penalty area to pass and head the ball, and even take throw-ins.

A 4-0 win against Burnley was the first of 21 unbeaten home games in the Second Division and, by January, Charlton were briefly top of the table, having attracted 32,000 for a 2-2 draw with West Ham. On Easter Monday, 46,713 saw Spurs beaten at The Valley and after a 3-1 win at Upton Park, where winger Harold Hobbis scored from the halfway line, Seed's team needed only a draw from the final game at home to Port Vale, who had to win to avoid relegation.

A 1-1 scoreline brought promotion for the second successive season, Hobbis finishing top scorer with 23 and earning two caps on England's summer tour.

Bartram's influence was huge the following season in the top division, where he played every game and the team conceded just 13 goals in their 21 home matches, losing only to Arsenal. The old Woolwich residents returned to their former manor in October to inflict a 2-0 defeat and end an unbeaten home run of 18 months' duration. Denis Compton scored the second goal in front of a crowd of 68,160, The Valley's capacity having been extended by concreting the huge east terrace with 132 steps.

By the time of the return game in February, a 1-1 draw watched by 60,568, Charlton were top of the table and only then did they falter, suffering a 5-0 defeat at Derby and allowing Manchester City to take the lead. City, unbeaten from Christmas onwards after sitting in mid-table, held on to win the title by three points, Charlton assuring themselves of second place ahead of Arsenal by beating Brentford 2-1 on the final day.

The Derby defeat and a 6-1 loss to Wolves in November notwithstanding, it was defensive strength that underpinned what is still their highest ever position in the top division. Scoring 58 was the worst return of any team in the top 12, but only Arsenal could match the 49 conceded. Seed had sold Ralph Allen to Reading, believing he was one of the few who would not be capable of another step up in class, and the lack of a real scorer was illustrated by George Tadman, a £1,000 signing from Gillingham, finishing top of the list with only 11 goals.

Seventeen years on from the Kent League, it was still an astonishing achievement, as was the level of crowd support, which in February 1938 reached a new high of 75,031 for the drawn FA Cup fifth-round tie against Second Division Aston Villa.

It is difficult to imagine that Charlton could have achieved as much had Henry Norris not moved the Woolwich club north of the river two decades earlier, but when Arsenal regained their title in 1938 Charlton were only six points behind them in fourth place. In the final season before the war, they finished three points above them in third.

Goalscoring improved to 65 and then 75 and how much greater might it, and Charlton's history, have been had Seed succeeded with an audacious transfer bid in November 1938? That month, he offered Stoke City £13,000 for an unsettled Stanley Matthews, which would have been close to the world record just set by Arsenal for Bryn Jones.

Whether Albert Gliksten would actually have coughed up seems unlikely. 'Have you gone mad?' he asked his manager, who was then told by Stoke that there would be no sale at any price. Charlton's chairman also refused to countenance a new stand at that time and claimed once war was declared that, like signing Matthews, it would have been 'money down the drain'.

* * * * *

For **Brentford** as well as Charlton, this became the most successful period in history. Despite a surprise title win in the 1918/19 war-time London Combination, thanks in part to guests like Cardiff's captain Fred Keenor, Brentford had similarly modest beginnings, joining Crystal Palace, QPR , Millwall and the rest in the new Third Division of 1920.

League football started with a 3-0 defeat by Exeter, in which Patsy Hendren and Jack Durston were both missing owing to a crucial Middlesex match against Surrey at Lord's. The most eagerly awaited and best- attended games in that inaugural season were the two Christmas fixtures against QPR, watched by a total of 41,379 spectators – although both were lost.

While Rangers were chasing Palace at the top of the table, Brentford struggled at the other end and were forced eventually to apply for re-election with Gillingham, the only team beneath them. Both survived but the experience prompted the club's directors to release their hold over team matters and appoint a new manager, Archie Mitchell, the experienced QPR centre-half.

In a difficult decade, ninth place in 1922 was the only top-ten finish, which hardly hinted at a sudden improvement at the start of the Thirties. It began with an extraordinary record during 1929/30, becoming the first team since the expansion to four divisions to win every home game.

The manager by then was Harry Curtis, a former Football League referee who was in charge at Gillingham for three years, then held the same position at Brentford from 1926–49 and was voted the club's greatest manager in 2013.

Whether or not it was due to his close observation from refereeing days, Curtis could certainly spot a player and especially a goalscorer. In 1929, he signed the former Spurs centre-forward Billy Lane from Reading, who scored a record 33 goals in that historic season.

As promotion became a real possibility on the back of immaculate home form, a new record crowd of 21,966 turned out to see Fulham beaten, like all visitors before and after them. At 5-1, it was one of the easier games. Happily, the full set was completed with a 3-0 victory over their other local rivals QPR, with more than 18,000 present. The full home record was 21-0-0, with goals of 66-12.

Alas, Plymouth Argyle, although beaten 3-0 at Griffin Park in January, had a much better away record and denied the Bees promotion by seven points.

After third place next season, the disappointment of finishing fifth in 1931/32 led Curtis to offer his resignation. It was rejected and the following season he revamped the team and earned the longed-for promotion.

Beating QPR 3-2 at White City was the best of starts, followed by six more wins in succession. Centre-forward Jack Holliday from Middlesbrough proved a hugely successful replacement for Lane, who joined Watford and in 1933 scored a historic hat-trick in under three minutes against Clapton Orient. Curtis later brought him back to Brentford as assistant and Lane also managed Brighton from 1951–61.

Lane's Brentford record of 33 league goals did not last long, however. Holliday beat it by four and went on to become the club's third-highest goalscorer of all time behind 1950s combo Jim Towers and George Francis.

At Luton in February, Holliday scored all Brentford's goals in a 5-5 draw and followed up with four in a 7-3 win over Cardiff.

Appropriately, it was Holliday who scored the winner in the 2-1 success at Brighton that confirmed the Bees would finish top ahead of Exeter and Norwich.

His 27 goals the following season ensured fourth place, only a point shy of promotion after a crucial late-season loss at Millwall. But in 1934/35 came a second promotion in three years.

West Ham were beaten 4-1 for the second successive season early on. In the new year, a new high of 26,079 saw Newcastle dispatched 3-0 and the 8-0 win over Port Vale on Easter Saturday set another record. Two days later, a 3-2 win at Bradford Park Avenue after being 2-0 down cemented promotion to the top division for one of the capital's least fashionable clubs with three games to spare.

To West Ham's annoyance, one of those games was lost at Bolton in front of more than 46,000, enabling the Lancashire side to pip the Hammers for the second promotion place on goal average. Holliday had continued on his merry way with 25 goals, giving him 90 in three seasons.

What followed was more even extraordinary than before: fifth place and then two sixth positions in the top division, the first of those seasons making the Bees the top London club, a point above Arsenal.

For their debut season at the highest level, further ground improvement took the capacity above 30,000 and a new record crowd of 33,481 was soon set to see Huddersfield Town beaten.

Setbacks including a 5-1 defeat at home to Sunderland, the eventual champions, and a 6-1 loss at Grimsby brought relegation concerns, but the board responded by making money available to Curtis, who again demonstrated his ability to spend it wisely by securing Scottish international centre-forward Dave McCulloch from Hearts. He was able to take some of the weight from Holliday, scoring a goal a game in his 26 matches as the former Middlesbrough man moved to inside-forward.

Thus fortified, a strong second half of the season followed and by remaining undefeated in the last 12 games, including a 2-1 win over Chelsea (33,468) and a 1-1 draw at Highbury, Brentford achieved what would remain the highest finish in their history. A famous season finished with league runners-up Derby County beaten 6-0 at Griffin Park, McCulloch (Scotland's centre-forward against England at Wembley that year) scoring four times.

In addition, they had beaten the champions Sunderland 3-1 away as revenge for the heavy home defeat and achieved the first of several notable results against FA Cup winners Arsenal, 2-1 at home.

Early the following season, 1936/37, Curtis's team again took three points out of four from Arsenal, as well as beating newly promoted Charlton 4-2. The two London rivals still finished above them, both in the top three, despite McCulloch's 31 goals.

Brentford were being talked about as never before, although less desirable publicity followed a tour of Germany when their players were photographed giving the Nazi salute before a game against Schalke 04.

In 1937/38, not only was sixth place maintained but a rare FA Cup run extended as far as the quarter-finals, leading some to describe it as the best season of all. George Eastham, an England international and father of the future Arsenal midfielder, was signed from Bolton, and a 5-2 win over Charlton in mid-October took Brentford to the top of the table.

They were still there going into the start of the FA Cup programme in January, which brought victories over Fulham (3-1) and Portsmouth (2-1), watched by 36,718, then Manchester United (2-0). The quarter-final brought a fourth successive home draw against Preston and another record crowd of 37,586, who saw luck run out in a 3-0 defeat.

As often happens during a cup run, league form faltered and although Arsenal were beaten twice over Easter, the results neither deprived the north Londoners of the title nor kept Brentford any higher than sixth when the final two games were lost.

The good times ended the following season, during which McCulloch (for £9,500 to Derby) and Eastham were sold. Gates dropped and the team sank to the bottom of the table in autumn, before recovering to ensure safety in 18th place.

Arsenal – again – Charlton and Chelsea (who finished 20th) were all beaten at Griffin Park, but in the final game of the season at Highbury (footage of which was used in the film *The Arsenal Stadium Mystery*), the home team at last achieved some revenge with their first win over the troublesome Bees in eight attempts. Nobody managed ten goals and the last home gate was under 13,000. Brentford had peaked, but what a peak it was.

* * * * *

Thus **Chelsea** were eclipsed by less fashionable western rivals in what was overall a poor decade for the club. The Twenties too had been distinctly mixed, only delivering intermittently the sort of results merited by huge crowds, even in Division Two.

Under long-serving Scottish manager David Calderhead, they were relegated from the top division in 1924, returning six years later with three of Scotland's 1928 'Wembley Wizards' in the side. While Alex James was inspiring Arsenal towards their dominant decade, Hughie Gallacher and Alex Jackson were attempting to do the same for Chelsea with less success and unhappy endings. Both joined the club in 1930, from Newcastle and Huddersfield respectively, linking up with defender Tommy Law, who had also played in the Scots' sensational 5-1 win at Wembley, where the mercurial Jackson scored a hat-trick from outside-right.

Gallacher, the feisty, diminutive centre-forward – a more talented David Speedie perhaps – ended up as top scorer for four seasons running with 14, 30, 19 and 16 goals in league and cup, despite regular suspensions.

While James's Arsenal were champions three times and runners-up once in those four campaigns, however, Chelsea's finishing positions were 12th, 12th, 18th and 19th. In each of the last two seasons, they avoided relegation by only two points and in November 1934 Gallacher, declared bankrupt after a costly divorce, was sold to Derby County. He committed suicide in 1957.

Jackson, having been made captain, was transfer-listed after ordering drinks for the whole team on room service at a

Manchester hotel. He departed for non-league football with Ashton and then Margate in 1932, the year of Chelsea's best cup run for a dozen years. As previously mentioned, they went as far as the semi-final, beating West Ham and Liverpool along the way, but failed to join Arsenal in the final, losing 2-1 to Gallacher's old club Newcastle at Leeds Road, Huddersfield.

After Leslie Knighton, once an undistinguished manager of Arsenal, succeeded a disenchanted Calderhead, the best effort in the league was eighth place in 1935/36, during which the club's all-time attendance record was set with a crowd of 82,905 for the derby against Knighton's former employers.

In autumn 1937, his team beat Brentford to lead the table briefly but then won only two of the next 22 games and ended up tenth. It summed up the decade when the Blues ended the last full season before the war in 20th place, this time a single point above relegation.

* * * * *

Local derbies against **Fulham** stayed on hold for the first four seasons after the First World War, during which time Chelsea's nearest neighbours were mostly what they had been before it, a solid mid-table Second Division side. Under Phil Kelso, another former Arsenal manager, the Cottagers then slumped into the bottom three in 1923/24 and he left.

Former player Andy Ducat, an England international at both football and cricket, was therefore in charge for the resumption of hostilities with Chelsea but in the four seasons that the teams met, they were involved at opposite ends of the table. Although benefiting from big crowds in the derbies at home and away, Fulham failed to win a single one of the eight games and the meetings ended with their relegation in 1928.

Joe Bradshaw was manager by that time and despite Sid Elliott scoring 26 goals, a dreadful away record meant they had only South Shields below them. One consolation came in the FA Cup run of 1926, when both Everton and Liverpool were beaten before a 2-1 quarter-final defeat at home to Manchester United in front of almost 29,000.

The only other meetings with Chelsea in the inter-war years turned out to be in the cup, in one of which Fulham finally managed only their second success in 14 derbies dating back to 1910. It was one of the worst records between any two London clubs and subsequent fixtures have not greatly improved it.

At least Fulham returned to the Second Division in 1931/32, a campaign that began with a 5-3 win over Coventry and continued in high-scoring fashion. By the end of it they had scored 111 times, 43 of them in 39 games by Frank 'Bonzo' Newton from Stockport County, setting a new club record. He was backed up by 32 by Jim Hammond as Torquay were beaten 10-2 and Thames (of whom more shortly) 8-0.

Twelve months later, Fulham were only half a dozen points away from preceding Charlton's feat of going from the Third Division straight to the First. They scored as many goals (78) as the Second Division champions Stoke, but had Spurs in front of them too and so were denied another promotion.

Even in the lower divisions Fulham had two England internationals, Albert Barrett and Len Oliver, among their half-backs. South African forward Frank Osborne, later to manage them, had won the club's first England cap in 1922 before being sold to Spurs. In 1933, outside-left Johnny Arnold played for England against Scotland, becoming a double international like former manager and Surrey batsman Ducat, as he had opened the batting against New Zealand at Lord's in 1931. Yet Arnold was only picked once at each sport.

In the remaining years until the war, Fulham reverted to mid-table status and found first Brentford and then Charlton beating them into the top division.

* * * * *

A few miles north, **QPR** found it impossible to climb any higher than the Third Division South. From a promising Football League debut in 1920/21, in third place and with the bonus of a famous 2-0 FA Cup win at home to Arsenal, they slowly subsided into mid-table and worse, ending up bottom and forced to apply for re-election twice in three years from 1924–26 after Arthur Chandler was sold to Leicester, whose record goalscorer he became.

A change of colours from unlucky green to blue and white hoops brought an improvement culminating in third place in 1930, when George Goddard scored 37 goals, but finance was a perennial problem.

Although 20,000 had watched the Arsenal cup tie and would turn up for games against fellow West Londoners, the average was less than half that number, prompting a move up the road to White City stadium for the 1931/32 season.

A 3-0 loss in the first game to Bournemouth, watched by a crowd of 18,907, followed by only one win in the next dozen matches dampened enthusiasm before a run of wins re-ignited it. For Leeds United's visit in the FA Cup third round in January 1932 the crowd was 41,097, which remains a club record.

In two seasons at the new venue, however, while continuing to maintain Loftus Road, a loss of some £7,000 was reported and the experiment was discontinued.

It did not help that closest rivals Fulham and Brentford were champions in those two years and although there were no relegation worries in the remaining seasons until the war, Charlton and Millwall also made the jump while Rangers' best efforts were finishing fourth twice and then third in 1938, having led by nine points at one stage. But their time would come, soon after the war.

* * * * *

The frustration for **Crystal Palace** in this period was that having made a spectacular start to their Football League career, becoming the first-ever Third Division champions in 1921, they were relegated within four years and spent the rest of the inter-war period vainly attempting to reach such heights again.

Palace's first league match, on 28 August 1920, may have come fully 15 years after they originally applied, and brought a long trip to Merthyr Town for a 2-1 defeat, but they recovered and overcame a two-week ground closure after fans came on to the pitch to protest at Southend's physical approach in a 3-2 defeat in November. Millwall were beaten twice, with 18,000 at The Nest for the home game, and an even bigger crowd saw Manchester City knocked out of the FA Cup before defeat by Hull.

From early in February, Palace then went unbeaten in 16 games, two of them drawn over Easter against closest rivals Southampton, who finished five points behind them. Scotsman John Conner led the way with 29 goals.

Manager Edmund Goodman, who had taken the job as far back as 1907, stayed until 1925 then reverted to secretary when four seasons in the bottom half of Division Two ended in relegation by a point in 1925.

The highlights of that period came in the FA Cup, above all in a stunning 6-0 third-round win at Everton in 1922, a result that has to be compared to the semi-final win over Liverpool 68 years later for dramatic impact.

John Whibley headed the first after four minutes and Bert Menlove made it two before half-time. After Everton's expected rally, Palace broke out to score four times more in last 20 minutes, through Conner twice, Menlove and Alan Wood.

It was arch-rivals Millwall who prevented any further glory, winning a replay at The Den in the next round. Two years later, First Division clubs Tottenham, the 1921 winners, and Notts County were knocked out in the final season at The Nest, where crowds had dropped to 6,000.

Nearby Selhurst Park, a former brickfield, was bought for £2,750 and built at a cost of more than ten times as much to yet another Leitch design, but with a huge bank behind one goal.

League performances had been nothing like the cup heroics and after finishing 14th, 16th and 15th before leaving The Nest, Selhurst was the venue for a drop from the Second Division that would take almost 40 years to reverse.

The opening game at the new ground, in August 1924, was a 1-0 defeat by The Wednesday, watched by a healthy 25,000, which turned out to be the highest crowd of a season that collapsed after Christmas when centre-half Jimmy Hamilton and principal goalscorer George Whitworth were injured.

Whitworth had been signed from Northampton after impressing while guesting for Palace in war-time and was good for 16 or 17 a season, totalling 50 in his 118 appearances before joining The Wednesday as relegation loomed.

After a decent enough start, Palace were fifth in November but only one of the final 14 games was won (against Chelsea) as the predicament steadily worsened. Home defeats by Fulham and Oldham in the last two matches proved crucial, Stoke finishing one point clear to save themselves.

Back in the Third Division South, an ordinary league campaign (13th place) was again salvaged by the FA Cup, in which Chelsea were beaten 2-1 in the fourth round before a record attendance of 41,586 that would stand until 1969. Centre-forward Percy Cherrett opened the scoring and inside-forward Alf Hawkins added a second just before half-time, with Chelsea only able to respond through a late goal by Albert Thain.

The powerful Cherrett was bought from Plymouth Argyle after the first four games in the lower division had been lost and he went on to score 65 times in 81 games.

Like all clubs, Palace were involved in a number of high-scoring games when the offside rule was changed for that season. Cherrett scored in the extraordinary 5-5 draw at home to his old club in November and made it seven in four cup ties when Palace visited Manchester City in the fifth round after beating Chelsea. His team put four past goalkeeper Jim Goodchild, but unfortunately the First Division side scored 11 – seven of them before half-time.

Selhurst staged a full international between England and Wales in March 1926, but although Palace improved and were normally a top-half team, the home crowd's hopes for a return to a higher grade failed to materialise.

Three second places were as close as they came. In 1928/29, it was Charlton who beat them to it on goal average, despite Palace defeating them at The Valley in March during a 17-game unbeaten run.

Two years later, Palace were eight points behind promoted Notts County despite a record haul of 46 league goals plus eight in the FA Cup by centre-forward Peter Simpson. Signed from Kettering Town, he hit a hat-trick on his debut against Norwich in September 1929 and finished that season with 37 from 35 matches. His eventual total before joining West Ham in 1935 was 165 in 195 appearances.

Regular changes of manager had no effect, Palace's third runners-up position not being achieved until the last season before the war, three points behind Newport.

* * * * *

For **Millwall Athletic**, who dropped the second part of their name in 1925, it was a time of establishing solid and occasionally over-excitable support in New Cross, rewarded with good home results and some FA Cup history.

The Den's reputation, both good and bad, was confirmed from the start of the club's Football League career. Their opening Third Division game in 1920, a 2-0 win over Bristol Rovers, watched by 25,000, was the first of 11 at home before Bob Hunter's team even conceded a goal.

More alarmingly, there was serious trouble there against Newport County in October, when the visiting goalkeeper – brave man – leapt into the crowd and was knocked down by a punch. The FA closed the ground for two weeks.

Not surprisingly, Millwall finished that inaugural season with the division's second-best defensive record, but a failure to score more goals meant ending up no higher than seventh.

When Palace, having moved on up as champions, returned to The Den for an FA Cup replay the following season, 35,000 packed in to see the Lions win. They went as far as the quarter-finals, beating Charlton by a year as the first Third Division team to progress that far, before losing to eventual winners Huddersfield Town.

For three seasons, it was a lack of goals that held them back in the league, the club's own match programme bewailing at one point: 'At some future date we hope to score a goal when playing at The Den.'

Things improved with third place in 1924, when promotion was on the cards as league leaders after 38 games. Taking no more than two points from the remaining four matches allowed Portsmouth to finish top, however. Plymouth were second, in the third year of their astonishing run of six successive years as runners-up in a division from which only one team were promoted.

That sequence concluded in 1927, with Millwall third again and putting down a marker for promotion the following year with another fine FA Cup run. Twice knocked out by Huddersfield earlier in the decade, they took revenge against the reigning First Division champions and then beat that season's Second Division winners Middlesbrough 2-0 as 44,250 watched the visitors miss two penalties.

In the quarter-final, it was Wilf Phillips of Millwall who missed a costly spot kick at The Den, allowing Southampton to draw 0-0 and win the replay.

Among the favourites for promotion along with perennial bridesmaids Plymouth in 1927/28, the Lions were rampant, scoring 127 goals (a Football League-record 87 of them in 21 home games) and finishing ten points clear. England international Jack Cock, described as a 'matinee idol', joined from Plymouth and scored 25 goals, which was only third highest behind little John Landelles from Grays Athletic (32) and Phillips (26).

A 6-1 defeat at Brentford in September proved something of an aberration and promotion was confirmed by beating Gillingham 6-0 in April, the 11th time the team had scored five goals or more.

Passing Fulham, who went down that season, the Lions met up with Tottenham, Chelsea, Orient and then promoted Charlton before, in 1932/33, there was a resumption of derbies with relegated West Ham, one of which was won and one lost. Having apparently established themselves in the higher division, they then suffered one of those unforeseen drops from seventh place that season to relegation.

By the final Saturday, Lincoln were already doomed but Millwall were a point ahead of Manchester United, their visitors to The Den. Looking nervous from the start, the home side went a goal down in only six minutes and conceded again early in the second half, after a linesman appeared to have flagged for offside. United held out comfortably and so were spared by one point from dropping to the third tier for the only time in their history.

Millwall still had two dramatic seasons to come before the war, starting with the FA Cup campaign of 1937. Under Charlie Hewitt, a Durham man who had played for Spurs and Crystal Palace before the first war, they made the most of home advantage in beating Aldershot (6-1), Gateshead (7-0, still a record) and then Second Division Fulham 2-0 in the third round.

The Fulham game attracted over 32,000 and there were 10,000 more to see First Division Chelsea drubbed 3-0 by what one report called 'an inspired home team revelling in the heavy going'.

The luck of the draw held for the fifth round, albeit bringing top-class opposition in Derby County, First Division runners-up the previous season and fielding half a dozen internationals. Press photographs showed spectators hanging from every vantage point. The official attendance of 48,672 was dangerously high and remained the ground record for evermore.

They saw another heroic performance, Millwall this time coming from behind after conceding a long free-kick and winning the tie in the 88th minute with a 25-yarder from inside-forward Jimmy McCartney.

Like neighbours Charlton in 1923, Millwall had made the quarter-finals as a Third Division side. Astonishingly, they would go one better, making history by knocking out a Manchester City side destined to be English champions that season by 2-0.

After six successive home ties, the Lions could hardly complain at leaving their Den at last for a semi-final against reigning champions Sunderland, although they were not pleased by the venue, inaccessible Huddersfield. About 10,000 Londoners still made the trip north while 20,000 turned up for a reserve game at home to West Ham, where word spread of a sensation after barely ten minutes. Skipper Dave Mangnall, only declared fit after treatment by a Peckham herbalist, had scored his ninth goal of the cup run.

Once Sunderland equalised, however, they dominated the rest of the game and won it when Scottish international Patsy Gallacher headed in a free-kick. 'I know what beaten but not disgraced means now,' reported the *Sunday Express* correspondent.

Sunderland went on to win the cup by beating Preston at Wembley and Millwall, eighth in the Third Division South, built on the excitement generated by their heroics to launch a promotion drive the following season.

Inspired by former England international inside-forward Jimmy Richardson from Newcastle United, they hit the top after 34 games and going into the final day led by a point from Watford and Bristol City, who were both at home while the Londoners took thousands of supporters with them to lowly Exeter.

Missing the injured Mangnall, they fell behind early but recovered in style with a hat-trick by winger Sid Rawlings contributing to a 5-1 triumph.

The highlight of the following season back in the Second Division, where they finished just below West Ham and Fulham in 14th place, was a 6-1 win after trailing at half-time away to Manchester City. The ever-unpredictable City had been relegated a year after losing at The Den but winning the First Division title.

* * * * *

Most decades in the 20th century were a struggle for **Orient**, under their various names, and the Twenties and Thirties were as bad as any. During that period, whether in the Second or Third divisions, they finished in the top ten just twice and were beset by financial worries most of the time.

What success there was came early, with seventh place in Division Two in an eventful 1920-21 season that was also notable for a visit from the Prince of Wales (later King Edward VIII) on one of the first occasions that royalty had attended a Football League match.

He and his brother the Duke of York (later King George VI) had watched Tottenham's win at Chelsea in October. In choosing Orient to visit as a mark of respect for their sacrifices in the First World War, the Prince of Wales might have been expected to opt for the early-season game against Cardiff City, who were competing in the Football League for the first time. Instead he picked an April fixture against Notts County, creating such interest that there were 20,000 inside the Millfields ground and twice as many outside.

The Prince sat next to the Mayor of Hackney, Herbert Morrison, an Orient supporter and shareholder who went on to become Home Secretary and then deputy prime minister to Clement Attlee in the Labour government of 1945–51. To Morrison's delight, the home side won 3-0 and by drawing their final home game a week later ensured what would be their highest finish at that level for more than 40 years.

Apart from a famous FA Cup win over Hughie Gallacher's Newcastle United in 1926, watched by a record crowd of 31,400, and England caps for speedy winger Owen Williams (1922/23) and centre-half John Townrow (1925/26), there was little else to cheer. After three successive seasons in 20th place, the Os finally went down in 1929.

Supporters became used to seeing the better players regularly sold. Within a year or so of becoming internationals, Williams and Townrow both left, for Middlesbrough and Chelsea respectively, and in 1925 big centre-forward Albert Pape departed in one of the most unusual transfers of all time.

Having only joined at the start of the 1924/25 season, and scored 11 goals in 25 games, he was sitting in his Orient kit before the match at Old Trafford in February when informed that promotion-chasing Manchester United had not only signed him for £2,000 but wanted him to play for them that afternoon. So at 2.15pm, he reluctantly left his now former team-mates, pulled on a United shirt for the first time and was unkind enough to score their third goal in a 4-2 win.

New rent demands from the Clapton greyhound syndicate which owned the Millfields ground prompted a move to Lea Bridge, a short distance away, in 1930. After the FA ruled it needed alterations following a complaint by Torquay in November, Orient made headlines again by playing two Third Division games at no less a stadium than Wembley.

Unlike West Ham in 1923, there was no need for supporters to climb or tunnel in. With a good number of Brentford fans turning up, the first game attracted 8,319 but for the second against Southend the 'crowd' was 1,916.

It was at the end of that season that Herbert Chapman attempted to adopt the club as Arsenal's official nursery, placing young players there to give them league experience, much as clubs use the loan system today. As their chairman Sir Samuel Hill-Wood put it: 'We can and do find lots of promising young boys, but they must have somewhere to play and be taught. What we wanted was some club willing and good enough to teach our young players for us.'

The Football League, however, would only allow non-league clubs to become nurseries, so Arsenal turned instead to Margate, while Tottenham adopted Northfleet. Charlton later used neighbouring Bexleyheath & Welling.

Orient, left to stand on their own financial feet, struggled on. In 1933, their debts brought a threat of expulsion from the league and the Prince of Wales – three years away from becoming king – was among those who donated enough money to save them.

Before the end of the decade, another move was made, a couple of miles east to Leyton, where almost 15,000 – six times the final attendance at Lea Bridge – turned out for the first game at Brisbane Road (sometimes known at the time as Osborne Road).

Yorkshireman Ted Crawford, signed from Liverpool, proved a useful goalscorer with 73 in six seasons, before ending up after the war as a manager in Italy with Bologna and Livorno. Even with his goals, Orient's average position in the Thirties was no higher than 16th. The consolation was that they had survived a difficult decade – unlike another London league club.

* * * * *

With Arsenal, Tottenham, Clapton Orient, Millwall, Charlton and above all, West Ham all well established by the late Twenties, it did not seem particularly logical to launch another professional football club anywhere near east London. The failure of the huge Memorial Grounds, deserted by West Ham in 1904, also suggested that a vast new sports stadium, five years after Wembley had been built, was not the most sensible proposal.

The venue came first, constructed by a consortium of businessmen in Nottingham Avenue, Custom House just north of the Royal Victoria Dock and designed – almost inevitably – by Archibald Leitch. With an ambitious capacity of some 100,000, the West Ham Stadium was built to house two sports growing in popularity, greyhound racing and speedway, which were nevertheless not going to fill it on anything like a regular basis.

Hence the birth of **Thames Association FC** (shortened later to Thames), who played their first game against Brighton on 30 August 1928, a month after the stadium opened with a speedway meeting. For two years, the new team competed in the Southern League, which had been reorganised twice since its top-division clubs decamped *en masse* to the Football League in 1920.

From English and Welsh sections it split into eastern and western, Thames joining the former. They finished only 14th of 19 teams in their first season, then third the next season, behind Aldershot Town and Millwall reserves, after which they were elected into the Football League with 20 votes to Aldershot's 19. Merthyr Town failed to win re-election with only 14.

It was a bad time for Welsh clubs as the Depression began to hit mining areas particularly hard and in the space of five years, Aberdare Athletic, Merthyr and then Newport County all disappeared from the league (although Newport returned a year later).

So for the 1930/31 season, London gained its 12th Football League club, six of them competing in the Third Division South. With West Ham having a poor season, ten derbies ought to have helped the newcomers' gates. When Clapton Orient turned up for a midweek game in September, however, the attendance in the vast stadium was 3,278. That proved one of the better ones, the average over two seasons working out at 2,469. Three months after the Orient game the official gate for Luton Town's visit was 469, the lowest in Football League history.

Lacking drawing power or not, Thames did manage to win 13 of their games that first season, 12 of them at home, including victories over Orient, QPR and Brentford. That enabled them to finish above both Norwich City, who were re-elected, and Newport, who were not.

For the second season, the club's best-known player, Jimmy Dimmock, was signed from Spurs five years after his final England appearance, but Thames proved beyond help. Their away record was again dismal and winning just seven games in total meant finishing five points behind Gillingham at the bottom of the table. Cardiff (9-2), Norwich (7-0) and champions Fulham (8-0) contributed to the heavy total of 109 goals conceded and the final game of the season, a 1-0 defeat at Brentford on 7 May 1932, turned out to be the club's last.

Seeing the writing on the wall of their huge home, the directors did not bother to contest the re-election vote. Talk of a possible merger with Orient, which might have made some sense, came to nothing. The stadium survived until 1972, even though the West Ham speedway team went out of business from 1955–64 before reforming.

Thames, however unlikely to succeed in the long-term, had at least reached Football League level. No other London club would be elected for 45 years.

Interlude I

War (1939-45)

THERE may have been nothing more sinister than coincidence about the German passenger airship, the Graf Zeppelin, flying over Wembley while Arsenal were beating Huddersfield Town in the 1930 FA Cup Final. Within a few years, however, events in Germany were causing sufficient alarm to make an invitation to that country's football team to play England in December 1935 at Tottenham – an area with a strong Jewish population since the turn of the century – seem insensitive if not actually provocative.

The FA took the view, still being followed by many sporting organisations decades later, that sport and politics must be kept apart. They stuck so rigidly to it that successive summer tours in 1938 and 1939 included games away to Hitler's Germany and Mussolini's Italy, at both of which England's players were obliged to give the Fascist salute.

On the day of the White Hart Lane game, attended by a reported 10,000 German supporters, Jewish organisations and the TUC staged protests and there were 14 arrests. After England's 3-0 victory, the FA president Sir Charles Clegg apologetically told the official banquet: 'This is the first time the TUC has interfered in football and I hope it will be the last.'

At the Berlin Olympics the following year, Great Britain's football team (captained by Arsenal's Bernard Joy) gave the 'eyes right' rather than Nazi salute, which upset the hosts. But when England played there in May 1938 in front of Hermann Goering, Rudolph Hess and Joseph Goebbels, Sir Neville Henderson, the British ambassador, said the team should give the salute as a matter of good manners, just as he did when visiting Hitler.

Skipper Eddie Hapgood, one of five London players in the team, subsequently claimed to have argued in vain and to have believed the indignity added to the team's determination in denting German propaganda with a 6-3 win.

Italy were unpopular winners of the 1938 World Cup in France, where they faced demonstrations at a number of games. The 2-2 draw against them in Milan in May 1939 was the last match but two that England played before the war, the others on the same tour being a 2-1 defeat by Yugoslavia and then a 2-0 win in Romania, when West Ham's Len Goulden and Charlton's Don Welsh scored the last goals in official internationals until September 1946. The FA had been told by the Foreign Office that May fixtures would be safe as 'August will be the danger month', which proved to be only a couple of days out.

The day after the 1939/40 English season started on 26 August to lower gates than might otherwise have been expected, Poland played Hungary in Warsaw and lost – a prelude to a much more serious defeat for their city and country. Germany invaded on 1 September, by which time the first children were being evacuated from London.

On Saturday 2 September, the third matches of the league season were played to even lower attendances, especially in London. Arsenal beat Sunderland 5-2 in front of a second successive crowd of barely 17,000; Charlton had only 8,608 at The Valley to see Manchester United beaten; Chelsea lost at Liverpool and in the Second Division Spurs won 4-3 at West Bromwich, with a hat-trick from Johnny Morrison, leaving both the north London clubs unbeaten. Orient were too, after three draws, but Fulham had taken only one point from their three games.

On the Sunday morning, Spurs players reported at White Hart Lane but soon realised the scheduled game against Southampton the next day would not be played. At 11.15am, the Prime Minister had gone on the radio to announce that the country was now at war.

Aware of the controversy at the start of the First World War about professional football continuing while rugby and cricket stopped, the Government initially closed all places of entertainment, only to quickly decide that sport could be a useful force for maintaining morale. Games could go ahead as long as local police approved, with a 50-mile limit on travel and attendances restricted to half normal capacity, and no more than 15,000 in any case.

Early friendlies included West Ham attracting 8,000 to see them beat old rivals Millwall, but under 6,500 were at Chelsea to see Spurs beaten 4-2. The constant fear was of air raids during games, many of which were later abandoned for that reason.

On 8 September, FA and Football League representatives met to form the War Emergency Committee. Although half a dozen clubs, including Aston Villa and Sunderland, said they would not take part, most were willing to be involved in the Football League's plans, which involved ten regional groups, two of them in the South, also split geographically.

Thus Arsenal, West Ham, Millwall, Watford, Norwich, Charlton, Crystal Palace, Clapton Orient, Tottenham and Southend contested the more northern group until the start of February, finishing in that order. Arsenal, playing at White Hart Lane after Highbury was requisitioned for use as an air raid precautions centre, won the title by five points, starting much as they carried on by beating Charlton 8-4, Orient 6-1 and Palace 5-0; a goal-rush in which Denis Compton scored seven goals and his brother Leslie six.

The southern section, in finishing order, comprised QPR, Bournemouth, Chelsea, Reading, Brentford, Fulham, Portsmouth, Aldershot, Brighton and Southampton.

For the second half of the season, the split was different, and based on pre-war divisions; the stronger South C League being won by Tottenham from West Ham and Arsenal, with Chelsea and Portsmouth bottom. In South D for the former Third Division South clubs, Crystal Palace won from QPR, with Brighton last.

Arsenal, with 53 points, could claim to be the most successful club overall, although the two totals were not officially added together.

After a bad winter, the season was extended into June to allow a War Cup to be played. The burly Leslie Compton continued his successful conversion from full-back to centre-forward, adding six more goals to his 28 in 35 league games, but Arsenal were beaten in the third round by Birmingham.

West Ham then beat the Blues and won their semi-final against Fulham 4-3 to earn a place in the first war-time cup final at Wembley against Blackburn. Although national morale was hardly high after the evacuation from Dunkirk, 42,399 turned out to see the Hammers' winger Sam Small score the only goal.

The idea of banning guest players had proved impractical but, to their credit, West Ham fielded 11 of their own in the final, a team in fact strikingly similar to the one that had begun the season, which included future Football League managers Ted Fenton (Colchester, West Ham and Southend) and Archie Macauley (Norwich, West Bromwich and Brighton) .

At various times during the two league campaigns, the Hammers still used Arsenal internationals Hapgood (twice), Ted Drake (twice) and Joy (once). Not that Arsenal could complain as their own guest list during the seven war-time seasons featured more than 70 players, including West Ham's Goulden as well as Stanley Matthews, Stan Mortensen and Bill Shankly.

That list illustrates some of the difficulties of getting a team together, depending on who was in the country and if so, where. Arsenal's Welsh inside-forward Leslie Jones once guested for three teams in four days while on leave from the RAF. Others sneaked out to play even without a weekend pass, and an unknown player named only as 'Newman' (new man) became a regular feature on team-sheets.

It also meant that playing opportunities for the young and old abounded. Future England international forward Roy Bentley was 16 when he turned out for Bristol City (and was still playing in Chelsea's championship team of 1955). At the other extreme, elderly managers sometimes had to pull on their boots. Millwall's Bill Voisey, coach to the 1936 British Olympics team, did so at the age of 50 and Orient's Bill Wright, a former defender, appeared in goal when no-one else was available.

Large numbers were accepted to the PT training course at Aldershot, where the local club, previously regulars in the bottom half of the Third Division South, came to benefit more than anyone from a regular flow of internationals. At one time, they fielded the complete England half-back line of Cliff Britton, Stan Cullis and Joe Mercer.

For the 1940/41 season, which began amid the four-month Battle of Britain and the Blitz and encompassed the country's 'darkest hour' , a peculiar system was introduced that caused particular discontent in London and eventually led to a breakaway. Thirty-four teams in the South of England and 36 in the North played as many matches as they could fit in, with final tables, such as they were, decided not even on points average but goal average.

Thus Crystal Palace were deemed to be top of the southern regional league because their 27 games produced a goal average of 86-44 (1.955), as opposed to runners-up West Ham's 70-39 (1.795). But had average points, based on the conventional two for a win and one for a draw, been used, the Hammers had the better record (1.36 to 1.33). It included a 3-3 draw against Clapton Orient in which they could only find ten players.

Orient still finished bottom of the southern list after winning only one of their 15 matches. Their season was summed up in a 15-2 defeat by Arsenal in the London War Cup in which Leslie Compton scored ten times, six of them headers. Tottenham's Jackie Gibbons was another forward the Os had reason to curse. In four successive games against them between 21 December and 11 January, he scored a hat-trick every time as Spurs won 9-0, 7-0, 3-0 and 9-1.

Brentford lost to Reading in the London War Cup Final. In the second season of the national War Cup, Arsenal knocked out West Ham and Spurs on their way to a final against Preston that attracted a 60,000 crowd to Wembley, many of them in uniform. Denis Compton scored the equaliser in a 1-1 draw after his brother missed a penalty. Preston won the replay at Blackburn three weeks later in front of another good crowd of 45,000.

Unsurprisingly in the circumstances, attendances for run-of-the-mill league games were poor. In October that second season, only 300 watched Charlton lose 2-1 to West Ham and at the end of December 1940, with their crowds averaging barely 400, the Robins went into hibernation for eight months. 'The public don't want football, the directors don't want football, so why go on?' said manager Jimmy Seed.

The Valley, situated close to the docks and munitions factories, was one of several grounds hit by bombs. It still had to play host to neighbours Millwall in 1943/44 after The Den's main stand burnt to the ground in an air raid an hour after a match, when casualties might have been fearful. It was a year before a new temporary stand was ready.

Just before start of 1944/45, a flying bomb destroyed much of West Ham's South Bank and they had to play the first 14 games away. During that time, club officials also had to evacuate the West Stand and set up home in Green Street House, the Boleyn Castle itself.

Highbury, although no football was played there, was also hit, the North Bank being destroyed and the Clock End suffering. Chelsea suffered air raid damage and opened a temporary stand and although Wembley – possibly because it was a little further out of town – escaped, the FA offices at Lancaster Gate were badly damaged by a fire bomb, even though water was kept in the baths there as recommended by government guidelines.

After the unsatisfactory 1940/41 arrangements, the summer of 1941 was an important time for London clubs, who were shocked by the amount of travelling that would be required under the Football League management committee's plans for one Northern League and one Southern League, the latter ranging all the way from Norwich to Swansea.

With Arsenal's media-savvy George Allison playing a leading role as spokesman, the 11 London clubs, along with five others – Aldershot, Brighton, Portsmouth, Reading and Portsmouth – insisted they would start their own competition and were therefore expelled from the Football League. Not until April were they officially reinstated, paying a nominal £10 fine each.

In the meantime, the FA sanctioned a London League, in which Arsenal were again the most successful club. Fielding many of their pre-war stars like Hapgood, Male, Joy, Crayston, Bastin, Drake and the Compton brothers with reasonable regularity, they won the league ahead of Portsmouth and West Ham.

In 15 home games they scored 70 goals, including wins of 11-0 against Watford and 10-0 against Millwall in successive matches. No-one enjoyed himself more than centre-forward Reg Lewis. A Staffordshire man signed from nursery club Margate, already holder of the reserves' goalscoring record from 1938/39, he now chalked up an astonishing 42 in 23 games.

The team that proved their nemesis – just as in the immediate pre-war period – were Brentford, beating them twice in the league and then in the two-leg semi-final of the London Cup, the latter two games being watched by a combined 78,754. For the final at Wembley, almost 70,000 turned out to see Brentford, the previous season's beaten finalists, defeat Portsmouth.

From 1942/43, a regular pattern was set in which clubs competed in a Football League South (stretching no further than Southampton and Watford or Luton), plus a League Cup South, whose winners met their northern equivalent in the War Cup Final at Stamford Bridge (the southern final having been played at Wembley and attracting the bigger crowds).

Arsenal again topped the league in 1943, scoring 102 goals in 28 games (Lewis 33 in 22) and did the London double by beating Charlton 7-1 (Lewis four) at Wembley before a 75,000 crowd. In the national final, however, Blackpool defeated them 4-2, with Matthews guesting.

For the next two years, it was Tottenham who finished top of the league ahead of West Ham, losing only one match out of 30 (5-1 at home to Chelsea) in the second season. Charlton were the 1944 London Cup winners, beating Chelsea 3-1 in front of General Eisenhower before drawing the national final 1-1 with Aston Villa.

In April 1945, a huge gathering of 90,000 celebrated the imminent end of war at last by watching Chelsea beat Millwall 2-0 in the London final before they lost 2-1 against Bolton on their own ground a month after VE Day. It was a sign of the times that Chelsea fielded no fewer than eight guest players from other clubs, while Charlton's Sam Bartram was in goal for Millwall.

Attendances for league games had improved from the earliest days and patriotic fervour ensured some large turn-outs for internationals, which began early on. In November 1939, a game between Wales and England drew 28,000 to Ninian Park, Cardiff for a 1-1 draw in which 18 of the players were from London clubs, including the noted Walthamstow Avenue amateur Jim Lewis Sr.

In total, there were 40 England games, for which crowds included 105,000 at Hampden Park in 1943 to see Denis Compton score in England's 4-0 win over Scotland and 133,000 a year later for a 3-2 England win.

After VE Day on 8 May 1945, the Football League were keen for normal service to resume the following season but many of the clubs were concerned about availability of players and transport, and opted to continue for one more campaign on a strict regional basis.

Naturally, many of the 1939 players did not return because of age, injury or worse. The roll-call of about 80 professional footballers who died included Arsenal's Herbie Roberts, Bobby Daniel, Hugh Glass, Sid Pugh, Leslie Lack, Bill Parr and Cyril Tooze; Fred Fisher of Millwall; Fulham's John Tompkin and Dennis Higgins; Allan Thornley of Palace.

Among the survivors were two notable centre-halves: West Ham's Dick Walker fought in the paratroop regiment from El Alamein to Italy and was mentioned in dispatches more than once.

Alf Fields of Arsenal (a former West Ham schoolboy player) was also in North Africa and Italy with the Royal Artillery and won the British Empire Medal. They would be back. Many others were less fortunate.

Chapter 4

Austerity (1946-60)

A return to normality and huge upsurge of interest and attendances; Charlton reach successive FA Cup finals but only Arsenal and Chelsea are with them in the top flight until Spurs return and win the 1951 title at first attempt by pushing and running; Chelsea's first-ever title (1955) and European jaunt before West Ham and Johnny Haynes's Fulham join the top division; Palace and Millwall stuck in the new Division Four

AFTER the ravages of war and 71 major air raids on London, West Ham's programme for the opening home game of the 1945/46 season against Arsenal referred to the fixture with defiant good humour as 'Roofless v Homeless'. The bomb damage meant Upton Park was open to the elements all round, and their visitors were still playing at White Hart Lane.

It was one indication that normality was still a little way off. Another one was the rule allowing up to six guest players (later reduced to three), although the Hammers had no fewer than nine pre-war players in their side for the 1-1 draw.

More typically, Arsenal were much changed, men like Bastin, Male, Hapgood (for five games only) and Denis Compton not returning until later in the season, which helped explain their moderate record. Ted Drake, it turned out, had played his final match on the same ground five months earlier.

Missing from the West Ham line-up was Len Goulden, a regular goalscorer throughout the war years for club and country. Chelsea, determined to improve on pre-war performances, paid £4,500 for him in one of the first major post-war transfers, adding John Harris, the Wolves centre-half, for £7,000 and, more dramatically, centre-forward Tommy Lawton from Everton in November for £11,500, making him the second most expensive player after Bryn Jones.

Meanwhile, players who had made do with whatever they could get since 1939 were pushing for proper payment.

An Association Football Players Union had been founded as long ago as 1907 and came to the brink of strike action two years later before the principle of bonus payments was agreed. After the First World War, the maximum wage of £10 a week was actually reduced to £8 during the season and £6 in summer, a figure barely increased again until 1945.

According to the union, only ten per cent of players were on the maximum wage by 1939, when the close-season figure was increased to £7 per week. Lawton said in his autobiography that during 1938/39 as top scorer for champions Everton, while playing regularly for England (which paid extra), his total earnings were £531.

Not for another two years after the war did a national arbitration tribunal raise the maximum wage to £12 in the season and £10 in the summer, with a minimum for players over 20 of £7.

Once the football started, it turned out to be Midlands teams who dominated the upper reaches of the so-called South league, though not until Charlton had been top for almost five months. A crucial moment in their season occurred away to eventual champions Birmingham City when, at 1-0 down, goalkeeper Sam Bartram was called upon to take a penalty – and hit the bar. Failing to win any of their last three games, they finished third, a point behind Birmingham and Aston Villa, with Derby fourth, followed by West Bromwich and Wolves.

London came next as West Ham, Fulham, Tottenham, Chelsea, Arsenal and Millwall held positions seven to 12. Only Brentford were in the bottom half, foreshadowing a fall that would see them relegated the following season.

Only three London sides were in the Third Division sections, played as a 20-match league campaign and then a 16-match league followed by semi-finals and final. QPR were the best of the three, winning both northern sections, with Clapton Orient eighth and seventh of 11, while Crystal Palace were top of the first southern group and then fourth behind Bournemouth, who won the knockout section.

Attendances among a population hungry for entertainment amid the relief of peace quickly picked up, although it was that tremendous appetite that led to the worst crowd tragedy yet to strike the sport. At the FA Cup quarter-final between Bolton and Stoke in March 1946, an exit gate was opened so that a boy and his father could escape from the crush and thousands more supporters poured in. A wall collapsed, leaving 33 dead and some 400 injured.

The competition was played over two legs for the only time in its history in order to provide extra games and maximise income, which proved little help for Orient, early giant-killing victims in losing to Newport – not the team from South Wales but from the Isle of Wight, who then lost 12-0 on aggregate to Aldershot.

Arsenal and Spurs made surprisingly early exits, the former losing 6-1 on aggregate to West Ham after a 6-0 beating in front of the best crowd of the season at Upton Park (35,000). Tottenham's conquerors Brentford made the quarter-finals, also beating Bristol City and neighbours QPR, but lost 9-4 overall to **Charlton**, who were in sight of their first national trophy when they beat Bolton 2-0 in the one-off semi-final with two goals by left-winger Chris Duffy, the second a stunning individual effort after beating five opponents.

Derby qualified to meet them after seeing off Birmingham 4-0 in a replay watched by an astonishing 80,487 at Maine Road.

In a dress rehearsal at The Valley a week before the final, Derby cannily used two understudies for their star men and new signings, inside-forwards Raich Carter and Peter Doherty. Losing 2-1 did not matter to them and boosted Charlton's title hopes.

The final, watched by the King and Queen as well as a young Princess Elizabeth, was memorable for two reasons, as well as the quality of football by Derby. They thought they had won with eight minutes to play, Charlton's right-half Bert Turner diverting a shot by Dally Duncan into his own net after Bartram had punched out a cross. Barely a minute later, however, Turner took a free kick just outside the opposing penalty area which deflected in off Doherty to make the Charlton man the first to score for both sides in a final.

Just before extra time, Bartram held a shot by the powerful Jackie Stamps with unexpected ease – because the ball had burst. Not wanting a bounce-up in his own penalty area, the goalkeeper quickly threw it as far as he could towards the touchline, from where the resulting restart took place.

In extra time Derby proved superior, scoring through Northern Irish international (and future World Cup manager) Doherty, then Stamps (twice) for a 4-1 win: 'a glorious finish to a memorable game worth going miles to see' wrote the *News of the World* correspondent.

Back in the dressing room, Charlton's players and management made the losers' habitual optimistic noises about coming back to win the following season without knowing that, for once, it would actually happen.

* * * * *

The other highlight of the initial post-war season was the 1945 tour by Russian champions Moscow Dynamo – playing two of their four games in London – which attracted enormous interest and, by the end of it, reluctant admiration.

Little was known about their football, partly because it would be 1958 before England played the USSR for the first time. Grateful as the British public were for the Russian effort and sacrifices in the war just ended, mutual misunderstanding and suspicion were features of the two-week tour, which began with an FA delegation twice waiting at Northolt airport before being told the Russians were about to land – at Croydon.

The visitors' initial impression of an underwhelming reception ('without flags, music or flowers') was compounded by being billeted for the first night in Wellington Barracks because no hotel would take a booking without knowing their exact date of arrival. Even FA secretary Stanley Rous admitted the accommodation was unsuitable and Arsenal's chairman, Sir Guy Bracewell Smith, agreed to make the ballroom of his Park Lane hotel available.

A list of 14 requirements previously presented included having no more than one game a week, on a Saturday, playing the famous Arsenal, all meals to be taken at the Soviet Embassy and having their own referee for at least one match.

Despite those demands, the first of four scheduled fixtures was on a Tuesday afternoon against Chelsea at Stamford Bridge, not as Dynamo had wanted, at Wembley. Queues formed from early morning and by kick-off at 2.30pm far more than the official capacity of 75,000 were inside, able to read in their match programme (priced two old pence) that 'history is being made before our eyes today'.

After the visiting players had presented their embarrassed Chelsea counterparts (including two guest players from Fulham) with a bouquet each, those lucky spectators saw not only a piece of history but what the long-serving sports journalist Frank Butler described in the *Daily Express* as 'one of the most entertaining exhibitions of football ever seen on an English football field'.

Having led 2-0 through Len Goulden and Reg Williams, Chelsea were pegged back to 2-2, led again with a header by Lawton (whom the Russians said had only been signed to help beat them) and then conceded a late equaliser generally agreed to have been well offside.

Diplomatic draw or not, Dynamo impressed with their energy, flexibility and quick-passing into open spaces. Rous and the soon-to-be-appointed England manager Walter Winterbottom resolved that 'there was much to be learned from European football'.

Fixtures having also been arranged in Wales and Scotland, the next stop was Cardiff, where the Third Division South side were hopelessly outclassed and lost 10-1. Manager Cyril Spiers called Dynamo 'the finest team I have ever seen'.

The much-anticipated fixture against Arsenal at White Hart Lane (Highbury still being unavailable) was surrounded by controversy from the start and ruined in the end by that famous feature of London life – fog.

As many Arsenal players were still stationed abroad, more than half a dozen reinforcements were sought from Cardiff, QPR, Fulham, Bury, Stoke and Blackpool, the latter pair supplying Stanley Matthews and Stan Mortensen no less.

The Russians protested with some justification that manager George Allison feared a demoralising defeat and had not selected an Arsenal team at all. In the event, the respective merits of the two teams were hard to judge for a crowd of more than 54,000, so thick was the fog.

There is general agreement that the Arsenal XI led 3-2 at half-time after conceding a goal in the first minute and were eventually beaten 4-3 amid some debatable decisions by the Russian referee, one of which was to keep playing after Allison suggested abandoning proceedings. Matthews told the story of inside-right George Drury being sent off and simply wandering back on, joking that he couldn't find the tunnel. It has also been claimed that for 20 minutes Dynamo played with 12 men, though it must have been almost impossible to tell.

The tourists' unbeaten run continued in Glasgow, where 90,000 had a better view of them and watched an exciting 2-2 draw with a physically tough Rangers side. So 271,000 or more had attended the four games.

There should have been another to come but even as the FA were preparing to select an international-standard team for the final match, Dynamo suddenly upped and returned home, to be greeted as heroes.

It had been a fascinating trip all round, albeit one that caused George Orwell, no friend of organised games, to make his famous (and unfair) remark in *Tribune* that 'sport is an unfailing cause of ill-will'.

* * * * *

Britons could not get enough of it. In the 1946/47 season, Football League crowds reached more than 35,500,000 and in the following two years added almost six million more.

London played a big part, especially in the top division. Returning to Highbury at last from their enforced stay on enemy territory, Arsenal drew 60,000 for their first Saturday fixture (2-2 v Sunderland) and 63,000 for the next (0-1 v Derby).

Their visit to Stamford Bridge the following month (lost 2-1) attracted 56,432, and when they returned in January for a 1-1 draw in the FA Cup third round, the gate was 70,257. By the time Chelsea won the second replay at neutral White Hart Lane, the three cup games had been watched by more than 186,000. Charlton too packed them in for derbies, including 55,000 for the 2-2 draw with Arsenal.

All that was in a season when, far from challenging front runners like Liverpool, Manchester United, Wolves and Stoke, the London trio were in the bottom half of the table. That made it the first season since 1924/25 (and the last to date) that no team from the capital had finished in the top half of the highest division.

Charlton's compensation, aided considerably by the luck of the draw, came from another cup run. After wins at home to Rochdale and away to West Bromwich Albion, they beat Blackburn with a late goal by Tommy Dawson in the first FA Cup game other than a final to be televised. The February slush ensured it was no great advert for the sport. Preston, a higher placed First Division team, were then beaten 2-1 at The Valley in a bad-tempered sixth-round tie to set up a semi-final against Newcastle United at Leeds.

Newcastle had led the Second Division at Christmas, beaten Newport County by a record 13-0, and had Arsenal reject Len Shackleton plus a young Jackie Milburn in the side, leading many to regard them as favourites. They grew even more confident once word slipped out that half the Charlton team had woken up on the day of the game with symptoms of food poisoning.

At one point during the game, Bartram needed a hot poultice on his stomach after doubling up at a goal kick. Skipper Don Welsh blacked out in the dressing room afterwards but came round to recall that he had scored two goals in a 4-0 victory and that Charlton were back at Wembley.

Fortune favoured them a fortnight later when another Second Division side, Burnley, unexpectedly knocked out that season's First Division champions Liverpool 1-0 in a semi-final replay.

Burnley's strength was a defence that conceded only 29 goals in 42 league games, and the final was a dour one in which they kept Charlton comfortably at bay until the last six minutes of extra time, when Chris Duffy drove in from 12 yards. Until then, the most notable incident was the ball bursting for the second successive year, leading to questions about the quality of materials available in the immediate post-war years of rationing and austerity.

Charlton had the first major trophy in their history; although manager Seed did some damage to it by breaking the lid on his way to a council reception at Greenwich Town Hall. Fortunately, a local garage was able to solder the top back on.

The winning team was: Bartram; Croker, Shreeve; Johnson, Phipps, Whittaker; Hurst, Dawson, Robinson, Welsh, Duffy.

That day at Wembley turned out to be a high point for the club until they returned for a play-off final more than 50 years later. Despite several more years of big crowds and a commendable fifth place in 1953, there was never the sort of investment in either the vast ground or the team that Seed always maintained could have made Charlton the Arsenal of south-east London.

At the start of the 1956/57 season, they lost the first five games and after the last of them, 8-1 against his boyhood club Sunderland, Seed was dismissed. His transfer dealings over 23 years showed a profit of £115,000, the last sale being that of striker Eddie Firmani to Sampdoria for a British-record £35,000. As with the gate receipts from Valley crowds, which peaked at an average of 40,216 in 1948/49, it was never clear where all the money had gone.

Firmani, who had an Italian grandfather, was one of an extraordinary total of 13 South Africans Seed signed, including the versatile Scottish international John Hewie and Kent football-cricketers Sid O'Linn and Stuart Leary.

Having recommended that Colchester's player-manager Benny Fenton, a former Charlton captain, should succeed him, Seed was surprised to see trainer Jimmy Trotter given the job. It did not work out and at the end of the season they were relegated with Cardiff City.

An immediate return was on the cards ahead of the last day of the 1957/58 campaign, which Charlton went into on 55 points, level with the equally high-scoring West Ham and one ahead of the visitors to The Valley, Blackburn Rovers. But while their London rivals won 3-1 at Middlesbrough to clinch the title, Charlton let down a crowd of 56,535 by trailing 4-1 before rallying to lose 4-3 and finish third, a point short despite having won more games than anyone and scored the most goals, 107, of which 28 came from outside-left Johnny Summers.

Londoner Summers, signed from Millwall in 1956, was the principal figure in another game that season that the *News of the World*, never knowingly understated, called 'the most fantastic match of the century'.

The date being the last Saturday before Christmas, one of the smallest crowds of the season – 12,535 – turned up to see the visit of Bill Shankly's mid-table Huddersfield Town. It is tempting to wonder how many of them left once Charlton, with defender Derek Ufton (another Kent cricketer) taken to hospital, went 5-1 down after little more than an hour.

John Ryan (63 minutes) then pulled one back for the ten men before Summers, moved into the centre, added to his first-half goal with four more before the 82nd minute: 6-5 to Charlton. Huddersfield equalised four minutes from time but, in the final minute, Ryan took a pass from Fred Lucas to score Charlton's sensational seventh.

Shankly ripped into his side, which included future World Cup winner Ray Wilson at left-back, but although it was an era of rumours about players betting against their own team, there was no suggestion the result was anything other than genuine.

Brian Clough, however, had abundant suspicion when he scored a hat-trick for Middlesbrough three years later in another extraordinary game at The Valley that finished 6-6. Clough went to his grave believing that two Boro defenders, both sent to prison in a later match-fixing scandal, had bet on Charlton to win that day.

Regularly scoring 90 goals or more failed to earn promotion under Trotter, such was the weakness of the Charlton defence post-Bartram. Sam had retired aged 42 after a 2-0 win over Arsenal in March 1956 to become manager of York City and then Luton Town. He now has a road named after him by The Valley and a statue outside the main stand. The south stand was named after Jimmy Seed in the early 1980s.

* * * * *

Seed, always a nervous watcher of matches who would occasionally hide at the back of the stand, spoke in his autobiography about the strains of management and used Tom Whittaker of **Arsenal** as example.

Forced to retire from playing in 1925 after six years at the club, Whittaker studied physiotherapy and became head trainer under Herbert Chapman two years later. Regarded as the tactician to George Allison's front-man, he took over as manager when Allison resigned at the end of the 1946/47 season, in which Arsenal's final position of 13th was their lowest for 17 years.

The popular Whittaker was a success from the start of a triumphant 1947/48 campaign that began with six successive wins and ended with Arsenal as champions by seven points from Manchester United. Strikers Ronnie Rooke, signed from Fulham after guesting in the Moscow Dynamo game, and Reg Lewis had been two of the few successes in Allison's last season, scoring 50 of the 72 league goals, and they hit another 47 between them.

The players did not realise they were champions until, on the return journey from a 1-1 draw at Huddersfield, Denis Compton jumped off the train at Doncaster to buy the evening papers, which revealed that the only three teams who could have caught them had all lost.

Joe Mercer at wing-half was an important addition to the side, which remained a top-six team while achieving their next success in the FA Cup. A stunning third-round defeat at home to Bradford Park Avenue of the Second Division, captained by Ron Greenwood, was the one blot on the 1948 championship season and, after knocking out Tottenham 3-0 the following season but losing at Derby, Whittaker's team reached Wembley in 1950 – without leaving London.

Drawn at home in four successive rounds, their defence conceded only one goal until an exciting semi-final against Chelsea that went to two matches at White Hart Lane, watched by an aggregate of more than 134,000.

In the first one, Arsenal trailed 2-0 to goals by Roy Bentley but retrieved them from corners, the first one scored direct by Freddie Cox, a rare signing from Tottenham for £12,000, and the second taken by Denis Compton and headed in by brother Leslie, ignoring Mercer's instruction to stay back in defence. In the replay four days later it was Cox again, enjoying being back at White Hart Lane by scoring the only goal in extra time.

The cup final opponents were Liverpool, who came through their own very local derby in the semi-final by knocking out Everton.

Arsenal: Swindin; Scott, Barnes; Forbes, L.Compton, Mercer; Cox, Logie, Goring, Lewis, D.Compton.

In the league, the Merseysiders had beaten Arsenal home and away but at Wembley it was Lewis's day, his goal in each half decisive and helping earn him a place many years later on the mural of Arsenal heroes round the Emirates Stadium.

'No question of "lucky" Arsenal' headlined the *Sunday Times*, singling out for special mention 'Joseph Mercer' and centre-forward Peter Goring from Cheltenham Town, who was in his first season. At a time when Stanley Matthews was failing to win a coveted FA Cup medal (losing the final in 1948 and 1951), Denis Compton's success just a few days before his retirement was a hugely popular one.

Compton was in the press box for the *Sunday Express* as Arsenal lost the 1952 final 1-0 to Newcastle. Yet again, there were two semi-final matches at White Hart Lane against Chelsea, this time finishing 1-1 and 3-0, with Cox scoring three of the goals.

In the final, however, the regular Wembley injury jinx struck early, full-back Walley Barnes tearing ligaments when his studs stuck in the turf. No substitutes, of course, but even Newcastle's manager Stan Seymour admitted Arsenal were the better team on the day.

'Boys, I've never been so proud of you in victory as I am of you in defeat,' Whittaker told his men in the dressing room.

Leslie Compton played his final league game that season but the club had another notable football-cricketer in their ranks in Bristolian outside-right Arthur Milton, the last man to play for England at both sports. Other than his cap against Austria in May 1952, Milton's greatest football honour was Arsenal's championship success the following year, when he played 25 times in preference to Cox.

It was the tightest of triumphs in which the top five (including fifth-placed Charlton) were separated by only five points and the title was decided on goal average for only the third time in history.

After Cliff Holton, a tall young centre-forward with a fierce shot, scored all four goals away to Sheffield Wednesday at the start of March, Arsenal endured a bad run but recovered to emerge as the strongest challengers to Tom Finney's Preston North End.

In the *annus mirabilis* which brought an end to rationing, a coronation, the conquest of Everest, an Ashes triumph, Sir Gordon Richards' first Derby victory and a cup winner's medal at last for Matthews (Blackpool having knocked out Arsenal in the quarter-finals), Finney winning the First Division would have been widely welcomed.

Losing 2-0 at Deepdale in the penultimate game was not the setback it might have been for Arsenal, as they still held a narrow advantage on goal average going into the final round of matches. Helpfully, Preston played first, a 1-0 win over Derby leaving Arsenal knowing they would be champions if they won at home to Burnley two days later on cup final eve.

An added twist was that Burnley's goalkeeper and Preston's were brothers. If Des Thompson could keep a clean sheet at Highbury, or earn his team a draw, his older brother George would win a championship medal.

It was a nervous night on which the visitors scored first and last, but in between times Alex Forbes, leading scorer Doug Lishman and Jimmy Logie all beat the younger Thompson to win the game 3-2 and with it the title.

The following season, however, an unexpected decline set in right from the start. Having won none of the first eight games, which culminated in a 7-1 drubbing at Sunderland, and failed with an illegal approach to Matthews, Arsenal gambled unsuccessfully by signing the 34-year-old Tommy Lawton from Brentford and finished no higher than 12th.

Despite a younger team improving to ninth and fifth over the next two years, the strain took a shocking toll on Whittaker. Early in the 1956/57 season, he was admitted to University College Hospital suffering from nervous exhaustion and on 24 October he died of a heart attack aged 58 – two years older than Chapman when he was also killed by the job.

Successor Jack Crayston lasted less than two seasons, the second of them most notable for the last game played in England by Manchester United's Busby Babes before the Munich air disaster. Happily, Highbury's biggest crowd of the season, more than 63,500, was present to see United win a magnificent match 5-4 after Arsenal recovered from 3-0 down at half-time to 3-3.

Crayston resigned in May, frustrated at not having enough money to spend. Ron Greenwood, appointed coach, found the team 'set and stodgy in their ways' and although he helped former goalkeeper George Swindin achieve third place in 1959, the decade ended with Spurs and even Fulham above Arsenal in the table, and the former about to have their moment of glory, glory.

* * * * *

At the start of the Fifties too, Arsenal had found their thunder stolen by **Tottenham.** They may even have laid the foundations by providing a manager for their rivals soon after the post-war resumption. Joe Hulme, star winger from the 1930s team, was received and remembered more favourably at White Hart Lane than former Arsenal men Terry Neill or George Graham would be in later years and although he was unable to return Spurs to the First Division, the team he left behind in 1949 immediately achieved dramatic success under the man who replaced him.

Hulme's side finished sixth, eighth and fifth, as well as reaching the 1948 FA Cup semi-final. Arthur Rowe, Tottenham born and bred, then returned from his position as manager of Chelmsford City to the club he had captained as a ball-playing centre-half. His principles were succinctly summed up as 'push and run', demanding short passing and immediately moving into space to take a return.

Quick and simple were the watchwords, and Tottenham's football proved too quick for Second Division opponents throughout Rowe's first season. They went unbeaten from 27 August 1949 to 14 January and won the title by nine points even after slacking off in the last few games once it was assured.

Rowe added only one player to Hulme's squad, a certain Alf Ramsey, whom he encouraged to cut out his long passes and push forward from right-back while right-half Bill Nicholson covered for him. Goals were shared among four of the forwards while the fifth, the little cockney sparrow and future coach Eddie Baily, orchestrated from midfield.

Although First Division Sunderland had been swept away 5-1 in the FA Cup that season, questions were asked about how the new style would cope with better opposition when Blackpool won 4-1 at the Lane in the opening game of 1950/51.

Any doubters had their answer that autumn after a run of eight successive wins, including victories over Stoke (6-1), champions Portsmouth (5-1) and Newcastle (7-0). There were more than 70,000 at the Newcastle game, which skipper and left-half Ron Burgess called the finest performance he had ever seen.

The maximum wage was still only £14 a week, but Spurs players earned more £2 win bonuses than any other team as they sealed the title with the 24th of them that season, beating Sheffield Wednesday 1-0 with a goal by Channel Islander Len Duquemin in the penultimate game. A different sort of bonus was remaining unbeaten in eight derbies against Arsenal, Chelsea, Charlton and Fulham.

One handicap to push-and-run was the poor quality of pitches once bad weather set in. It was notable the following season that their defence of the title faltered during the winter months with seven defeats in a dozen games, including home losses to Charlton and championship rivals Arsenal.

Staying unbeaten from February onwards still left Spurs in second place, one ahead of Arsenal on goal average but four points short of winners Manchester United.

Arsenal's title triumph the following season, 1952/53, included a double over tenth-placed Tottenham, whose highlight was an FA Cup run that lasted nine games but fell one short of Wembley. Four times they were drawn away from home, needing a replay to dispose of Tranmere Rovers (9-1) and league runners-up Preston, plus two replays to see off Birmingham in the quarter-finals.

The semi-final was at Villa Park against Blackpool, with the nation rooting for Stanley Matthews and no doubt delighted when, in the last few seconds, Ramsey underhit a backpass and Jackie Mudie scored the winning goal. A mortified Ramsey never forgot it and years later took an Ipswich journalist out on to the Villa Park pitch to show him exactly how and where the mistake occurred.

As well as good pitches, push-and-run also required tremendous stamina and as Rowe's ageing team drifted downhill, he became the latest manager to feel the strain. He suffered a breakdown in 1954 and, after falling ill again in April 1955, offered his resignation.

Final positions of 16th, 16th and 18th (two points from relegation) told the tale of decline, but by 1956 new names were emerging under the management of the cheery Jimmy Anderson that would become famous ones in Tottenham history: Peter Baker, Danny Blanchflower, Terry Dyson, Ron Henry, Cliff Jones, Tony Marchi, Terry Medwin, Maurice Norman and Bobby Smith all played a part over the next two seasons as Spurs finished second to United, then third behind Wolves and Preston.

There was one more setback to come, albeit with a happy outcome. In October 1958 Anderson resigned, yet another victim of ill health, and made way as was always planned eventually for his assistant Bill Nicholson.

Nicholson's first game in charge, at home to Everton, was just about the most remarkable debut of any manager. Knowing the players inside-out after coaching them for four years, he made three changes to the side that had drawn 1-1 at Portsmouth the previous week, bringing back the crucial midfield creative hub of Blanchflower and little Tommy Harmer, and was rewarded with one of those scorelines that the teleprinters have to confirm in writing: 10(ten)-4.

The score was given added piquancy by being one of the catchphrases of the time, after the popular American television programme *Highway Patrol*. It did, however, also hint at shortcomings in the team: a feeble Everton side had conceded ten goals, yet still managed to breach the Spurs defence four times.

By the end of the season, Nicholson's team had shown equal facility for scoring and conceding goals, had fallen victim to the season's FA Cup giant-killers Norwich City and were 18th once more.

One year on, however, everything was falling into place. In reaching third position in 1959/60, only two points behind unexpected champions Burnley, the defence that had conceded 95 goals the previous season had let in a mere 50. The scoring rate (including a 13-2 FA Cup replay win over Crewe) had been maintained and crucially Dave Mackay, John White and Les Allen had been signed.

Greatness beckoned.

* * * * *

For **Chelsea** too, there was a First Division title at last, and never mind the knockers who pointed out that a modest 52 points would only ever have won it in two previous seasons out of 28.

They would not have been tipped as champions in 1955, even though the previous year's eighth place in Ted Drake's second season as manager was a huge improvement on what had gone before: a dismal post-war run of 15th, 18th, 13th, 13th, 20th, 19th and 19th.

In 1951 and 1953, they could easily have gone down. On the first occasion, a run of 14 league games without a win in the new year had war-time manager Billy Birrell's team virtually doomed. Winning the last four was the only possible way out and, in what was regarded as typically unpredictable Chelsea style, they did it.

Liverpool, Wolves, Fulham and Bolton were all beaten, although even then some fancy maths was required to confirm that the 4-0 victory over Bolton gave them a better goal average than Sheffield Wednesday, who had beaten the other relegation-threatened side, Everton, 6-0.

It did so by such a tiny margin that just about the most important result of the season turned out to have been the very first one, when Wednesday lost 4-0 at Stamford Bridge.

Two years later, with Birrell retired and the old Arsenal and England warrior Drake appointed after a couple of good seasons with Third Division South Reading, it was again necessary to win the last game in order to survive. Manchester City were duly beaten 3-1.

Drake, however, was credited with introducing a greater professionalism to the whole club, whose image he was also keen to change by ditching the Pensioners nickname.

The story of the Blues now took an upturn. England international Roy Bentley was already *in situ,* having taken over from Tommy Lawton as the most productive goalscorer and, in an improved 1953/54 campaign, he led the way again with 21 league goals but was well backed up by Johnny McNichol, Drake's first signing from Brighton, with 18.

An embarrassing 8-1 defeat away to champions Wolves suggested the defence still needed tightening, despite Ron Greenwood's arrival as centre-half from Brentford. But eighth place meant that for the first time since 1920, Chelsea finished as the top London club.

That may well have been the limit of their ambition for the following season, especially after four successive defeats in October, including a famous 5-6 loss at home to Manchester United. By mid-November, Chelsea had won only five of the first 17 games and nobody was thinking about the championship. Then things began to look up. Losing to Lawton's goal for Arsenal on Christmas Day at Highbury was one of few setbacks, although it cost Greenwood his place and he was soon off to Fulham.

The younger Stan Wicks came in and stayed in a side almost unchanged for the rest of the season as results continued to impress. Chick Thomson taking over from Bill Robertson in goal was one of the changes. Young Peter Sillett alternated with either John Harris at right-back or Stan Willemse on the left. The wing-halves were Ken Armstrong and Derek Saunders, the wingers Eric 'Rabbit' Parsons and Ken Blunstone. Bentley was centre-forward, captain and leading scorer for the seventh successive season, with McNichol also chipping in and only the number 10 (inside-left) shirt regularly swapped.

Seamus O'Connell, one of several amateur players past and present whom Drake used, wore it for three of the last four games. The first of them was at the Bridge on Easter Saturday against Wolves, pushing hard to retain their title. The gates were closed long before kick-off on a crowd of more than 75,000, who for 75 minutes saw no goals. Then England captain Billy Wright handled on the line and, amid tremendous tension, Sillett stepped up to hammer in one of his trademark penalties.

A precious goalless draw followed away to Portsmouth, who were also in contention, and a week later the final home game brought a 3-0 victory over Sheffield Wednesday with two goals by Parsons and another Sillett spot kick. The crowd invaded the pitch but were asked to hush until Portsmouth's result was confirmed. Soon came the jubilant announcement that they had failed to win at Cardiff and Chelsea's first Football League champions, sitting in the bath, had to pull on some clothes and salute their supporters from the main stand.

> **Chelsea:** Thomson; P. Sillett, Willemse; Armstrong, Wicks, Saunders; Parsons, McNichol, Bentley, O'Connell, Blunstone.

'After 50 inglorious years as football's laughing boys, Chelsea are League champions,' wrote the *Sunday Pictorial*. 'Their defeat of relegated Sheffield Wednesday assured them of their first major honour in the Golden Jubilee year of the club. No wonder manager Ted Drake bubbled over with pride and joy. There's no doubt that Drake, a former Arsenal and England centre-forward, has injected Chelsea with a never-say-die spirit.'

The *News of the World* reminded readers of what Drake had said on taking over in 1952: 'Don't expect me to make Chelsea into a successful team for at least three years.' He was bang on schedule.

Losing the final game 2-1 at Manchester United hardly mattered, even though it meant that only Arsenal in 1938 and Wednesday in 1929 had ever become champions with as few as 52 points from a 42-match programme.

Unlike that pair, who only won it by a single point, Chelsea were four clear of their nearest challengers Wolves, Portsmouth and Sunderland.

Of the ten defeats (the same number as champions Wolves the previous season), five came at the Bridge, but the average attendance there of 48,302 was and remains the highest in the club's history.

Decline was sharp and shocking, more so than in the case of Tottenham and Arsenal earlier in the decade. Champions in their Jubilee season, Chelsea immediately slumped to 16th position the following term, four points off relegation. The team that began with a 2-0 home defeat by Bolton was exactly the same one that ended the previous campaign. Drake soon began to make changes when only one of the first seven games was won, but an October improvement was not maintained and the run-in, apart from a 6-1 win over Everton, was dreadful. That game was watched by under 14,000 and, for a previous midweek game at home to Charlton, the gate was 8,473.

Half a dozen of the championship side left and it was another 12 months before a real reason to be cheerful: the advent of Jimmy Greaves. On the day of the 6-5 defeat by Manchester United, the bowler-hatted Chelsea scout Jimmy Thompson told Drake he had found 'the player of a lifetime' in a game for Essex schools. So he had. Fortunately for Chelsea, the 14-year-old Greaves did not support any of his local teams, preferring to watch amateur football, and although Tottenham and West Ham were aware of him, neither club was as persistent as Thompson. Initially paid £3 a week as a groundstaff boy, he scored 51 goals in his first season as a junior and more than double the year after.

It was time for the first team and once Greaves made his bow at White Hart Lane on the opening day of the 1957/58 season – with a debut goal, of course – he stayed in the side and added 21 more. The team finished no higher than 11th. There was one in each leg of the FA Youth Cup Final as well, but after drubbing Wolves 5-1 in the home leg Chelsea contrived to lose 6-1 at Molineux.

This became a theme. For all Greaves's goals, there was a fallibility to the rest of the team, especially in defence. As he scored 32 and then 29 in the next two seasons, including five in one game against both Wolves and Preston, Chelsea actually dropped to 14th and then 18th, conceding 98 and 91 respectively.

Winning the title in 1955 meant Chelsea should have become the first English team to take part in European competition.

Like the other major London clubs, they had played foreign opposition from early in the century, first travelling to Denmark in 1906. Arsenal hosted a Parisian XI as early as 1904 (see Chapter 1), Spurs toured abroad in 1905 and West Ham undertook a Spanish tour in 1922.

Once English clubs began installing floodlights, the trend for international friendlies grew and by 1954 there was serious talk of a major European competition. That autumn alone, Arsenal played at home to Grasshoppers of Zurich, Maccabi Tel Aviv and Spartak Moscow, as well as losing 5-0 away to Moscow Dynamo. More than 40,000 watched Chelsea draw with Red Banner of Hungary, Spurs hosted Wacker of Vienna and Rot-Weiss Essen, and Second Division West Ham were given a lesson when AC Milan won 6-0 at Upton Park.

Wolves pushed the debate along when manager Stan Cullis grandiosely called his team 'champions of the world' after heavily watering the pitch to help them beat Hungary's technically superior Honved 3-2 in the Molineux mud.

In April 1955, *France Football* magazine summoned 16 leading clubs to Paris, including Chelsea as England's only representatives, and although secretary John Battersby fell violently ill after eating oysters for lunch he was elected in his absence to a committee that arranged the first European Champion Clubs' Cup for the following season, pairing Chelsea with Djurgarden of Sweden.

Alas, the club had reckoned without the insular Football League management committee, which told them that taking part 'would not be in the best interests of the League'. Chelsea chairman Joe Mears was on that committee and reluctantly went along with the recommendation. Polish club Gwardia Warsaw took their place and in September 1955 the European Cup began with Hibernian representing Scotland but no English interest.

Mears, and a whole crop of London players, did not have to wait long for their chance, however. Only a fortnight after the

Paris meeting, Sir Stanley Rous helped organise a competition to be called the Inter-Cities Fairs Cup for European cities that held an international trade fair. Only one team per city was allowed, so Mears took charge of a **London XI** that kicked off continental competition for the capital on 4 June 1955 by winning 5-0 away to a Basle XI.

The team was:

> Ron Reynolds (Tottenham); Peter Sillett, Stan Willemse; Ken Armstrong (all Chelsea), Jim Fotheringham (Arsenal), Derek Saunders (Chelsea); Harry Hooper (West Ham), Johnny Haynes (Fulham), Cliff Holton (Arsenal), Eddie Firmani, Billy Kiernan (both Charlton).

QPR's Brian Nicholas replaced the injured Saunders before half-time, Holton scored a hat-trick and the other scorers were Firmani in the first half and Hooper in the second.

Winning all four games in a mini-group that lasted almost two years, London went on to defeat Lausanne 3-2 on aggregate in the semi-final, then came up against Barcelona in the final. Greaves and Jim Langley with a late penalty earned a 2-2 draw at Stamford Bridge, but in the return in May 1958 Barcelona – effectively the club side with one reinforcement from Espanol – were too strong, putting six goals without reply past Arsenal's Jack Kelsey.

Not surprisingly, the team had completely changed from the first match almost three years earlier, but a start had been made. For the second competition between 1958-60, Chelsea represented London, making their belated European debut by winning 3-1 away to BK Frem in Copenhagen on 30 September 1958, with Greaves inevitably among the scorers.

He scored two more in the second leg in November, watched by only 13,104, but was missing from the away leg of the quarter-final in May, when a Belgrade XI won 4-1 for a 4-2 aggregate success.

At Christmas, Greaves had been unsuccessfully tapped up by a Newcastle United director. Chelsea's fear for the new decade, with the maximum wage about to be lifted, was how long they could keep him.

* * * * *

Re-establishing **West Ham** as a First Division club took a long time. By May 1958, when they at last returned, no club had been in Division Two for longer than the Hammers' 26 years.

As we have seen, there were more pre-war survivors than for most teams, which proved a mixed blessing. Welcome as the sense of familiarity was, it soon became apparent that the ageing squad needed rejuvenating.

Not the least of reasons was that some of the best players had departed: Goulden, as mentioned, to become a star at Chelsea, 'ten goal' Joe Payne, one of the many whose career was ruined by the war, was forced into retirement after only ten games and wing-half Archie Macaulay moved to Brentford. Frank Neary from QPR did not solve the goalscoring void and although Bill Robinson, Charlton's FA Cup-winning centre-forward, was more successful, there were a couple of post-war seasons that finished uncomfortably close to what would have been a first-ever spell in the third tier.

The 1949/50 campaign, when Spurs topped the Second Division table, was one of them, in which the only three teams below the Hammers were QPR and relegated pair Plymouth Argyle and Bradford Park Avenue.

Ted Fenton – older brother of Benny – a local lad, former West Ham player and the manager during non-league Colchester United's FA Cup giant-killing season of 1947/48, was brought in as assistant and then successor to Charlie Paynter, ending the latter's 50 years of service at Upton Park.

He found it hard going during the early 1950s.

Slowly, however, the club's reputation for bringing through some of the best East End talent grew, thanks in large part to the work of the now retired Robinson and chief scout Wally St Pier. Although Manchester United's babes dominated the first five years of the new FA Youth Cup, the Hammers were semi-finalists in the second season, 1953/54, and beaten finalists in 1957 (against United) and 1959 (against Blackburn).

Eighth place in the Second Division in 1957, doing the double over Fulham and Orient in front of big crowds, also promised greater things, which were duly achieved the following season. In late autumn, only six points separated the top 15 clubs, but Fenton's re-signing of his former Colchester centre-forward Vic Keeble from Newcastle United in October enabled West Ham to establish themselves among the serious promotion contenders.

Keeble scored 23 goals in 32 games, inside-forward John Dick weighed in with 21 and the modern overlapping full-backs John Bond and Noel Cantwell added a remarkable dozen between them, all contributing to the only league campaign in which the club has ever reached 100 goals.

It was Bond, nicknamed 'Muffin' (as in Muffin the Mule), who hammered a crucial free kick past the Liverpool defence for the equalising goal in the penultimate game, watched by 37,750, and when Middlesbrough were beaten 3-1 at Ayresome Park on a gripping final day, the title itself was confirmed. Charlton missed out on the same afternoon with their home defeat by Blackburn.

Bond and Cantwell were two of the future managers also including Malcolm Allison, Frank O'Farrell, Dave Sexton and Jimmy Andrews who regularly adjourned after training to Cassettari's cafe on the Barking Road after training, moving salt and pepper pots around as they plotted the sort of radical new thinking that English football badly required in the years after the eye-opening shock of losing twice to Hungary in 1953/54 by 6-3 and 7-1.

Club captain Allison had joined from Charlton in 1951 after falling out with manager Seed and was a regular at centre-half for six years until an early-season game at Sheffield United in the promotion campaign, when he was struggling to run. Having kept room-mate and great friend Cantwell awake with his coughing that night, he was sent to the London Hospital to be told he was suffering from TB, would have to lose a lung and should forget about playing football.

Typically, Allison refused to accept retirement and believed after returning in the reserve team that he was on the verge of regaining a first-team place. Then came one of the seminal nights in West Ham history: Monday 8 September 1958 and Manchester United's visit to Upton Park.

Injuries meant the number six shirt was up for grabs and the contenders were Allison and a 17-year-old boy who regarded him as a hero and mentor, called Bobby Moore. Cantwell, asked for his choice by the manager, put friendship aside and suggested Moore, who was duly picked for a debut that drew rave reviews in the 3-2 victory. Allison never played another first-team game and retired the following month. Moore, born in Barking and educated at Tom Hood School in Leytonstone, went on to accrue 642 of them.

The squad barely needed strengthening to make an impression in the First Division. Welsh international inside-forward Phil Woosnam, who had been an amateur teaching physics at Leyton County High School, made the short trip from Orient in return for a £30,000 cheque and turned professional. Irish goalkeeper Noel Dwyer, who proved less reliable, was also signed.

Heads turned when in the double-header traditionally played over two midweek dates early in the season, West Ham took a win and a draw against champions Wolves. Winning four of the six London derbies and losing only at Chelsea (3-2), the Hammers finished an impressive sixth. John Dick scored even more heavily than before, with 27 goals to Keeble's 20.

In 1959/60, they were top of the table when travelling to Sheffield Wednesday at the end of November but, not for the first or last time, the winter mud slowed them. A 7-0 thumping at Hillsborough foreshadowed a decline to 14th place.

* * * * *

Beginning the first full season of national football after the war by losing 7-2 at Bury suggested **Fulham** might be in for hard times.

In fact, they beat West Ham back to the First Division by a good few years in what proved a false dawn.

The initial success began amid the darkness of a managerial death, when Jack Peart was suddenly lost in the early days of the 1948/49 season. Frank Osborne took over as general manager with another former player, Eddie Perry, taking charge of the team until Bill Dodgin Sr replaced him the following year.

Like West Ham in 1958, success stemmed from the signing of a goalscorer. For Vic Keeble read Arthur Rowley, acquired from West Bromwich Albion, but with none of Keeble's reputation. Having scored only four goals in ten games for the Midlands club, he hit 19 in 22. Three London derbies right at the finish could have undone Fulham's promotion push but by beating Brentford 2-1, West Ham 2-0 and drawing with Tottenham, they ended up a point clear of West Bromwich (the only visitors to win at Craven Cottage) and two in front of Southampton.

Rowley would go on to become the heaviest scorer in English football history, yet he was not a success for the Cottagers in the top division, scoring only eight times in Fulham's miserable total of 41 goals, which left them a mere five points clear of immediate relegation.

Rowley moved on to Leicester, where he was a huge success every season for years to come. Fulham struggled again, dropping one place to 18th – though still above neighbours Chelsea despite conceding the two defeats to them that enabled the Blues to stay up. In 1951/52, however, it was Fulham who made the drop, finishing rock bottom after another two losses to their nearest neighbours.

A changing team was overseen by new manager Dodgin, who introduced among others his son Bill Jr, Jimmy Hill from Brentford and left-winger Charlie Mitten, a former member of Manchester United's 'famous five' forward line, who arrived – once he had served a six-month suspension – via the outlawed Colombian League.

The Second Division proved far more fun, as well as allowing some promising youngsters to develop. Most notable among them were two inside-forwards who would prove a huge miss to their local clubs. Bobby Robson, a Newcastle fan, was lured to London by Dodgin's enthusiasm in the face of Tyneside's apathy. A schoolboy international Arsenal fan from north London called Johnny Haynes, influenced by his friend Tosh Chamberlain, also believed he would have a better chance of breaking through down by the Thames.

Haynes made his debut on Boxing Day 1952 at home to Southampton and within three years was an England regular as a Second Division player.

His forte was spraying passes to the flanks, which he practised by putting a towel down by the touchline and hitting long diagonal balls to land on it. Come match day, woe betide any winger – normally outside-left Chamberlain – who failed to make the most of them. The miscreant would be treated to a trademark glare from the hands-on-hips maestro and often a mouthful too, most notably one day when Chamberlain had decided to take a break and enjoy a cigarette handed to him by a spectator as the ball floated into touch.

Robson, a wing-half or inside-forward who loved to push forward and score goals, had to wait until November 1957 for his international recognition, by which time he had given up all hope of winning medals at the Cottage and signed for West Bromwich Albion.

He might have regretted the move had Fulham won the FA Cup that season, when they wasted a chance to reach Wembley by losing a semi-final replay at Highbury 5-3 to a Manchester United team that had been torn apart by the Munich air disaster. After a 2-2 draw at Villa Park, watched by almost 70,000, goalkeeper Tony Macedo's errors allowed United the win that all neutrals were hoping for, although Bolton Wanderers spoilt the fairy-tale by beating them in the final.

Fulham, normally in the top ten while scoring heavily, finished fifth that season as West Ham went up and then followed them the year after, which marked the emergence of another supremely promising youngster.

Former striker Bedford Jezzard, leading scorer for five successive seasons in the early 50s, had taken over as manager. He picked 17-year-old wing-half Alan Mullery to play his first game in the 5-2 home win over struggling Leyton Orient in February 1959, when his idol Haynes scored a hat-trick and the *Evening Standard* reporter wrote: 'Mullery...is surely an England star of the future.'

* * * * *

Struggling or not at that particular time – they rallied after that seventh successive defeat to avoid relegation comfortably – **Leyton Orient** had at least returned to the Second Division after 27 years.

Their name had changed in 1946, nine years after taking over the Brisbane Road ground from the amateurs Leyton, and a much-needed change of fortune began with the appointment in August 1949 of Alec Stock.

Briefly a professional with Charlton and QPR, the bubbly former Dartford Grammar School boy made his name as player-manager of non-league Yeovil when they knocked First Division Sunderland out of the FA Cup that year (before losing 8-0 at Manchester United).

It was slow progress initially in the Third Division South, despite two excellent FA Cup runs. Winning away to Everton and Birmingham in 1952 led to a new ground record of 30,000 for the 3-0 defeat by Arsenal. Two years later, 'little' Orient were on the verge of the semi-final, but in front of 31,000 visiting Port Vale of the Third Division North scored an early goal and clung on to it with their near-impregnable defence, which that season conceded only 21 goals – 29 fewer than any other club in the four divisions.

Helped by chief scout Stan Berry, Stock recruited particularly well from various amateur clubs, successful signings including Ken Facey (Leyton), Vic Groves and Len Julians (both Walthamstow Avenue), Ron Heckman and Stan Charlton (both Bromley), skipper Stan Aldous (Gravesend) and goalkeepers Dave Groombridge (Hayes) and Pat Welton (Chislehurst).

Several of those players formed the backbone of the side that finished runners-up to Bristol City in 1955 and immediately launched another promotion challenge the following season.

Supporters feared it would be ruined by the familiar sale of leading players when, in October, Arsenal swooped for both full-back Charlton and centre-forward Groves, paying £30,000. In their next home game, Orient crushed Crystal Palace 8-0, following up with 12 goals in the three subsequent games and not looking back until the title was assured with the 2-1 home win over Millwall in late April.

Fittingly, the winning goal that day was scored by Tommy Johnston, the only serious rival to Laurie Cunningham as the club's greatest player and – judged purely on achievements for Orient – a more influential one. A craggy Scot who wore a bandage on the arm that nearly had to be amputated after a mining accident, he had joined in February from Newport County. The signing was made by Les Gore, the loyal trainer who took over for the first of six stints as caretaker manager when Stock departed for Arsenal as an assistant to Tom Whittaker. He returned in disillusionment after 53 days, in time for the promotion push.

Heckman and Johnny Hartburn, the left-wing pairing, scored 43 of the 106 league goals, but in the higher division it was Johnston who excelled. Ever-present in the first year, he scored 27 times as the team finished 15th and, in 1957/58, rattled in 35 in 30 games before promotion contenders Blackburn snatched him away for a derisory £15,000.

In one extraordinary spell from the end of November 1957, he scored 19 times in ten games, including two hat-tricks and four against Rotherham on Christmas Day. Adding another eight after his transfer to take Blackburn up to the First Division with West Ham, he was the country's leading scorer for the season.

Stock left again, this time for a few months with AS Roma, but his third spell from March 1958 to February 1959 was unhappier and ended just as Johnston returned. This may not have been coincidental for it was ebullient chairman Harry Zussman who wanted him back.

The Scot was always happier playing for caretaker Gore, and enjoyed another two and a half seasons, and 52 more goals, ending with a club record 123 in 190 games. Twenty five of them came in 1959/60, when Orient finished in the top ten and started to introduce half of the team who would produce their greatest ever season two years later.

* * * * *

Stock moved on to **QPR**, where he would eventually achieve great things at a club that had started strongly after the war, quickly winning promotion to Division Two for the first time in 1948 but lasting only four seasons.

Runners-up to Cardiff City as the Third Division South resumed, Rangers began at a gallop the following season, with ten wins and two draws from the first dozen games establishing them firmly at the top before the one extended blip in the autumn.

Even in that period they beat Bournemouth, who would become their nearest challengers but still end up four points in arrears. Swindon and Orient were the only teams to win at Loftus Road, where promotion was secured with a goalless draw at home to Swansea in front of 27,757. Cyril Hatton, signed from Notts County, top-scored with 25 league and cup goals and Welsh international wing-half Ivor Powell was such an influential figure that Aston Villa paid £17,500 for him later that year.

Both men figured prominently in an exciting FA Cup run in which First Division Stoke City were beaten 3-0 and Derby were held 1-1 in the quarter-final before a 5-0 defeat in the replay.

During the fifth-round win over Luton, wooden fencing collapsed under the weight of numbers in a 30,000 crowd, although there were no serious injuries. A limit of 28,000 was set for the Derby tie, for which there was so much interest that some 60,000 applications were received and many supporters demanded that the club should accept Tottenham's offer to stage the game at White Hart Lane.

Manager Dave Mangnall, the former Millwall forward appointed in 1944, understandably insisted on rejecting the offer and his decision was justified by what *Pathe News* called a 'stupendous fight' against the team who finished fourth in the top division that season. Hartburn, later of Orient, put Rangers ahead before Scottish international Billy Steel equalised.

It was therefore a memorable 50th year for the club, founded in 1898, but in four seasons in Division Two goals were hard to come by, the highest position was 13th and relegation came in 1952. A winning start at home to West Ham proved illusory and despite winning three of the last four games, Rangers were bottom of the table from mid-February onwards.

Mangnall paid with his job and Jack Taylor took over for the remainder of the Fifties, which were a struggle. Not until 1957 did they make the top half of the table, when future England international Ron Springett's goalkeeping was an important factor. At the time the two regionalised divisions were split for the 1958/59 season, Rangers were only a few points away from joining Crystal Palace and Millwall in the new Division Four.

They managed 13th place in the new league, after which Taylor left for Leeds, to be replaced by Stock. Better days lay ahead.

* * * * *

West London rivals **Brentford** not only qualified for the new Third Division but had been just a couple of points short of promotion back to Division Two in 1958, apparent victims of a fix, of which more later.

The immediate post-war years brought hard times for them, bringing an end straightaway to their only period in the top division. Harry Curtis, manager since 1926, was still in charge 20 years later, but soon had to sell boy wonder Leslie Smith to Aston Villa and found a fine start to the 1946/47 season quickly deteriorating.

A dreadful run of one win in 15 games until Boxing Day was followed by an even worse period. From the start of February there was one win in 17, 2-1 away to Leeds, the only team to finish below them.

Len Townsend's eight goals made him top scorer and the final game was a home defeat by Arsenal, whom the Bees had had the mockers on for so long. They went down by eight points.

Starting the next season with a humiliating 5-0 defeat by Fulham suggested, correctly, that life would not be easy downstairs. Two bad seasons ended in 15th and then 18th place, the latter only a point away from another relegation despite a record 8-2 win over mid-table Bury, in which Scottish inside-forward Peter McKennan scored five times.

That was the first game in charge for Curtis's replacement Jackie Gibbons, a former Tottenham amateur who continued to play in attack and recruited former Bradford team-mate Ron Greenwood to shore up the defence. McKennan's goals also inspired a run to the FA quarter-finals, where his old club Leicester silenced the record crowd in Griffin Park history of 38,678 by winning 2-0.

Greenwood enjoyed 'three wonderful years' at the club, where he became captain and persuaded young wing-half Jimmy Hill to take over as the players' union representative.

The forthright Hill left for Fulham in March 1952 after a row with the manager, in which he supported Greenwood but had too much to say about it to the press. Greenwood stayed longer before joining Chelsea and was influential in persuading the board to sign Tommy Lawton for £16,000.

The former England striker put thousands on the gate but was not quite the success the club had hoped for, either as centre-forward or briefly as player-manager once Gibbons left in 1952 after three years of improved performances and top-ten finishes, with Billy Dare invariably top scorer. Before that, 17-year-old future England international Peter Broadbent emerged as a potential star, but Brentford benefited only to the tune of his bargain £7,000 transfer fee to Wolves.

Dropping to 17th in 1953 was a warning and after Lawton took the opportunity for a last hurrah in the First Division with Arsenal the following autumn, Bill Dodgin Sr, arriving from Fulham, could not prevent relegation along with Oldham.

Dodgin lasted until after the 1956/57 season, by which time the most encouraging sign was the emergence of the greatest combination of strikers in the club's history. The powerful Jim Towers arrived first, making his mark in 1954/55 with 16 goals. George Francis, another local boy who had often played against Towers in schoolboy football and did national service with him, was given a debut in February that season.

Their partnership came close to securing promotion in 1958, when Towers beat the existing club record with 29 goals and Northampton and Norwich were both beaten 7-1. Brighton, Plymouth and Swindon were involved in the shake-down with the Bees, only one team as ever winning promotion, but the outcome left a nasty taste.

Brentford drew away to both Plymouth and Brighton in April as well as winning their last three games, including the Albion's visit to Griffin Park. Crucially, however, Brighton had two matches in four days on either side of that game, both against lowly Watford, who were already destined to drop into the new Fourth Division and had little to play for.

Brighton went into the second of those needing a draw to go up and the referee reported suspicions about exactly how hard Watford were trying in a 6-0 defeat.

Two years later John Meadows, Watford's captain at the time, told the *Daily Mail* in a front-page story: 'Some Watford players and myself shared £110 between us from the Brighton players at the end of the season to bend a home and away match with them.'

Brighton's captain Glen Wilson was quoted as telling the paper: 'This sort of thing goes on all the time.'

Thus Brentford finished only second, and the following year, with Towers breaking his own scoring record, they were third behind Plymouth and Hull. The 1959/60 season was Francis's best with 31 goals, but it ended in sixth place. Sadly, the best of the 'Terrible Twins' and the team was behind them.

* * * * *

While south London rivals Charlton were lording it in the top division in the post-war years and drawing huge crowds, Millwall and Crystal Palace saw plenty of each other in the Third Division South – frequently in desperate circumstances. At one point, the pair even finished bottom in successive seasons, relying on the prevailing old pals act to secure re-election to the Football League.

Millwall, one of those clubs badly hit in football terms by the war, had resumed after it in Division Two but lasted only two seasons, finishing 18th and then bottom. In the latter season, not for the first or last time, the FA closed The Den for one game just before Christmas because of bad crowd behaviour. The locals might have wished it shut on the February day that Bury, in relegation danger themselves, won 7-1 there.

Charlie Hewitt, a successful Millwall manager from 1936– 40, left Orient to return to south London and experienced the extremes in his eight-year tenure until 1956: bottom in 1950, runners-up to Bristol Rovers in 1953 and 22nd in his final season, truncated when he was sacked in January.

Goalkeeper Malcolm Finlayson, destined to be a league champion and FA Cup winner with Wolves, was responsible for the division's best defensive record in that runners-up season, but was also still around when 100 goals were conceded in 1956. Only by winning the last three games did the Lions condemn Palace to apply for re-election instead.

Two years later, Millwall never looked likely to make the cut for the new Third Division by finishing in the top half of the table. Not even a return to management for the estimable Jimmy Seed could drag them higher than 23rd place and the first season of Fourth Division football ended two places below Palace in ninth.

* * * * *

Palace's record over the same period was even worse. In 12 Third Division South seasons, they were only once in the top half (seventh in 1949/50) and their average placing was 18th. Bottom in 1949 and 1951, they were only one place off it in 1956.

Not surprisingly, the turnover of managers was high. Noted former Arsenal men Ronnie Rooke and Laurie Scott had a go as player-managers and there were even joint bosses for a while in Charlie Slade and Fred Dawes after Rooke resigned.

Goalscoring was generally a problem and would have been worse without Albert 'Cam' Burgess from Chester, who scored three on his debut against Orient in 1951/52 and the following season claimed three hat-tricks in four games. He totalled 40 goals in 50 matches.

FA Cup defeats by clubs like Great Yarmouth and Bishop Auckland helped neither morale nor finance.

Palace should still have avoided the Fourth Division but from a good position in 1957/58 slipped just below the halfway mark, costing former Spurs goalkeeper and Cardiff manager Cyril Spiers his job.

More optimistic signs were the debuts of teenage forward Johnny Byrne and goalkeeper Vic Rouse, both of whom played in the record 9-0 win over Barrow in October 1959. New manager George Smith had Palace in the top eight for the first two seasons in the fourth tier, Byrne emerging as one of London's many Sixties stars in the making.

Chapter 5

Glory days (1961-70)

A new era as the maximum wage is abolished and Haynes becomes the first £100-a-week English footballer; Spurs become first club this century to complete league and cup double; European football grabs the imagination and brings trophies to swinging London; Moore, Hurst and Peters (plus Cohen) win the World Cup; even Leyton Orient make the top division while QPR win League Cup at Wembley; but hooliganism on the rise with London clubs to the fore.

B Y the summer of 1961, goals and wages were both on the increase but the former had peaked and the latter were taking off with no end in sight. Season 1960/61 produced the highest scoring of the post-war era, with 1,724 goals in the First Division alone, at an average of 3.73 per game. Ten years later, it had dipped to the lowest ever: 1,089 at 2.36.

In each of the two campaigns at the end of the Fifties, five Football League teams had scored 100 goals or more. For 1960/61 it was seven, including Tottenham (115), Fourth Division runners-up Crystal Palace (110) and the team above them, Peterborough United, whose astonishing first season of league football brought 134 goals in 46 games (52 of them to Terry Bly, the centre-forward signed from Norwich for just £5,000). Others in the capital only just missed out on a century: Chelsea scored 98 but conceded 100, Charlton's figures were 97-91 and Millwall's 97-86.

It was a good time for any forwards on a goals bonus and was about to get considerably better. The maximum wage had crept up every couple of years from £14 in 1951 to £20 (£17 in summer) in 1958, where it remained. It was a nice round figure that clubs were not keen to increase, even though they risked losing top players abroad, as Leeds United and Charlton had done with John Charles and Eddie Firmani respectively.

Jimmy Hill, mentioned in the previous chapter as a feisty midfield performer for Brentford and Fulham, became chairman of the players' union in 1957 and linked demands for a wage increase with reform to the iniquitous 'retain and transfer' system, under which a club retained a player's registration after his contract ended. If he did not wish to re-sign, they could simply keep him without paying any wages.

The newly named Professional Footballers' Association – a title thought up by Hill to convey greater dignity – became heavily involved in the case of George Eastham, Newcastle's gifted little inside-forward, who had asked for a transfer at the end of his contract in 1960. As Newcastle refused, he declined to play, taking a job in Surrey with the future Fulham chairman Ernie Clay, until a move to Arsenal for £47,500 was finally agreed three months into the new season.

Emboldened by this success, the PFA pushed for the abolition of the maximum wage, although Hill feared that members would accept an offer increasing it to £30. There were so many strings attached that they refused to, and at three regional meetings in December 1960 voted by 694-18 to issue a month's notice of intention to strike.

With Hill using his journalistic contacts to good effect, the players' case attracted more sympathy than might have been expected and in January the Football League backed down. The maximum wage was abolished, but the clubs then refused to back an agreement to outlaw the retain-and-transfer system.

The plaque at St Andrew's Church, Fulham Fields, commemorating the club's foundation as St Andrew's, claimed for 1879.

Weary Gunners: A Kentish Independent *cartoon commiserates with the over-worked Woolwich Arsenal after five First Division games in eight days, in December 1904.*

Clapton Orient, 1905, the year they met Chelsea in London's first Football League derby.

Pensioner meets Cockerel: Chelsea v Spurs, 1909.

Was it the 'white horse' final: or an over-developed film, as PC George Scorey later told friends?

'Pass him down the front': helping hands at Upton Park, 1930.

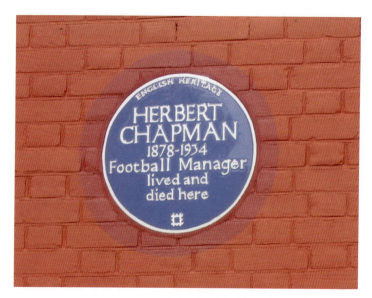

English Heritage plaque to 'the first modern manager' at his home in Hendon.

CHELSEA FOOTBALL & ATHLETIC CO. LTD.

Official Programme

Directors :—Capt. J. H. MEARS, R.M. (Chairman), J. E. C. BUDD,
C. J. PRATT, H. J. M. BOYER, L. J. MEARS.
Manager-Secy. :—Wm. BIRRELL.
Ground :—STAMFORD BRIDGE, S.W.6.   'Phone :—FUL. 3321.

COMMEMORATING THE FIRST VISIT OF A
RUSSIAN CLUB TO ENGLAND.

CHELSEA F.C.
v.
DYNAMO F.C.
(MOSCOW)
(U.S.S.R. CHAMPIONS)

·Tuesday, November 13th, 1945·
KICK OFF 2.30 P.M.

ДОБРО ПОЖАЛОВАТЬ!

Мы—Директора, игроки-спортс-
мены и публика футбольного клуба
Челси, сердечно приветствуем Вас—
персонал и игроков Московского
футбольного клуба «Динамо».

Мы приветствуем Вас как чемпи-
онов Вашей страны и надеемся, что
Ваше пребывание здесь будет для
Вас приятным.

WELCOME !

We, the Directors, players and
supporters of the Chelsea Football
Club, extend a hearty welcome to
the Officials and players of the
Moscow Dynamo Football Club.
We congratulate you as Champions
of your Country and hope that
your stay in this Island will be a
happy one.

PRICE TWOPENCE

The Russians are coming (part I): a 3-3 draw at Stamford Bridge, 1945.

First European adventure – a London XI take on a Frankfurt XI in the 1955 Fairs Cup.

The young maestro: schoolboy international Johnny Haynes, 1950.

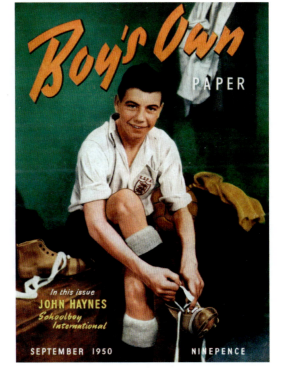

A 12th win in 13 games (with one draw) to start the 1960/61 season for Tottenham; this one by 4-0 at Nottingham Forest.

Unusual informality from the bowler-hatted Bill Nicholson as Spurs celebrate winning the First Division, 1961.

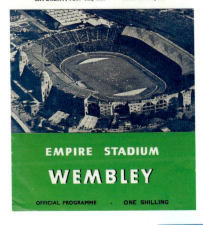

THE FOOTBALL ASSOCIATION CHALLENGE CUP COMPETITION

FINAL TIE
LEICESTER CITY
v
TOTTENHAM HOTSPUR

SATURDAY, MAY 6th, 1961   KICK-OFF 3 p.m.

EMPIRE STADIUM

WEMBLEY

OFFICIAL PROGRAMME   ·   ONE SHILLING

Double up: Leicester City unable to prevent history being made.

'Little' Leyton Orient make the top division, and start against Arsenal, 1962.

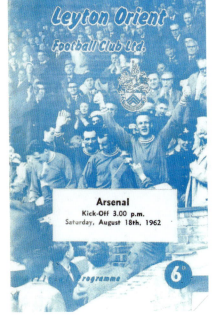

Leyton Orient
Football Club Ltd.

Arsenal
Kick-Off 3.00 p.m.
Saturday, August 18th, 1962

Programme

6ᵈ

LEYTON ORIENT SUPPORTERS CLUB

A SPECIAL MEETING

WILL BE HELD
IN THE MAIN SEATING STAND
AT
LEYTON STADIUM

on SUNDAY 20th November, 1966, at 11 a.m.

DIRECTORS AND OFFICIALS OF THE LEYTON ORIENT
FOOTBALL CLUB WILL BE IN ATTENDANCE
including Mr. Arthur Page and Mr. Dick Graham

ALL THOSE INTERESTED IN LEYTON ORIENT
WHETHER MEMBERS OF SUPPORTERS CLUB
OR NOT ARE INVITED

ADMISSION BY THIS TICKET ONLY

But four years on, Orient summon supporters to discuss the latest financial crisis.

The Dons win at Wembley, 1963, on the day Eddie Reynolds headed their four goals.

THE FOOTBALL ASSOCIATION CENTENARY YEAR

-1863-   -1963-

AMATEUR CUP   FINAL TIE

SUTTON UNITED

v

WIMBLEDON

OFFICIAL
PROGRAMME

ONE
SHILLING

WEMBLEY

EMPIRE STADIUM

SATURDAY, MAY 4th Kick-off 3 p.m.

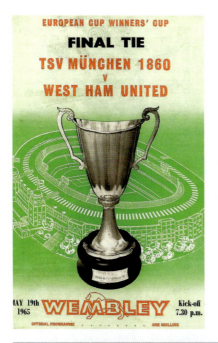

Their finest hour? Manager Ron Greenwood believed so of West Ham's 1965 Cup-Winners' Cup triumph.

QPR manager Alec Stock was told he had signed 'a clown' in Rodney Marsh. Supporters found no cause for complaint. And Stock signed him again, for Fulham.

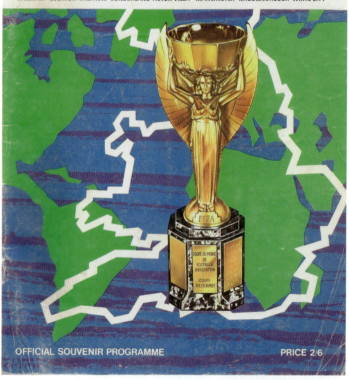

OFFICIAL SOUVENIR PROGRAMME   PRICE 2/6

*The World Cup comes to London: official
tournament programme.*

*All for ten shillings
(50p): a standing ticket
at the tunnel end.*

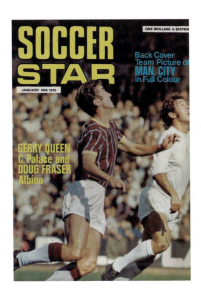

*Queen in tussle at Palace:
Gerry Queen (later of Orient)
makes the* Soccer Star *cover,
1970.*

*A rare day in the
spotlight for Brentford:
Wembley, 1985.*

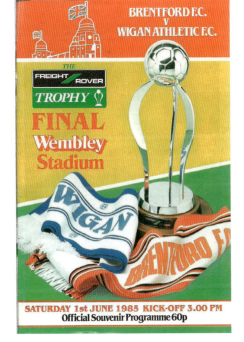

Valley of weeds, 1988: but Charlton Athletic would return home in triumph four years later.

Liverpool smashed: the short-lived London Daily News *celebrates Wimbledon's win at Anfield, March 1987.*

Best of enemies: Tottenham's Clive Allen, PFA Player of the Year, and Arsenal's Tony Adams, Young Player of the Year, separated by Sir Stanley Matthews, 1987.

The odd couple: Barnet manager Barry Fry and chairman Stan 'king of the touts' Flashman, on their way to the Football League, 1990.

Millwall look west before leading the way with a new stadium in 1993.

Millwall celebrate their Docklands roots, as well as days out in 2004 for the FA Cup Final and UEFA Cup.

FOOTBALL *Bates' 20-year reign as chairman of Premiers.*

Chelsea are sold to Russian oil baron for £60m

BY DAVID HELLIER

CHELSEA FOOTBALL CLUB, the glamorous but highly-indebted and loss-making west London Premiership team, was yesterday sold for nearly £60m to a Russian businessman by Ken Bates, its chairman of more than 20 years.

Bates, who has expanded the company that owns the team into other areas of business such as hotels, a travel agency and a sports club, has sold his shareholding for around £17.5m.

The Russian businessman, Roman Abramovich, who is one of the major shareholders in Sibneft, one of Russia's largest oil companies, is making an offer at 35p a share which has been accepted already by more than 50 per

he was a "keen follower of sport and international football."

In May 2003, Sibneft announced a merger with Yukos Oil, Russia's second largest oil producer, to create Russia's largest oil company and the world's fourth largest oil producer. More recently Abramovich has become tied up in politics – he recently became governor of Chukotka in north-east Russia.

In his purchase of Chelsea Village, the holding company that owns Chelsea Football Club, Abramovich is being advised by Citigroup, the giant US banking group.

The takeover comes at a

cused the management of lacking ambition and there are suggestions that he too could be on his way.

In spite of this, Bates and the team manager Claudio Ranieri have managed to take the team to the brink of qualification for next season's lucrative European Champions' League – a qualifier must be overcome first – and some kind of financial stability will be widely welcomed by the club's players and supporters.

Last year Chelsea Village reported a loss of £16.6m and in the latest six-month period – up to the end of December 2002 – the group reported a half-year loss of £11.3m as it has struggled to fill its hotels, restaurants and sports club

The Russians are coming (part II): Roman Abramovich takes over at Chelsea, 2003.

Arsenal bid farewell to Highbury (1913–2006).

London's first champions of Europe: Chelsea, 2012.

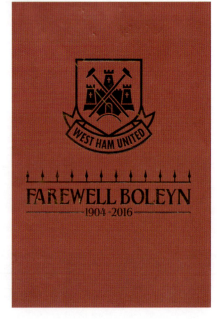

Last orders at the Boleyn for Manchester United's eventful visit, 2016.

The High Court eventually did it for them in the case of 'Eastham v Newcastle United (1964)' when the system was declared a restraint of trade. Some clubs continued to impose an unofficial maximum of their own but Fulham – hardly the richest in the country – famously agreed to the rash promise chairman Tommy Trinder had made to pay England captain Johnny Haynes £100 a week. The floodgates had opened, even if dressing-rooms were hardly yet awash with money.

* * * * *

In the late-1950s, an article in *Charles Buchan's Football Monthly* asked: 'The Double: Is It Possible?'

With Manchester United's Busby Babes failing to achieve it when mid-table underdogs Aston Villa beat them in the 1957 FA Cup Final (albeit after putting United's goalkeeper Ray Wood out of action with a shocking challenge), the implication was that to win both league and cup in the same season might be beyond any 20th century team.

The impression hardened when Stan Cullis's Wolves, apostles of direct play and champions for two successive seasons, missed the hat-trick by just a point in 1960 before winning the FA Cup.

Others had come close, including Newcastle in 1905, champions who lost the final, Herbert Chapman's Arsenal, runners-up in both in 1932, as were Wolves seven years later. In 1954, West Bromwich won the cup but were four points short in the league. Logically, the Double should have been perfectly possible. An outstanding championship-winning team just needed that element of luck that most cup sides enjoy somewhere along the road.

From early on in the 1960/61 season, it was apparent that Bill Nicholson's **Tottenham Hotspur** were likely to be outstanding champions. Indeed, they could and perhaps should have won the title a year earlier.

The Double team was effectively in place from December 1959, when Nicholson had much the better of the deal that brought inside-forward Les Allen from Chelsea in exchange for Johnny Brooks to play alongside another former Stamford Bridge man, the burly, fearsome Bobby Smith. Even before Allen's arrival, Spurs had hit the top of the table, unbeaten after 12 games when they routed the champions Wolves 5-1 in October, with four goals from Smith.

The winter mud, of which there was plenty, had no adverse effect. Allen scored five in the 13-2 FA Cup rout of poor Crewe, who were 10-1 down by half-time. Unexpectedly it was spring when Spurs faltered, two home defeats in three Easter days by Manchester City and Chelsea (with a Greaves goal) costing them the title, which unfashionable Burnley took with 55 points to Wolves' 54 and Tottenham's 53.

A significant change after the City defeat was to drop 'Tiny' Tommy Harmer, a mesmerising dribbler full of feints and swerves but now 32, and move the elegant John White, signed from Falkirk, from outside-right to inside-forward.

The possibilities were made clear in a final defiant 3-1 win away to Wolves, denying Cullis's team the Double, and from that day the following season's team was set in something close to stone. In the league and cup programme of 49 games, the same 11 players would play at least 35 each.

Like most teams of the time, Spurs essentially played a 3-3-4. Scottish international Bill Brown (£16,500 from Dundee) was in goal and the full-backs were Londoners Peter Baker and Ron Henry, with six-footer Maurice Norman (£18,000 from Norwich) in between them.

In contrasting skipper Danny Blanchflower (£30,000 from Aston Villa) and Dave Mackay (£30,000 from Hearts), Spurs had one of the finest of all wing-half partnerships. White (Falkirk, £20,000) flourished once moved inside from the wing, where former Swansea City pair Cliff Jones (£35,000) or his understudy Terry Medwin (£18,000) played on the right and the little jockey's son Terry Dyson (free) on the left. Smith (Chelsea, £18,000) led the forward line with Allen (Chelsea, player-exchange) alongside him.

If the fees seem absurdly cheap, those for Blanchflower, Mackay and Jones were all records for their particular position at the time. The Tottenham board, while traditionally parsimonious, stumped up for Nicholson when necessary. As for the rest of the squad, it was tough being a Spurs reserve for the 1960/61 season. In addition to the 12 players mentioned, only five others were used, of whom three made but a single appearance and the other two (wing-half Tony Marchi and centre-forward Frank Saul) stood in half a dozen times each when Mackay or Smith were injured.

Harmer, not called upon at all, soon gave up hope and in October moved to Watford, although he would have a huge part to play later for Chelsea. By the time he left, Spurs were well on their way, winning their first 11 games – a record for any division – and then four of the next five as well.

Bogey team Manchester City forced a draw at White Hart Lane but not until the trip to Hillsborough on 12 November were Nicholson's team beaten, by 2-1.

The result gave heart to Wednesday, closest pursuers – if that is the word – to Tottenham, who responded by drubbing Birmingham 6-0, then slipped up in a classic against champions Burnley, who came back from 4-0 down to draw.

There was a comfortable Christmas double over West Ham, 2-0 and 3-0, and a ten-point lead going into the new year before Arsenal were beaten 4-2 in front of the season's best crowd of 65,251. Only after that was there a blip, a run of only two wins in seven games, successive defeats by Cardiff and Newcastle causing an irate Nicholson to claim 'they've become lazy'.

By Easter Sheffield Wednesday, unbeaten since early December, had cut the gap to three points, and incredibly it seemed that Spurs might throw the title away for a second successive year. The response was to win all three Easter matches, two of them against Chelsea, then ensure the title by defeating runners-up Wednesday 2-1 under the White Hart Lane floodlights after falling behind.

A home defeat by West Brom on the final day meant Spurs only equalled rather than beat Arsenal's 1931 record of 66 points, although their total of 31 wins was a new record and 115 goals remains the best haul in the top division since the war. Smith scored 28 of them, Allen 23 and winger Jones 15 from 29 games.

'The hard work of manager Mr Bill Nicholson and his great team has its first reward, and England has a worthy representative in next season's European Cup,' wrote John Camkin in the *News Chronicle*. 'And now on to the Cup Final and the double!'

As Spurs were so far ahead in the league when the FA Cup third round took place in January, winning both competitions was already being widely discussed. 'Another Bid For That Cup And League Double' was the headline in London's *Evening News* even before an unexpectedly difficult 3-2 win over Charlton of the Second Division.

Beating Crewe in the fourth round was rather more straightforward, visiting goalkeeper Brian Williamson ensuring the score was kept to single figures this time, at 5-1. Aston Villa were next and after winning a dress rehearsal in the Midlands 2-1 in the league, Spurs returned a week later to go through 2-0.

The sixth round brought Second Division opposition but turned out to be the toughest tie of the whole cup run, and one that could have ended all hopes of history. Away to Sunderland, in front of a passionate Wearside crowd of over 60,000, Spurs looked comfortable with Cliff Jones' first-half goal, only to concede an equaliser and prompt a pitch invasion by hundreds of fans.

Blanchflower wrote later that the noise from the Roker Roar was 'unbearable' and that he had never seen such excitement anywhere. He somehow managed to keep his troops calm enough to force a replay, which was won 5-1.

The semi-final against Burnley was one of those that would have been better kept for Wembley (as it was the following year). Three times in little more than ten years, Tottenham had lost a semi-final at Villa Park, all to a late goal, but this time fortune smiled on them in a flattering 3-0 win earned by goals from Smith (2) and Jones.

That game was long forgotten by the time of the final, which took place seven weeks later, by which time Spurs were champions and history was there for the taking. Opponents Leicester City were a top-six side who had won at White Hart Lane for the past two seasons, but they needed three games to win the semi-final against Sheffield United, the Second Division runners-up. Tottenham were clear favourites.

Football Monthly's prediction that the final 'may well be one of the best since the war' proved well wide of the mark, although to be fair the magazine's preview included the proviso and hope that the usual Wembley injury jinx did not strike again.

That was exactly what happened after only 18 minutes when Allen caught full-back Len Chalmers, who wrenched his knee and was a passenger for the rest of the game. (Substitutes were still four years away).

It still took Spurs 69 minutes to score, Smith swivelling to beat Gordon Banks, and when Dyson, the smallest player on the pitch, headed a second the FA Cup and with it the Double were won.

Tottenham: Brown; Baker, Henry; Blanchflower, Norman, Mackay; Jones, White, Smith, Allen, Dyson.

Could a Treble have followed the following season? In 1961/62, Tottenham were close on three fronts, yet achieved only one-third of their objectives.

The new-fangled Football League Cup was not one of them. Spurs had been one of five clubs who did not enter the inaugural competition of 1960/61 and in their case did not do so for another six years. For 1961/62, Nicholson considered his side had enough on their plate as defending champions in two competitions and they would also be, as the *News Chronicle* had predicted, worthy representatives in the European Cup.

He was not pleased, however, with the way the league campaign began: six defeats by the end of November, including an early one at West Ham. With Bobby Smith scoring only two goals, then suffering from injuries, drastic action was required and that same month Tottenham's directors sanctioned the signing of Jimmy Greaves from AC Milan.

At Chelsea, the young Greaves had grown increasingly frustrated as his astonishing scoring record showed no sign of earning any medals. In 1960/61, he surpassed his previous best with 41 league goals yet Chelsea were not even in the top half of the First Division table, and went out of the FA Cup at home to Tottenham's rabbits Crewe.

When Italian clubs agreed to admit more foreigners for the 1961/62 season, Greaves (Milan), Denis Law and Joe Baker (Torino) and Gerry Hitchens (Inter) all agreed to leave England. Despite the maximum wage having just been abolished, Italian money still seemed too good to turn down. But Hitchens, the blond Aston Villa and England centre-forward, was the only one of the quartet to settle, staying for eight years at various clubs.

Greaves, having second thoughts, tried desperately to get out of the deal even before he signed off in typical fashion by scoring all four goals against Nottingham Forest in his final match. That proved impossible and he spent most of his six months in Italy dreaming of a return.

It came about quicker than expected when Milan signed the Brazilian Dino Sarni and realised they could make a quick profit on Greaves, who was duly sold to Tottenham in November for £99,999 – almost 25 per cent more than they paid for him.

Nicholson did not want him labelled Britain's first £100,000 footballer, but need not have worried. A relieved Greaves returned to London happy to accept a £60-a-week basic wage, scoring (of course) in his first game for Spurs reserves – watched by 14,000 at Plymouth – and then claiming a hat-trick on his first-team debut at home to Blackpool on 16 December.

On his return to Stamford Bridge for the Boxing Day fixture, he was warmly applauded and scored in the first of a double in four days over his former club that meant Spurs were back challenging near the top of the table.

Had they beaten Ipswich by two goals at frosty White Hart Lane in March instead of losing 3-1, Spurs would have been champions again on goal average. Instead, Alf Ramsey's East Anglian underdogs emulated the Tottenham of 1951 by winning the title a year after promotion from the Second Division, an extraordinary double for Ramsey as player and manager.

There was frustration too in the European Cup. From being 4-0 down in an hour away to Gornik Zabrze in the first round ('I was bloody upset with our players,' Nicholson recalled), Spurs recovered to win 10-5 on aggregate. They then beat Feyenoord and Dukla Prague before Greaves became eligible for a memorable semi-final against holders Benfica that was tantalisingly close to producing the greatest glory, glory night of all.

For the away leg, Nicholson's strategy of playing Tony Marchi as an extra defender failed as Spurs conceded twice early on in a 3-1 defeat, in which Smith and Greaves both had 'goals' disallowed. Worse, Jose Aguas scored early in the second game after Greaves had another effort dubiously chalked off.

For the rest of the game Spurs, in their all-white European strip, were magnificent, as were the 64,000 crowd. Smith scored just before half-time and Blanchflower just afterwards, but at 3-4 on aggregate Spurs hit the post or bar three times without managing to find an equalising goal.

'Benfica survived 90 minutes of football hell that would have destroyed any other team on earth,' wrote Ian Wooldridge in the *Daily Mail*. The Portugese champions, it should be said, also hit the bar and had one effort disallowed. They went on to beat Real Madrid 5-3 in one of the greatest of European finals, which Tottenham could only watch in frustration.

All of which left the FA Cup and a final against Burnley, who had finished one point above Spurs despite losing 4-2 at White Hart Lane. Greaves had scored eight goals on the way to Wembley and he added another within three minutes of the start. Jimmy Robson equalised in the second half but Smith restored Tottenham's lead within a minute and Blanchflower, cool as ever, converted a penalty.

So the cup was retained but amid thoughts of what might have been, which were exacerbated at the start of the new season. Spurs played away to champions Ipswich in the Charity Shield, belatedly worked out how to deal with Ramsey's tactics and won 5-1.

Ipswich finished 17th and then bottom the following season, while Spurs were runners-up to Everton despite scoring 111 goals – almost 30 more than the champions – and became the first British winners of a European competition when they took the Cup-Winners' Cup in some style.

Scotland's Rangers were beaten in what was inevitably dubbed the Battle of Britain and fears about the loss of Mackay for the final against Atletico Madrid were forgotten in a 5-1 triumph in Rotterdam.

Tottenham: Brown; Baker, Henry; Blanchflower, Norman, Marchi; Jones, White, Smith, Greaves, Dyson.

Despite Greaves' exceptional goalscoring, there was only one more Sixties season in the top three. In 1966/67, he put his bitter personal disappointment ('a bloody horrible year') at missing out on England's World Cup triumph behind him, scoring 31 league and cup goals as Spurs finished four points behind champions Manchester United. But the campaign is remembered more for victory in the first Cockney cup final, when Chelsea were beaten 2-1 at Wembley with Jimmy Robertson and Frank Saul scoring before a vain, late reply from Bobby Tambling.

'Spurs won their fifth FA Cup victory in five finals, their third of the sixties, in a slightly one-sided yet always entertaining match,' reported the *Sunday Telegraph*. 'If not quite playing as they pleased, they dictated the game for all but a few sporadic anxious moments.'

> **Tottenham:** Jennings; Kinnear, Knowles; Mullery, England, Mackay; Robertson, Greaves, Gilzean, Venables, Saul.
>
> **Chelsea**: Bonetti; A Harris, McCreadie; Hollins, Hinton, R.Harris; Cooke, Baldwin, Hateley, Tambling, Boyle.

The last playing links with the Double side were effectively cut in 1968, when Mackay left for Derby County (where he would win the title as player and then manager), Cliff Jones went to Fulham and Saul joined Southampton in part-exchange for Martin Chivers.

* * * * *

Chelsea, meanwhile, were becoming a force again, the epitome of the 'Swinging City' that *Time* magazine first identified in April 1966.

There were a grim couple of years to start the decade nevertheless as Greaves finally departed for Italy in May 1961 after scoring 132 goals in 169 games. His four years at the club ended sourly, when they suspended him for refusing to join a post-season tour, which cost him an England cap – and probably a goal or two – in the 8-0 romp against Mexico.

Without him, the team unsurprisingly dropped from mid-table to the bottom, actually conceding fewer goals but scoring 63 instead of the previous season's 98.

Tommy Docherty arrived as player-coach from Arsenal in September 1961 and replaced Drake as manager the following month. Regenerating the squad took time, and relegation could not be avoided, but Chelsea's victories in the FA Youth Cup in both 1960 and 1961 offered him plenty to build on.

Goalkeeper Peter Bonetti, the Harris brothers Allan and Ron, Terry Venables, Bert Murray and Bobby Tambling all played in one or both of those finals, and in the side which won immediate promotion in 1962/63, and then finished in the top six of the First Division.

The veteran inside-forward Tommy Harmer became known as 'Tummy' Harmer after scoring the only goal with what might politely be called his abdomen in the crucial penultimate game of the Second Division campaign away to promotion rivals Sunderland. Three days later, Chelsea won the final game at home to Portsmouth 7-0 to finish above the Wearsiders on goal average, Tambling having scored four to give him 37 for the season.

Stamford Bridge still had a huge capacity and in January 1964 there were 70,123 present to see Tottenham – Greaves and all – beaten in an FA Cup replay.

The following season was Docherty's best of all. With centre-forward Barry Bridges, new signing George Graham and the ever-reliable Murray and Tambling all reaching double figures in the league alone, Chelsea topped the table in April before falling away to end up third. They reached the FA Cup semi-final, where they lost to Bill Shankly's Liverpool, and won the Football League Cup by beating Leicester City in one of the last two-legged finals (3-2, 0-0).

That was Docherty's one and only trophy, though he was close again in 1966 and 1967, losing the FA Cup semi-final and then final, plus the semi-final of the Fairs Cup (a 5-0 humbling by Barcelona). The broken leg suffered by dazzling young centre-forward Peter Osgood at Blackpool in October 1966 was a huge handicap, for Tony Hateley, powerful in the air but a very different sort of player, did not do enough to justify a £100,000 fee.

Transfers like that one, and the £70,000 signing of vintage Scottish dribbler Charlie Cooke, while Venables and Graham were shipped out to north London, ensured that 'The Doc' kept Chelsea in the headlines. There was a feeling, however, that it would all end in tears and so it did. Already warned about his conduct by the club early in 1967 after some newspaper remarks concerning the directors, he upset them again in October by incurring a month-long FA ban for abusing an official on tour in Bermuda and was given little option by the board but to resign.

Dave Sexton, previously a Chelsea coach before managing Orient and coaching at Arsenal, returned from Highbury to oversee a very different but even more successful regime. Quiet to the point of introversion, he was an outstanding technical coach who also brought important players to the club like long-throw specialist Ian Hutchinson and his old Orient defender David Webb.

Webb it was who scored one of the most famous – and scruffiest – goals in Chelsea history on 29 April 1970 to win the FA Cup Final replay against Leeds. The Blues had been sixth, fifth and third in Sexton's three seasons, during which Don Revie's ultra-professional, unloved Leeds were fourth, first and second.

The mutual dislike between the teams is sometimes said to stem from the 1967 semi-final when Leeds had a goal unreasonably disallowed, but it went back further than that. John Giles said in his autobiography that the day he decided to become a player who would euphemistically 'look after himself' was in September 1964, when a tackle by Chelsea's Eddie McCreadie at Stamford Bridge put him on a stretcher and out of action for four weeks with a knee injury.

Almost six years on, both men were still looking after themselves, along with people like Billy Bremner, Jack Charlton and Norman Hunter on one side, and Ron Harris, Osgood and Hutchinson on the other. Unfortunately Alan Hudson, who might have added to the levels of finesse, was injured. In a highly entertaining 2-2 draw on a heavily sanded Wembley pitch, Webb was tormented by Eddie Gray, so for the replay Sexton moved him into the centre of defence and replaced him at right-back with Harris, who was never going to stand for such liberties.

> **Chelsea:** Bonetti; R. Harris, Dempsey, Webb, McCreadie; Hollins, Cooke, Houseman; Baldwin, Osgood (Hinton), Hutchinson.
>
> **Leeds:** Harvey; Madeley, Charlton, Hunter, Cooper; Bremner, Giles, Gray; Lorimer, Clarke, Jones.

'Players from both sides were cut down by awful tackles and referee [Eric] Jennings was content to wag the odd reproving finger,' wrote Brian James in the *Daily Mail*. Jennings gave 46 fouls – 35 of them against Chelsea – and let plenty more go.

After Mick Jones put Leeds ahead, an unmarked Osgood equalised because Jack Charlton had started chasing a Chelsea player 'who whacked me in the thigh with his knee'. Webb became the hero in extra-time by scoring with his face from Hutchinson's huge throw.

'We feel sorry for Leeds,' said fellow-defender John Dempsey, whose tongue might just have been in close proximity to his cheek. On the same night, Manchester City won the European Cup-Winners' Cup, which would become Chelsea's target the following season.

* * * * *

Having reached the First Division in 1958, **West Ham** were about to embark on the most successful period in their history. The disappointment was that a squad of so much talent under such an innovative manager never came close to winning the league championship.

That manager was Ron Greenwood, selected to take over in April 1961 after Ted Fenton's 11-year reign came to an abrupt end. Did the directors, who had originally placed him on sick leave, panic at the prospect of relegation? It was certainly an erratic season, including results like a 6-0 win over Arsenal, a 5-5 draw at Newcastle and 6-1 loss at Manchester United.

Greenwood, coaching Arsenal (although not for the Upton Park drubbing) and the England Under-23 team, was upset that the Highbury board made no attempt to keep him when he clearly had his sights on the manager's job there. But he was impressed by the quality of West Ham's playing staff, despite their final league position of 16th, and in the following season lifted them to eighth.

There were three key changes during 1962 that proved of long-term benefit. Although he had a strained relationship with Bobby Moore, Greenwood had recognised the youngster's quality since schoolboy days and unlike others did not regard him as either a centre-half or a wing-half. He made a crucial decision for West Ham and England before a game against Leicester in the 1961/62 season by telling Moore to drop back a little alongside centre-half Ken Brown. 'Play deeper and play loose,' Greenwood said.

It was an inspired move and within a few months England manager Walter Winterbottom accepted Greenwood's recommendation to take the 21-year-old to the World Cup finals in Chile, where he played every game.

In the spring of that year, West Ham paid a British-record £65,000 for Johnny Byrne, a mobile and skilful centre-forward whose 30 goals had helped Crystal Palace win the Fourth Division the previous season and earned him an England cap as a Third

Division player. He struggled at first but improved dramatically the following season once Greenwood made another brilliant positional change, turning Geoff Hurst from a workaday wing-half the other players used to laugh at ('a bit of a carthorse,' Moore called him) into an international-class striker.

Following a dreadful start in 1962/63, bottom of the table after losing 6-1 at home to Spurs and then 2-0 at newly promoted Leyton Orient, Hurst took the number 10 shirt. After beating Liverpool, West Ham immediately reversed the Spurs score by winning 6-1 at Manchester City.

Moore, Hurst and Martin Peters were now established and by the end of the season – concluded with another 6-1 win over relegated City – West Ham were a comfortable 12th and, if not championship material, were becoming a dangerous cup team.

After getting past Fulham, Swansea and Everton with one-goal victories in the FA Cup, they went out at Liverpool 1-0 in the quarter-final, but the following season, 1963/64, brought two long runs.

In the League Cup, where they had not progressed beyond the second round in three previous attempts, Orient, Aston Villa, Swindon and Workington were beaten before Christmas. The semi-final was lost over two legs to Leicester (3-4, 0-2), but by that time the FA Cup, never yet won, was creating greater excitement.

The draw was favourable, producing three successive Second Division opponents in Charlton, and yet again Orient and Swindon, and ten goals were scored in seeing them off, half of them by Hurst. 'Budgie' Byrne, never known to voluntarily stop talking, was actually outscoring his partner at that stage and claimed two of the three that beat Burnley before West Ham's fortune seemed at last to be hiding and the bubble about to burst. The two Second Division sides through to the semi-final, Preston and Swansea, were paired with each other, leaving the Hammers to take on the Manchester United of Best, Law and Charlton.

On the Saturday before the game, United left out all three – injured, Matt Busby claimed – for a league match at Upton Park and still won 2-0, prompting goalkeeper David Gaskell to tell a couple of home players that they need not bother turning up for the semi-final.

He was doubtless as shocked as his team-mates and their thousands of supporters at Hillsborough when West Ham, the supposed southern softies and exponents of the beautiful game, adapted to the cloying mud much better than the Busby boys and beat them 3-1. The first two goals came from Ronnie Boyce and the third from Hurst after a classic pass from Moore that presaged, had anyone known it, the final seconds of the World Cup Final.

Having used the same team in every round, Greenwood was not going to change for the final against Preston, which meant disappointment for Peters. He had been dropped after the extraordinary 8-2 home defeat by Blackburn on Boxing Day, whereupon the manager brought in the more physical Eddie Bovington for the return two days later – which West Ham won 3-1.

Bovington was thus one of the seven players beginning with the letter 'B' lining up against a Preston side who had finished third in the Second Division and fielded the youngest finalist to date in 17-year-old Howard Kendall.

West Ham: Standen; Bond, Burkett; Bovington, Brown, Moore; Brabrook, Boyce, Byrne, Hurst, Sissons.

Preston: Kelly; Ross, Smith; Lawton, Singleton, Kendall; Wilson, Ashworth, Dawson, Spavin, Holden.

Despite being clear favourites, the Londoners found themselves twice behind, Moore admitting afterwards that Preston had dominated the first half. Doug Holden put them ahead after Jim Standen, West Ham's Worcestershire cricketer, could only parry a shot from Alex Dawson. John Sissons, a winger who never lived up to Greenwood's estimation of him as a better prospect than George Best, equalised but before half-time the burly Dawson headed Preston back in front.

Hurst's header seven minutes into the second half only just crept over the line and extra time was looming when he forced the ball out to Peter Brabrook on the right for a cross headed in by an unmarked Boyce.

The club's first FA Cup triumph brought a place in the European Cup-Winners' Cup and the tests that Greenwood had always wanted against continental opposition and coaches. An improved 1964/65 league campaign ended in ninth place, with Byrne (25) and Hurst (17) again prolific scorers, and by the time it finished the Hammers were on the verge of a European final.

Along the way, they beat La Gantoise (2-1), Sparta Prague (3-2) and Lausanne (6-4), and then in a tight semi-final Zaragoza (2-1, 1-1). In the second leg in Spain Greenwood, ahead of his time as usual, played with not so much a 'false nine' as no centre-forward at all, leaving two attackers wide and pulling two deeper. Knowing the final was to be played at Wembley proved just the spur for his team to hold on in the face of a sustained assault.

Byrne missed that game and the final with an injury suffered playing for England, but the sturdy Brian Dear made sure of being his replacement by scoring five in the 6-1 win over West Bromwich at Easter. Alan Sealey, secured from Orient in exchange for centre-forward Dave Dunmore, had taken over the right-wing spot from Brabrook, so with Joe Kirkup at right-back and Peters back in favour, there were four changes from the previous year's visit to Wembley.

West Ham: Standen; Kirkup, Burkett; Peters, Brown, Moore; Sealey, Boyce, Dear, Hurst, Sissons.

The whole team – though not their manager, who was in church being confirmed – travelled to watch TSV 1860 Munich qualify for the final by winning a play-off against Torino. At that time, they were the senior team in Bavaria, Bayern Munich having been ignored when the Bundesliga was formed in 1963 and not due to join it until the 1965/66 season.

Perhaps Italian opponents would have played far more defensively at Wembley, but the Germans contributed to an outstanding game in which West Ham were simply too good for them, giving Greenwood his proudest 90 minutes as a club manager. 'We proved that football at its best is a game of beauty and intelligence,' was his verdict on a 2-0 win secured by a double from Sealey. Sadly, the winger's career was effectively ended in his early 20s when he broke a leg falling over a bench during pre-season training that summer.

Before the end of the decade, there were two more semi-finals and a losing final. The last four of the following season's Cup-Winners' Cup comprised three teams who were top of the table in their respective countries – Liverpool, Celtic and Borussia Dortmund – plus the Hammers, who found Dortmund too good for them, as did Liverpool in the Hampden Park final.

Two months later Dortmund's Hans Tilkowski, Lothar Emmerich and Siggi Held were back in London for the World Cup Final, where the West Ham trio, backed up by the capital's other representative George Cohen of Fulham, this time had the better of them.

England stayed at the Hendon Hall hotel in Barnet and although one match in the London-based group, between Uruguay and France, took place at White City (because it was a scheduled greyhound night at Wembley), Alf Ramsey's team had the significant and unprecedented advantage of playing every game at their national stadium.

There was personal disappointment for Tottenham's Greaves, injured in the final group game against France, but Hurst replaced him to head an un-Greaves-like goal and win the quarter-final against Argentina (from a cross by his room-mate Peters, who called it 'a West Ham goal') then score his famous hat-trick in the final, with two assists from Moore, while Peters added the other goal.

Alf Garnett, the bigoted star of the television sitcom *Til Death Us Do Part* (played, ironically, by Spurs fan Warren Mitchell), was not the only West Ham supporter who believed his club won the World Cup.

At club level, however, there was further frustration in two annoying League Cup defeats by West Bromwich Albion. In World Cup year, it was the last final to be played over two legs. After winning the home match with a very late Byrne goal, Greenwood's team suffered one of their occasional defensive collapses and at The Hawthorns were 4-0 down at half-time, eventually losing 4-1.

The following year, a semi-final loss by 4-0, 2-2 to the same team removed the possibility of a capital cup final at Wembley – two months before Spurs and Chelsea made history by competing for the FA Cup. Instead it was Albion who went through to meet QPR.

A small consolation was that as well as knocking out Tottenham (1-0) and Arsenal (3-1) that season, West Ham's 7-0 demolition of a full-strength Leeds United in the fourth round was regarded by many spectators as the finest exhibition they had ever seen.

In a way, it summed up Greenwood's West Ham, who on any given day could produce a performance like that, but in the league they did not beat Leeds once in the next 14 meetings.

* * * * *

For much of the decade, **Arsenal** did not so much swing as totter around and occasionally fall down flat. The most embarrassing point was surely a wet Thursday night in May 1966 when for the first of two home games in three days, and with Liverpool's European Cup-Winners Cup final live on television, just 4,554 turned up to watch the 3-0 home defeat by Leeds.

It was the lowest league gate since Plumstead days at the start of the century and, even at that time, would have been sniffed at most weeks. Unusual circumstances or not, the pitiful attendance also reflected Arsenal's form – one win since January. They finished 14th in the table, one place lower than the previous season, and it was no surprise when manager Billy Wright returned from holiday to be informed his time was up.

Wright had been appointed four years earlier when George Swindin resigned, the board having foolishly let Greenwood, his natural successor, leave for West Ham the previous season. It was a gamble, for the former Wolves and England captain had no managerial experience except for a short spell with England's Under-23 team.

He inherited a side not without talent, like the contract rebel George Eastham, but languishing in mid-table while neighbours Tottenham were collecting the trophies and superlatives. Needing a goalscorer after David Herd was sold to Manchester United, Wright did well in the summer of 1962 to secure Joe Baker, returning like Greaves and Law from an unhappy spell in Italy, and was rewarded with 31 goals in the Anglo-Scottish striker's first season, which Arsenal finished in seventh place.

Third highest scorers in the division, they seemed to have something to build on but in Wright's remaining three seasons could do no better than eighth, 13th and 14th.

In the second of those campaigns, there was a humilating FA Cup defeat by Third Division Peterborough United, while new signing Frank McLintock from Leicester recalls going to bed after his debut asking 'what have I done?' Within 18 months he had requested a transfer, which the club prudently turned down.

So to the sporting summer of 1966 when, as London prepared for the World Cup, 46,000 turned up at Highbury to see the capital's Henry Cooper come close to knocking out Cassius Clay in a world heavyweight title fight. (A young apprentice called Charlie George helped erect the ring in the centre of the pitch.)

Arsenal made headlines too and stunned their players by naming the club physiotherapist Bertie Mee as the new manager. Like Tom Whittaker's similar promotion almost 20 years earlier, it worked better than could have been imagined, not least because he employed two outstanding first-team coaches in Dave Sexton and then Don Howe, while imposing new discipline off the field.

Although Eastham was sold to Stoke, some excellent new signings arrived in Chelsea's George Graham (swapped for striker Tommy Baldwin) and the Huddersfield left-back Bob McNab. In successive seasons, the team finished seventh and ninth and forged a reputation too as cup fighters, which was where the first success came.

In 1968, there was a second successive FA Cup fifth-round defeat by Birmingham City but only after a Wembley appearance in the Football League Cup Final against Leeds. It was a grim spectacle, which Don Revie's side won 1-0 with a goal by left-back Terry Cooper, finally taking a first major trophy, which they would follow with the league title a year later.

By that time, Arsenal were only three places behind them, the league table illustrating how functional football was becoming as Sixties glamour faded. Leeds won the league by scoring just 66 goals in 42 games, but conceding only 26. Arsenal's figures in fourth place were 56-27, John Radford top-scoring with 15.

There was League Cup disappointment again when, after coming through two brutal semi-final games against Spurs with Radford's goals (1-0, 1-1), Arsenal delighted most of the nation by losing to Third Division Swindon Town 3-1 in extra time on a Wembley pitch so bad that after 90 minutes Don Howe appealed in vain to the referee to abandon proceedings.

The consolation was that fourth place earned a return to the Fairs Cup, in which they had played two rounds in 1963. Six years on, it was a far stronger Arsenal who went all the way to the final past Glentoran, Sporting Lisbon, Rouen, Dinamo Bacau and Johan Cruyff's Ajax, the previous season's European Cup runners-up.

Amid a disappointing league campaign, this time with only 51 goals scored, Europe became the focus of the season and a 3-0 win at home to the Dutch side in the semi-final was one of their very best performances.

Charlie George, a brash, long-haired teenager from nearby Holloway School, had only just established himself in the side when he scored two of the goals.

Trailing 3-0 in the first leg of the final away to Anderlecht with a few minutes left, Arsenal appeared to be in line for another set of runners-up medals.

Ray Kennedy then headed an invaluable away goal as a substitute for his fellow teenager George, and after considering matters in the showers, McLintock returned to rouse his team-mates by telling them they would pulverise the Belgians in the return, battering them with crosses.

A *Daily Telegraph* journalist, given exceptional dressing-room access before the second leg, reported George being physically sick with nerves, defender Peter Simpson smoking and drily advising 'just treat it like a cup final' and Howe urging 'hit them hard and do it quick and when you've done it, pick them up'.

Eddie Kelly, another of the younger brigade, scored after 25 minutes, and 20 minutes from time, as McLintock had predicted, the visiting defence fell victim to a cross, sent over by McNab and headed in by Radford. With the away goals rule having been introduced a few years earlier, two would have sufficed, but Sammels added a third for good measure.

Celebrations of this first trophy since 1953 were unrestrained. 'Highbury housed the greatest knees-up in the history of British football last night,' wrote Peter Batt in the *Sun*. 'They climbed goalposts, formed giant snake-like lines to dance the conga and inevitably massed together in front of the main stand for a Cockney knees-up that would have sent even Mother Brown scurrying under the table.'

'The players realise this is only an interim step,' Mee told the press.

Indeed, with only one change, the team would be the one that emulated Tottenham's Double 12 months later.

> **Arsenal:** Wilson; Storey, McLintock, Simpson, McNab; Sammels, Kelly, Graham; Armstrong, Radford, George.

* * * * *

Four other London clubs played First Division football in the Sixties, three of them for the first time in their history.

Leyton Orient's was the most romantic tale and stemmed from the epoch-changing events of 1961: Johnny Carey, shockingly sacked by Everton but still Republic of Ireland manager, was lured to east London but Tommy Johnston declined to take a pay cut and left as the only player to have scored more than 100 goals for the club.

Dave Dunmore, swapped for the unfortunate Alan Sealey, was Carey's first-choice centre-forward and became a fine leader of the line as a team that finished 19th the previous season suddenly began to click. A 5-1 win away to Walsall early on was one of five wins in six games and drawing 3-3 at Anfield with the runaway leaders Liverpool, clearly the best side in the Second Division, was soon followed by nine successive wins, putting them right up with Bill Shankly's side.

Only then did they stumble, losing games either side of a heroic FA Cup effort against 1960 league champions Burnley, and with one match left Sunderland sneaked ahead for the first time on goal average.

The programme for the final game at home to Bury had a front-cover picture of Carey and his trademark pipe, and correctly pointed out that it was a season when 'deeds have far exceeded expectations'. Orient did their bit on the day with two goals by inside-left Malcolm Graham, but it would not have been enough if Sunderland won at relegation-threatened Swansea.

BBC Radio, sharing the general opinion that Sunderland were favourites to go up, chose that game for their second-half commentary and a roar around Brisbane Road told the players that the Welsh side had equalised. With plenty to play for themselves, they hung on and Orient, astonishingly, were promoted.

The strength of the team was clearly in defence, conceding fewer goals than Liverpool, who scored 30 more. Goalkeeper Bill Robertson, a championship winner with Chelsea seven years earlier, had taken over from Frank George in mid-season but skipper Stan Charlton, former Busby Babe Eddie Lewis, and the half-back line of Malcolm Lucas, Sid Bishop and Cyril Lea missed just two games between them.

Not untypically of the club and manager, it was decided to give the same players a chance in the First Division, although Charlton urged Carey in vain to sign an extra striker like Southampton's George O'Brien. For a while they thrived, losing narrowly to

Arsenal on the first day in front of 26,300 and beating West Ham, Manchester United, Everton and Fulham in September to sit halfway up the table.

But once injuries struck, there was trouble ahead. From 29 September at Craven Cottage through the long winter of 1962/63, Orient did not win another league game until Easter Monday at Bolton. The added experience of eventual recruits Malcolm Musgrove from West Ham and Wolves FA Cup winner Bobby Mason did not help and the main interest long before the end was which of the Manchester clubs would go down with them. United survived, beating the Os on the last day at Old Trafford, and City made the drop instead.

Carey could not resist an offer to stay in the top division with Nottingham Forest and, under Benny Fenton, Orient reverted to their status as a lower-half Second Division team, only to lose that too. Dave Sexton resigned his first managerial job before the 1965/66 season ended in relegation with Middlesbrough. The Brisbane Road match between the pair in April attracted a crowd of just 2,286.

The club could still produce good young players like defenders David Webb and Paul Went, who moved on to Southampton and Charlton respectively, but after Dick Graham's austere regime, Jimmy Bloomfield's spell as player-manager almost brought relegation to the Fourth Division in 1968/69, when the final game at home to Shrewsbury had to be won (and was, 4-0).

Yet the following season, with Bloomfield now concentrating on management, was inspired, a mixed team of youngsters (Tommy Taylor, Dennis Rofe, Barrie Fairbrother) and veterans (wingers Peter Brabrook and Mark Lazarus) romping to the Third Division championship.

* * * * *

QPR's rise to the First Division, scarcely less romantic than Orient's, was inspired by the manager they gained from them. When Alec Stock left the Os for the third time, after Tommy

Johnston was re-signed against his wishes in February 1959, he was not out of work for long, moving across to West London that summer to succeed Jack Taylor.

It was slow progress there, which made the eventual success all the more satisfying, although it was to end with Stock's callous dismissal.

Rangers had spent almost all the Fifties in the middle or lower half of the Third Division South and the new man soon had them moving upwards, Brian Bedford's goals helping them to eighth place in 1960 then third, missing out by two points, and fourth, three points away.

To the fury of Brentford fans, Stock was able to buy the twin strikers George Francis and Jim Towers and although neither stayed long, Bedford remained prolific, with the goals tally 93 and then 111. Meanwhile, defensive stalwart Tony Ingham completed an extraordinary run of 247 consecutive league games towards his eventual club record of 519.

There was a lull of three seasons in the bottom half of the table from 1962–65, including another unsuccessful spell up the road at White City, where one crowd was little more than 3,000. Results might have cost many managers their job. The board kept faith and were rewarded handsomely as Stock, always on the lookout for a player and particularly keen on Londoners, began rebuilding under new chairman Jim Gregory, a London car dealer whose approaches to his favourites Fulham had been rejected.

Mark Lazarus, signed from Orient in 1960 then sold to Wolves and Brentford before being re-signed from both, was back at the Bush for his third spell. Les Allen, squeezed out at Tottenham by Jimmy Greaves, joined in July 1965, as did Jim Langley from Fulham, a club Stock believed had a tendency to 'throw away bargains'.

He picked up his greatest one there in March of a successful 1965/66 season by paying £15,000 for Rodney Marsh, confined to the reserves, and was told he had signed 'a clown'.

The younger element included the Morgan twins from Chingford, Roger and Ian, forwards given debuts as 17-year-olds.

Stock would tell them to switch sides regularly in order to confuse defenders who could not tell them apart.

The side that would create QPR history had been built by the summer of 1966, having finished third behind Hull City and Millwall. From the start of the following campaign, they were far and away the outstanding Third Division team and one of the very best of all time at that level.

Worries that a lengthening run in the Football League Cup would impede progress towards the title proved unnecessary. On they went in the cup competition, past Colchester, then Aldershot, Swansea and higher-division opposition in Leicester and Carlisle.

The 4-2 victory over the former, a top-half First Division team, showed serious intent and when Carlisle were knocked out too, the realisation dawned that Rangers were two legs away from the new venue for the final: Wembley.

Birmingham City, midway up the Second Division, were given a goal's start in the first minute and demolished 4-1 on their own ground, making the home game a formality that ended with a 7-2 aggregate.

West Ham's failure against West Bromwich Albion in the other semi-final meant that Wembley would not see an all-London final, and when the First Division side led 2-0 at half-time – both goals scored by former Rangers winger Clive Clark – an anti-climax was in the offing. In the dressing-room Stock laid into his players, picking on Allen and Marsh in particular. The transformation was spectacular. Roger Morgan headed one goal, Marsh drove an equaliser from the edge of the penalty area and nine minutes from time Albion goalkeeper Dick Sheppard failed to hold a loose ball and Lazarus pounced for the winner.

In the *Observer*, John Arlott wrote: 'The first Third Division club to play at Wembley did themselves credit. QPR, with a jaunty flourish of individual abilities which have separated them from the rest of their division, surprised, surely, even themselves and their supporters.'

QPR: P.Springett; Hazell, Langley; Keen, Hunt, Sibley; Lazarus, Sanderson, Allen, Marsh, R.Morgan.

WBA: Sheppard; Cram, Williams; Collard, Clarke, Fraser; Brown, Astle, Kaye, Hope, Clark.

By that time, early in March, Rangers had lost only two league games, and although three more defeats followed in April there was never any doubt where the championship was going.

What was less expected was the following season's triumph. Winning five of the first six games, however, despite a series of injuries, confirmed they would be a team to reckon with. Dave Clement and Allan Harris – brother of Chelsea's 'Chopper' – became regulars in defence, with Ron Springett, who had swapped clubs with brother Peter, behind them. A meagre 36 goals conceded was much the best in the division.

Allen and Marsh both missed almost 20 games, which restricted the number of goals scored, but come the final game away to Aston Villa, Rangers needed a win to make the First Division for the first time. Trailing at half-time, they were still only drawing with four minutes to play. Then a cross was whipped into the Villa area and full-back Keith Bradley, under pressure from Marsh, knocked it into his own net.

The season and that final day took a lot out of Stock, an asthma sufferer and, on his own admission, 'a worryguts'. At the start of the new season, the club's first-ever at the highest level, doctors ordered him to take three months off and he watched with increasing anguish as his team slumped to the bottom of the table after 13 games without a win. On the day he returned to work in November, chairman Gregory, who had already offered the job to his assistant manager Bill Dodgin, told him he was sacked.

Tommy Docherty, exiled for a year at Rotherham United, took over before falling out with Gregory after only 28 days, and Les Allen, who never wanted to be a manager, reluctantly took on the job. Results remained just as bad for the rest of the season and the totals of four wins and 18 points were the worst since the top division was expanded in 1919.

Chastened, Rangers settled back to life in the middle of the Second Division.

* * * * *

As QPR's star was briefly in the ascendancy, so that of neighbouring **Fulham** was going the other way, despite resisting the efforts of Tottenham and others to lure away their maestro.

Johnny Haynes had made his debut as early as 1952 and, having helped propel them to the First Division seven years later, soon became used to a relegation fight. From an impressive tenth place in their first season, 1959/60 (despite a 9-0 humbling by Wolves), Fulham missed the drop by four points and then one in successive years.

Any lengthy absence for Haynes always meant problems and his longest began in October 1962. Four months after captaining England at the World Cup in Chile, he was badly hurt in a car crash in Blackpool and missed most of the season. Yet the campaign proved that Fulham were not quite a one-man team. Despite two other broken legs and further injuries to Alan Mullery and Bobby Robson, they managed to win eight games in a row when the ice and snow finally cleared, and unlike Orient stayed up comfortably.

Haynes openly admitted he was not quite the same player again. He never returned to the England team, Arsenal's George Eastham taking the number ten shirt. While finishing 15th in 1963/64, Fulham lost Mullery to Tottenham (in order to pay for covering the Hammersmith end of the ground) and also played their part in the great Boxing Day goals extravaganza. On the day that West Ham lost 8-2 at home to Blackburn, west London saw Haynes and company thrash Ipswich, the champions 18 months earlier, 10-1 with hat-tricks for Graham Leggatt (in four minutes) and Bobby Howfield. Being Fulham, they managed to lose the return two days later 4-2.

The next two seasons were a struggle as well, missing relegation by one place each time, and in 1968 the apparently inevitable could no longer be delayed. Ninety-eight goals were conceded, seven of them at West Ham and five at Everton in their final match in the top division for 33 years.

Robson, back from a brief spell in Vancouver, had taken over as manager and was bitterly upset at being dismissed a few months into the following season, which ended in a second successive relegation after Haynes, never seriously interested in management, took over as caretaker.

He made way for Bill Dodgin Jr, whose father had been in charge 16 years earlier, and the decade ended more optimistically, in fourth place behind the Third Division champions Orient and with a record 8-0 away win at Halifax. Haynes played his 657th and last game in January of that season, a 1-1 draw at home to Stockport County.

* * * * *

For the other west London club, **Brentford,** the supposedly swinging Sixties was the decade that almost killed them.

In 1962, they became the first club to have dropped from the First Division to the Fourth, all in the space of 15 years. The exile lasted only a season, the Fourth Division title being won the following year after some heavy investment, with the inside-forward trio of John Dick, Johnny Brooks and Billy McAdams scoring 67 goals between them from a total of 98.

But by 1966, they went down again and soon afterwards supporters were shocked to hear that ambitious and successful QPR were proposing a takeover of their neighbours and a move to Griffin Park.

The *Evening Standard's* Bernard Joy inadvertently started the football rolling when he wrote in a piece about ground-sharing that Rangers and Brentford would be natural bedfellows. QPR's chairman Jim Gregory bit, and began discussions with his opposite number at Brentford, the Nottingham Central MP Jack Dunnett.

According to Denis Signy, a journalist who had become general manager at Brentford and sat in on the talks, Rangers were to buy Griffin Park for £220,000 and were to sell Loftus Road to the local council for £310,000. Alec Stock (QPR) would manage the merged club, with Billy Gray (Brentford manager) and Bill Dodgin (QPR) as his coaches.

Just like 20 years later (see Chapter 6), when Fulham were in Gregory's sights, it was the furious reaction of supporters that scuppered the plan. At a public meeting Dunnett, later president of the Football League, had to call the police to restore order. Denounced as the villain, he sold control of a relieved and reprieved Brentford in February 1967 to a consortium led by Ron Blindell.

Finances were tight and, as Rangers stormed on to the First Division, their neighbours remained marooned in the Fourth, but with their own identity preserved.

* * * * *

Crystal Palace were the other London side to follow QPR and Orient in reaching the top division for the first time in their history during the Sixties, a decade that in their case began in the bottom tier.

Only the outstanding Peterborough United side, scorers of 134 goals in their first season of league football, prevented Palace becoming Fourth Division champions in 1960/61. Scoring 110 times (30 of them by Johnny Byrne) while finishing runners-up was impressive enough. So was an attendance of 37,774 for the Easter derby with Millwall (lost 2-0) and the season's average of 19,020, both of which remain a record for the division.

Byrne's inevitable departure the following season and Arthur Rowe's resignation as manager following ill health led to a new tougher, but successful era begun by the formidable Dick Graham and carried on by Bert Head.

Graham, the archetypal 'sergeant-major' figure, liked hard work and robust football, which in 1964 paid off with promotion back to the Second Division after 39 years. Despite losing the opening game 5-1 at Coventry, Palace should have beaten Jimmy Hill's side to the title, but they failed to win any of the final seven games and missed out on goal average.

The same rugged approach served them well at the higher level, with four seasons in the top half before another step up in 1968/69. Bert Head had re-signed Byrne, well past his peak, and he moved on to Fulham before the promotion season, in which Charlton were among the contenders to go up with a Derby County side revolutionised by Brian Clough.

After losing an FA Cup replay at The Valley in January, however, Palace were beaten only once more, by Blackpool, for the rest of the season and finished a comfortable six points clear of their neighbours. Goalkeeper John Jackson, young midfielder Steve Kember and Scottish defender John McCormick all played in every game, having cost £1,500 between them. Jackson's namesake Cliff was top scorer with 18, followed by Mark Lazarus, enjoying success at yet another London club.

Like Fulham before them, Palace would find the top division a regular struggle, but they had made it.

* * * * *

That promotion chase proved to be the honourable exception in a decade of mediocrity for **Charlton.**

Relegated in 1958, they spend the whole of it in the Second Division, fourth place in 1964 and third behind Palace five years later being more than balanced by worries about dropping down another level on three or four occasions. Meanwhile, the Gliksten family were still reluctant investors after the chairmanship passed to 23-year-old Michael in 1962, and supporters came to expect that leading players like Marvin Hinton (to Chelsea, 1963), Mike Bailey (Wolves, 1966), Billy Bonds (West Ham, 1967) and Len Glover (Leicester the same year) would be sold.

In 1961/62, when Jimmy Trotter gave way to Frank Hill, they were bottom at the halfway stage and only rallied late in a season most notable for the versatile Scottish international John Hewie playing four games in goal, none of which were lost. That summer, Johnny Summers, the five-goal hero of the 7-6 victory over Huddersfield, died of cancer, aged 34.

The following season was the closest of all the escapes, requiring wins from both the last two games to stay up. A 2-1 success over Southampton did not come until the final minute and then a loser-goes-down match at Walsall was abandoned at half-time because of flooding before Charlton returned to win 2-1.

The introduction of promising youngsters like Keith Peacock, plus the return from Italy of Eddie Firmani, who later became manager, offered some optimism that petered out in poor seasons midway through the decade with finishing positions of 18th 16th and 19th. Not surprisingly, crowds dropped to below 14,000, which the board justified as reason to accept almost £130,000 in total for Bonds and Glover.

The 1969/70 campaign cost Firmani his job and once again only victory in the final match, at home to Bristol City, prevented relegation. It would not be long in coming.

* * * * *

While Charlton were stuck in the Second Division, **Millwall** went through a far more interesting decade of ups and downs, ending it above their neighbours in two seasons out of three despite having started in Division Four.

It was Charlton's most venerable manager, Jimmy Seed, in charge at The Den until 1959, after which the club tended to change managers and divisions every other year for a while.

Reg Smith, a pre-war Millwall and England winger, was recruited from Falkirk for the 1959/60 campaign and began in sensational style with the team unbeaten until their 20th game, equalling Liverpool's record from the start of a season. From that base, they should have reached the Third Division but too many games were drawn and Watford beat them by four points to the fourth promotion place.

Peter Burridge from Orient proved a star signing, with 34 and then 22 goals, his second season helping to bring the Fourth Division title under Ron Gray, promoted from assistant manager when Smith was sacked after a heavy FA Cup defeat. Burridge was then controversially sold to Palace and Gray in turn served under two years, being replaced after seven successive home defeats in autumn 1963 by Nottingham Forest's 1959 FA Cup winner Billy Gray, initially as a player-manager.

Come the end of the season and having risen four places off the bottom, Millwall needed a favour from QPR in the form of victory over relegation rivals Barnsley. It was not forthcoming, the 2-2 draw sending the wounded Lions back where they had begun.

They did not stay long, finishing not only as runners-up to Brighton the following season in a tight five-team race but second behind Hull City in the Third Division 12 months after that. The spectacular achievement was based on a solid defence now featuring Alex Stepney in goal and at full-back fellow Londoner Harry Cripps, destined to grow into such a New Cross legend that most Millwall supporters would forget, or ignore, the fact that he had once won the FA Youth Cup alongside Bobby Moore at West Ham.

In attack Len Julians, formerly of Orient and Arsenal, was enjoying an Indian summer with 38 goals over the two seasons and Scot Hugh Curran supported him before being snatched away by Norwich City in January 1966.

Millwall's other great strength as they rose to and consolidated in the Second Division was their home crowd, terrifying many an opponent who stepped gingerly up the narrow tunnel behind the goal. In 44 home games during the two promotion seasons, the team conceded only 28 goals and were unbeaten.

By the start of 1967, with Benny Fenton the new manager, that unblemished home run had been extended to 59 games. It was clearly going to be an unhappy day when it ended, which came in unfortunate circumstances on 14 January.

Charlton and Palace had been unable to succeed at The Den earlier in the season, the latter's visit attracting over 28,000, and Millwall were third in the table and starting to dream of an unprecedented third promotion when lowly Plymouth Argyle went 2-0 up at half-time and clung on for a 2-1 win. They had the team bus stoned for their trouble, which was hardly the first time the club's supporters had disgraced themselves.

There were ground closures in 1920 (see Chapter 3), 1934, 1947 and 1950, and attacks on opposing players or officials in 1965 (against Walsall), 1968 (Birmingham) and 1969 (QPR).

In November 1965, the tabloid press had a field day ('Soccer Marches To War') when a dummy hand grenade was thrown from the Millwall end into the Griffin Park net being guarded by Brentford goalkeeper Chick Brodie. Nine months after the Plymouth incident, another home defeat, by Aston Villa, led to referee Norman Burtenshaw being knocked to the ground. The FA ordered the walls around the pitch to be made taller, and the Referees' Association threatened to boycott The Den .

Fights among rival spectators dated back as far as the early 20th century, a West Ham-Millwall game in September 1906, when 'free fights were plentiful', often being cited. The big difference from about 1963 was that crowds of like-minded supporters began standing together at games, chanting and singing.

A personal memory from that year is joining a large group of away supporters without any great trepidation on the North Bank of both Arsenal and West Ham. Those areas, however, soon became very much the prized territory of home fans – plus the boldest of infiltrators, who would attempt to 'take' the home end. According to an academic study on *The Roots of Football Hooliganism* (Routledge Press, 1988), 'trouble in and around London grounds gathered momentum in and around 1967'. It was going to get a lot worse.

Interlude II

Non-league football

Thriving non-league scene in London from the start despite competition from a dozen professional clubs; from Casuals in the first Amateur Cup Final (1894), the capital supplies almost 20 different winners; leading amateurs appear as late as 1955 in Chelsea's title-winning team; 100,000 watch Amateur Cup finals at Wembley featuring teams like local rivals Walthamstow Avenue and Leyton, Barnet and Enfield; after the FA abolish amateurism in 1974, Barnet and Wimbledon go on to achieve Football League status while mergers eventually propel Dagenham & Redbridge to the same level.

AS recounted in Chapter 1, professionalism was legalised by the FA in 1885. A proposal that only amateurs should compete in the FA Cup was doomed to fail and Old Etonians were effectively the last amateurs to win it in 1882. Corinthian FC were not the only ones who wanted no part of the paid new world, eventually merging (in 1939) with the like-minded Casuals to form Corinthian Casuals, while almost all the present-day London professional clubs had amateur roots (Chelsea being a notable exception).

From the many and various local leagues dotted around the capital, the stepping stones to the Football League for the most ambitious clubs were the London League (founded 1896) and Southern League (1894). Amateurs also played in both competitions but those less interested in full-time football tended to opt for the Isthmian League (1905) and Athenian League (1912). Officials at that level did love a classical title and the Spartan, Delphian, Hellenic, Corinthian and Aetolian leagues all followed.

Before all of that, however, came knockout football with the FA Amateur Cup, played nationwide as early as 1893. In that first year, there were as many as 81 entries. **Old Carthusians**, the former pupils of Charterhouse School, who won the FA Cup in 1881, beat Bishop Auckland (founded by Oxbridge theological students in the North East, hence their light and dark blue colours) in the semi-final and in the first final at the Athletic Ground, Richmond on 7 April 1894 they met Casuals, who had beaten the Sherwood Foresters.

The Carthusians came through by two goals to one in what *The Standard,* forerunner of London's *Evening Standard,* rightly called 'the first trophy of its kind'. There were an estimated 4,000 spectators, including the Duchess of York, who 'remained to the end, apparently enjoying the game'.

A year later, the holders lost their trophy in the final to Middlesbrough, another fixture presaging how the South East and North East would come to dominate the competition. Before amateurism, and with it the Amateur Cup, were abolished in 1974, the Oxbridge team Pegasus were the only side from outside those two areas to win the trophy more than once. The others who did so were four teams from the Northern League (Bishop Auckland, Crook Town, Middlesbrough and Stockton) and nine from London – Barnet, Bromley, Clapton, Enfield, Hendon, Ilford, Leyton, Leytonstone, Walthamstow Avenue – plus the Old Carthusians.

Almost all those London clubs date back to the 19th century. **Ilford** competed in the inaugural London League of 1896/97.

They were then among the clubs who sent representatives to discuss a new, strictly amateur competition and became founder members of it when the Isthmian League was born in 1905.

London Caledonians, Clapton, Casuals, Civil Service and Ealing Association joined them in a competition still thriving today, albeit with title sponsors and a slightly less austere approach. Originally, there was no trophy for the winners and the motto was *honor sufficit*.

Unusually, the same six clubs stayed for a second season when Ilford went from top to bottom. A shake-up then brought in Dulwich, Bromley and Leytonstone among others in the next two seasons, plus Woking in 1911.

In nine years before the war, London Caledonians were champions five times, Bromley twice, Clapton and Ilford once each.

The Scottish exiles **London Caledonians**, playing at Caledonian Park, Holloway, remained in the league until 1939 before disbanding. They added only one more title but won the Amateur Cup in 1923, the London Senior Cup (first played for in 1883) and Middlesex Cup five times each, and lost to some notable clubs like Wolves and Huddersfield in the FA Cup.

Clapton, pre-dating Clapton Orient and with no connection to them, have two claims to fame: the first club recognised by the FA as having played abroad (in Belgium, 1890) and the longest continuously used ground in London, from 1888 at the Old Spotted Dog behind the disused pub of the same name in Upton Lane, Forest Gate – some distance from Clapton, where they spent barely a year after being formed.

Founder members of the Southern League, the 'Tons' found life among the Football League wannabes financially demanding and happily stayed in the Isthmian League from 1905 to 2007 before settling for a lower grade of football.

Winning the Amateur Cup five times, like Crook Town, was a proud achievement beaten only by Bishop Auckland's ten.

Cray Wanderers claim a record of their own for longevity as the capital's oldest surviving independent club (just about qualifying as Londoners by virtue of their home in the London Borough of Bromley).

Documentary evidence is thin, but the club is believed to have started with labourers building the railway viaduct at St Mary Cray in 1860. The original ground is now the Star Lane cemetery, Cray having shared Bromley's Hayes Lane stadium since 1998.

Second to them for longevity until disbanding in 2011 were **Leyton**. Founded in 1868, they were Amateur Cup winners twice in succession in the 1920s and losing finalists at Wembley in a local derby with Walthamstow Avenue in 1952.

Mergers followed with Wingate (1975) and Walthamstow Pennant (1995) but after Leyton Pennant became Waltham Forest, a 'new' Leyton at the old Hare and Hounds Ground in Lea Bridge Road were granted an order in the High Court as 'the unincorporated club formed in 1868'.

Between the wars the other strongest Isthmian League teams, all of whom won the title two years running, were Ilford, St Albans, Nunhead, Wimbledon (twice) and Leytonstone. **Nunhead**, in south-east London, played from 1888–1941 and claimed Denis Compton as a young player in 1934/35 at grounds now used by Haberdashers' Aske's school in New Cross, the alma mater of England internationals Scott Parker and Shaun Wright-Phillips.

The Athenian League, meanwhile, became established as the second strongest all-amateur tournament in the region, helping to uphold the South East's reputation against the North East.

Amateur Cup finals were largely played in the two regions, depending on the finalists, and were hosted between the wars by Arsenal, Millwall, Chelsea, Crystal Palace and West Ham among others.

After the Second World War, amateur football benefited as much as the professional game from the desire for entertainment, and with Barnet (1946) then Leytonstone (1947 and 1948) emerging as winners in front of good crowds varying from 49,000–57,000 at Stamford Bridge and Highbury, it was decided to take the final to Wembley.

Bromley had the honour of winning the first final there, 93,000 watching them beat Romford 1-0 to add the cup to their Athenian League title. For a few seasons thereafter, a capacity crowd regularly turned up for the final.

For a long time, standards were high enough for the best amateurs to play comfortably at Football League First Division level. And while the maximum wage was in force, those with a good job – plus, quite probably, a little 'boot money' to help them along – were better off to resist a professional contract.

We have mentioned (Chapter 3) Bernard Joy, of Casuals, Fulham and Arsenal, the last amateur to play for the full England team. Chelsea's championship-winning squad of 1955 contained two amateurs in Seamus O'Connell, a cattle-farmer from the North East and Amateur Cup winner with both Bishop Auckland and Crook Town, plus centre-forward Jim Lewis Jr, who won 49 England amateur caps with **Walthamstow Avenue** and scored 40 goals for Chelsea. Also from the Avenue, and captain of the 1952 Amateur Cup Final winners, came wing-half Derek Saunders, who moved to Stamford Bridge a year later and did turn professional.

That followed one of the club's greatest achievements, a 1-1 draw away to Manchester United in the 1952/53 FA Cup fourth round, with England cricketers Trevor Bailey and Doug Insole also in the side. The prolific Lewis, who once hit a hat-trick in three successive games, scored the equaliser ten minutes from time and got both Avenue's goals when they lost the replay 5-2 at Highbury in front of 46,000.

The Avenue, alas, were swallowed up in the mergers that eventually led to the creation of Dagenham & Redbridge (see Chapter 8). So were old rivals **Leytonstone,** founded in 1886 and Isthmian League champions seven times in nine seasons from 1938–52, as well as Ilford.

Barnet (Chapter 7) and Wimbledon (Chapter 6) eventually joined the professional ranks in the 1960s, as did Wealdstone in 1971, but Hendon and Enfield, other amateur stalwarts and great rivals of each other and Barnet, remained as such until the term was abolished.

Enfield, founded in 1893, were dissolved in 2007, six years after supporters dismayed by the move to Borehamwood formed Enfield Town, since when outsiders are entitled to be confused by the original club's re-emergence as Enfield 1893.

Hendon supporters took over their club in 2010, happily continuing the long history begun in 1904 and continued under the names of Christchurch Hampstead, Hampstead Town (featuring both Compton brothers in the 1930s), Hampstead, Golders Green and, from 1946, Hendon. They played at Claremont Road from 1926–2008 before sharing with Wembley FC.

In an article written in 1973 asking who was the greatest amateur player of all, the former England amateur team manager and sportswriter Norman Creek, whose football memories stretched back to playing for Corinthian in 1919, mentioned Walthamstow's Jim Lewis. But his choice was Edgar Kail of **Dulwich Hamlet**, who won three caps with the England senior team in 1928/29, for his 'combined ability as a ball player and marksman'.

Dulwich feature prominently in a list of London's Amateur Cup winners during the 20th century, which could be said to provide a rough-and-ready guide to the leading clubs:

Clapton 5; Dulwich Hamlet 4; Bromley, Hendon, Leytonstone 3; Enfield, Ilford, Leyton, Walthamstow Avenue 2; Barnet, Casuals, Kingstonian, London Caledonians, Wealdstone, Wimbledon 1. It does not stretch geographical boundaries very far to include Surrey's Walton & Hersham and Woking (one win each).

Among those who were runners-up at least once are Barking, Dagenham, Hayes, Romford and **Sutton United**, the last named founded in 1898 and most famous for their 1989 FA Cup victory over Coventry City, the 1987 winners. Thirty years earlier, **Tooting & Mitcham** almost created as big a sensation by leading Nottingham Forest 2-0 in the third round at Sandy Lane. The First Division side came back to equalise and went on to win the cup. Tooting's victory in the 2016 London Senior Cup, first competed for in 1882/83, meant they joined Ilford as the most successful side with seven wins each.

From 1974, the FA Trophy, which had started in 1969, became the principal knockout competition for all non-league clubs. The North dominated early on and it was the 11th edition, in 1980, before Dagenham took the trophy south, followed later by Enfield, Wealdstone, Woking and Kingstonian.

Although Wimbledon, Barnet , Dagenham & Redbridge and then AFC Wimbledon all made it to the Football League (see Chapters 6, 7 and 8 respectively), London non-league clubs do not find it easy to compete for spectators and sponsorship with the large number of senior clubs. When a 20-strong national non-league competition known as the Alliance Premier began in 1979, it was notable that only Barnet and Wealdstone came from the capital.

Enfield later won it twice, while Woking and **Welling United** (started as a youth team in 1963) also managed long stints at that level, joined more recently by Bromley and Sutton, but all on small crowds.

Not far from Welling in the Surrey Quays area, **Fisher Athletic,** founded as long ago as 1908 and named after a Catholic martyr, stayed in the Conference from 1987–91, at one time under the managership of none other than Malcolm Allison, as well as the even more colourful Dogan Arif.

Moving to share with Dulwich at Champion Hill, they suffered severe financial problems and were wound up in 2009 with debts of around £250,000 before a new club, Fisher FC, emerged.

For many others lower down the football pyramid, survival is sufficient. **Corinthian Casuals** remain true to the heart of Pa Jackson, founder of the Corinthians in 1882, their website summing up the club's philosophy: 'The aims of the Club are to promote fair play and sportsmanship, to play competitive football at the highest level possible whilst remaining strictly amateur and retaining the ideals of the Corinthian and the Casuals Football Clubs.'

The London FA, founded in 1882, controls about 2,000 clubs and a quick glance at any number of London parks every weekend, let alone the broader acres of Hackney Marshes, Wanstead Flats or

Wormwood Scrubs, would confirm that genuine amateur football continues to survive and – for all the problems of refereeing shortages, occasional violence and abusive spectators – to flourish.

Chapter 6

Transition (1971-90)

The mighty are fallen as old guard of managers depart (Greenwood, Nicholson, Sexton, Mee); Arsenal emulate Tottenham's Double but Spurs, Chelsea, West Ham all relegated before Spurs revive as foreign influx begins; QPR peak; Palace make the top division; the 80s become a dire decade for football as crowds plummet everywhere; success in south London as Charlton, Millwall, Palace and Wimbledon all reach Division 1; QPR try to merge with Fulham while Charlton have to leave home; eight London clubs in the top division before football changes forever.

A T the end of the 1970/71 season, London's *Evening Standard* published a special edition celebrating the capital's remarkable triumphs: Arsenal's league and cup Double, Chelsea's European Cup-Winners' Cup, Tottenham's Football League Cup. To suggest that within a few years, the latter pair would be relegated and all three, plus West Ham and the top London league club QPR, would change managers, would have been risible.

Yet the early-to mid-1970s marked not so much the end of an era as the end of three or four of them all at the same time, with revered trophy-winning managers moving out or up at Chelsea, Tottenham and West Ham, all in the space of a few weeks, and Arsenal following suit less than two years later.

QPR, who had finished higher than any other club in the capital in 1973/74 for the first time in their history, joined in the mayhem and, by the end of the calamitous 1974/75 season, there was no London side in the top ten of the First Division for only the second time since 1925. Early in October, the bottom three teams in the First Division table had been Chelsea, Spurs and Arsenal.

If there was a connecting factor behind this upheaval, it was the changing nature of society as reflected in football. The old guard of managers and former players from the days of the maximum wage, national service and an age of deference frequently found modern life exasperating. To a short-back-and-sides, £20-a-week (if that) generation, players' and supporters' behaviour – as well as the hairstyles, clothes and musical preferences of both – were equally bewildering.

'Players have become impossible,' said a disenchanted Bill Nicholson after leaving Tottenham. 'They talk all the time about security but are not prepared to work for it.' New signings coming to London, he said, wanted a minimum of £7,000 'under the counter'.

Sir Alf Ramsey was the first major managerial figure of this generation to go, sacked by the FA in March 1974. The next sensations were further north, Bill Shankly suddenly resigning at Liverpool in mid-summer, before Brian Clough, who had been drummed out of Derby County and failed at Brighton, took over his arch-enemies Leeds United.

At West Ham, Ron Greenwood decided with rather odd timing that he would move upstairs and let the more pragmatic John Lyall become team manager for the third match of the new season. He just neglected to tell the directors, who read about it in the press and were not best pleased but agreed with the plan.

Nicholson, dismayed when Tottenham fans rioted in the UEFA Cup Final second leg away to Feyenoord in May 1974, lasted only five games into the season, resigning as the team lost every one.

Next to go the same month was Gordon Jago, who had taken QPR back into the First Division and finished eighth at the first attempt. Then Dave Sexton was dismissed by Chelsea, where he had fallen out with star players Peter Osgood and Alan Hudson. He was out of work for only a few weeks before replacing Jago, who moved to Millwall in place of Benny Fenton, sacked on the same October day as Sexton.

'The fatality rate among London managers is now reaching farce proportions,' wrote Peter Blackman in the *Standard*. 'With results in London so poor, no manager can feel safe.'

The changing of the guard was complete in the summer of 1976, when Arsenal's Bertie Mee moved out and Terry Neill, briefly Nicholson's controversial replacement at Spurs, took over.

* * * * *

It had all begun so well. Despite having finished no higher than 12th in 1970, **Arsenal** were confident of building on their Fairs Cup triumph to become championship contenders.

The start was difficult, with Peter Simpson, Jon Sammels and Charlie George all badly injured and out for months. A crucial game, paradoxically, was the 5-0 defeat away to Stoke City at the end of September, which skipper Frank McLintock believes was the turning point of the season. There was no panic.

Team spirit had been exemplified ten days earlier when the players stuck together in a violent fist fight outside the banquet following a draw away to Lazio in the Fairs' Cup. After the Stoke debacle, Mee called a team meeting and the free-for-all was this time verbal, but without bitterness.

The manager then selected an unchanged side for the next seven games – until Simpson and Sammels were fit to return – of which five were won and two drawn. Arsenal did not lose again until January, against Huddersfield, and further losses at Liverpool and Derby left them seven points behind Leeds.

From then, it was a race between the two, complicated by Arsenal having games in hand. Unlike Leeds, sensationally beaten by Colchester United, they made progress in the FA Cup, but every game from the fourth round to the semi-final required a replay, further complicating the fixture list. In April, Arsenal played eight league games, winning the first six to go top then losing what appeared to be a critical one, at Elland Road to a Jack Charlton goal. Taking revenge on Stoke courtesy of substitute Eddie Kelly's goal in a tense penultimate game meant they would still be champions with a win or a goalless draw at Tottenham, of all places, two nights later. The team that had finished against Stoke took on a strong Spurs side unbeaten in 11 games and pushing to finish third.

> **Tottenham:** Jennings, Kinnear, Knowles, Mullery, Collins, Beal, Gilzean (Pearce), Perryman, Chivers, Peters, Neighbour.
>
> **Arsenal:** Wilson, Rice, McNab, Kelly, McLintock, Simpson, Armstrong, Graham, Radford, Kennedy, George.

Unbeaten run or not, Tottenham's home game in the previous midweek against Huddersfield attracted fewer than 20,000 people. For the championship decider, there were probably more than that locked out. It was impossible to count them, so the *Daily Express* estimated 50,000.

Arsenal's journey from the South Herts golf club in Totteridge took four times as long as normal and preparations were rushed. The game plan, re-instituted after the September drubbing at Stoke, was to keep things tight for 20 minutes, although on this occasion 'silencing the crowd' of 51,992 was not an option.

Chances were evenly spread and with three minutes left Arsenal looked like achieving the goalless draw that would leave them level on points with Leeds, but with a fractionally better goal average of 70-29 (2.41) against 72-30 (2.40).

Then Radford's header was turned aside by Pat Jennings, George Armstrong retrieved it and crossed for Ray Kennedy to squeeze a header past Jennings and covering left-back Cyril Knowles and in off the crossbar.

The goal actually made no difference in the sense that one for Spurs would still give Leeds the title. They went for it furiously, goalkeeper Bob Wilson taking a kick in the head before the final whistle confirmed Arsenal as champions for the first time since 1953. Their supporters invaded the pitch and, commendably given the climate of the time, police described crowd behaviour as 'magnificent' all round.

Tottenham's chagrin was all the greater in the knowledge that their 1961 Double was now in serious danger of emulation ten years on. Only Shankly's Liverpool, who had knocked them out in a sixth round replay, could prevent it and theirs was not a vintage side. Fifth in the league, with one win and one defeat against Arsenal, they had scored just 42 goals in 42 games – including only 12 away from Anfield – but for the second time in three seasons conceded a miserly 24. New-fangled hand-held calculators would not be required to keep score at Wembley.

> **Arsenal:** Wilson, Rice, McNab, Storey (Kelly), McLintock, Simpson, Armstrong, Graham, Radford, Kennedy, George.
>
> **Liverpool:** Clemence, Lawler, Lindsay, Smith, Lloyd, Hughes, Callaghan, Evans (Thompson), Heighway, Toshack, Hall.

'The non-event of the century' *The People* newspaper called it, which hardly did justice to the historic achievement of the winners, even if the game itself was goalless and eminently forgettable until the start of extra time. When Steve Heighway, one of Liverpool's two university graduates, beat Wilson at his near post two minutes after the start of the extra half-hour, Arsenal needed all their famed resilience to keep the dream alive.

Nine minutes later they equalised, the goal being credited on the day to George Graham but later given to Kelly. In the 111th minute Charlie George, a genuine local hero, smacked in the winner and fell flat on his back with arms outstretched. It was an iconic celebration that could just as well have been exhaustion in the team's 64th game of the season. At Islington Town Hall following the next day's triumphal procession, Frank McLintock, Footballer of the Year, fell asleep.

Mee's team suffered a grievous blow when the outstanding coach Don Howe was allowed to leave for an unsuccessful period as manager of his former club, West Bromwich Albion. They had two more years as trophy contenders before succumbing to the London malaise.

As defending champions, they failed to figure in one of the First Division's tightest ever finishes, with Clough's Derby County succeeding them, a single point ahead of Leeds, Liverpool and Manchester City. Leeds beat Arsenal 1-0 in a poor centenary FA Cup Final, but failed by that one point to emulate their Double. The European Cup brought two easy victories and then a third-round defeat by the emerging Ajax (1-2, 0-1).

One final title challenge to Liverpool in 1973 petered out in April after a shock FA Cup semi-final defeat by Second Division Sunderland. By that time, McLintock and fellow-Scot Graham had both left, for QPR and Manchester United respectively.

The following season three-up and down was introduced, which Mee believed led to an increase in the negative football gaining hold everywhere. He could not have believed that Arsenal would be involved in two successive relegation struggles, in 1975 and '76, as he revamped the squad with a mixture of the proven – Alan Ball and Terry 'Henry' Mancini – plus three young Irishmen, David O'Leary, Liam Brady and Frank Stapleton.

It was Mee's successor Terry Neill, from the other side of the Irish border, who reaped the benefit of the latter trio after taking over in the summer of 1976 and spending heavily on England internationals Malcolm Macdonald and Alan Hudson. From 16th and 17th, Neill lifted the side back into a regular top-eight spot, although seven points behind the 1981 champions Aston Villa was as close as the new Arsenal came to a title challenge.

Where they excelled was cup football, reaching three successive FA Cup finals and playing in Europe four times in five seasons. Unfortunately, two of those Wembley finals were lost to underdogs in Bobby Robson's Ipswich Town (1978) and Second Division West Ham (1980).

Four days after the West Ham loss, Neill's team suffered another cup final defeat, this time on penalties to Valencia in the European Cup-Winners Cup, a tournament for which they had qualified by winning the extraordinary 1979 domestic final against Manchester United.

Apparently coasting at 2-0 with four minutes to play after goals by Brian Talbot (a member of Ipswich's winning team the previous year) and Frank Stapleton, Arsenal were shocked when United drew level with two in under two minutes through Gordon McQueen and Sammy McIlroy. The resilience of the Double team eight years earlier was then demonstrated when a weary Brady, undisputed man of the match, fed Graham Rix for a cross that Alan Sunderland poked home. The last three goals had come in two minutes 50 seconds.

> **Arsenal** (4-4-2): Jennings; Rice, O'Leary, Young, Nelson; Price (Walford), Talbot, Brady, Rix; Stapleton, Sunderland.
>
> **Manchester United** (4-4-2): Bailey; Nicholl, McQueen, Buchan, Albiston; Coppell, McIlroy, Macari, Thomas; Jordan, J.Greenhoff.

Slipping to tenth place in 1982/83 and losing both domestic cup semi-finals to Manchester United was a warning to Neill and when Walsall of the Third Division won at Highbury in a League Cup game with historic echoes the following November, Howe took over as manager. He left in March 1986 after learning that, in an example of most un-Arsenal-like behaviour, the club had offered his job to Barcelona's Terry Venables.

Venables had agreed to join at the end of the season but then pleaded domestic problems. He ended up at Tottenham instead 18 months later and the Arsenal job went to his great friend George Graham. Graham, who had done good work at Millwall, was a disciplinarian fitting the Arsenal profile. He began with two successive League Cup finals, beating Liverpool with Charlie Nicholas's goals and losing to Luton Town, built a rock-solid defence by endless repetitive practice and remedied a lack of goals by signing Alan Smith from Leicester City.

Youngsters like Tony Adams, David Rocastle, Michael Thomas and Paul Merson, all signed as schoolboys, progressed through the ranks and after finishes of fourth and sixth, a serious championship challenge seemed possible in 1988/89.

Norwich City were the surprise pacemakers, top at Christmas before falling away as Arsenal took over. Reigning champions Liverpool, only sixth at that stage, then put together one of their famous spring runs, winning 13 games out of 14 and drawing the other amid all the trauma of the Hillsborough tragedy in which 96 of their supporters died.

It meant that they would retain the title, and win the Double, unless Arsenal, three points behind, could win at Anfield by two clear goals on Friday, 26 May. The match should have been played in April but events at Hillsborough meant that Liverpool did not play any league matches for three weeks and had to fit in six during May.

Having seen off Wimbledon, QPR and West Ham in quick succession, scoring nine goals in the process, they were heavy favourites to disappoint a fourth London side, especially one who had lost their last seven games at Anfield and not won there since 1974.

> **Liverpool** (4-3-3): Grobbelaar; Nicol, Ablett, Hansen, Staunton; Houghton, McMahon, Whelan; Aldridge, Rush (Beardsley), Barnes.
>
> **Arsenal:** (1-4-3-2) Lukic; O'Leary; Dixon, Bould (Groves), Adams, Winterburn; Rocastle, Thomas, Richardson; Smith, Merson (Hayes).

Graham's plan was to play a pressing game: deny Liverpool the luxury of their intricate close-passing, 'make them kick it long' at his big centre-halves, of whom there were three, with David O'Leary employed as a sweeper behind the towering Steve Bould and Adams.

The manager said he would be happy with a scoreless first half and then a goal early in the second half, which was exactly what materialised. Smith glanced it in with the deftest of headers and suddenly Liverpool, for whom going behind at home would normally unleash an attacking storm, were unsure whether to stick or twist.

In the last minute John Barnes, true to his instincts, decided to beat a hobbling Kevin Richardson instead of heading for the nearby corner-flag, but lost possession. The ball went back to the goalkeeper, who calmly threw out to Lee Dixon, from where two smart passes found Smith and then Thomas. The 21-year-old Londoner got a lucky bounce off Steve Nicol's shoulder and beat Bruce Grobbelaar for the most dramatic finish yet to any league season, all in front of a television audience of eight million benefiting from ITV's exclusive contract for live games (see next chapter).

Just like Paul Gascoigne's tears a year later in Turin at the World Cup semi-final, it has been described as the moment that changed English football. From the misery of the Eighties, the only way was up.

* * * * *

In an era notable for potential ground sharing, the most sensational proposal was that between north London's two great rivals. In late-November 1977, there were serious discussions between Arsenal and Tottenham about selling their grounds and building a new one at Alexandra Palace. On 2 December, the *Daily Express* published a photograph under the headline 'Spurs, Arsenal launch the Grand Alliance' showing the two boards of directors sitting on opposite sides of a table, looking a little sheepishly at the camera.

The *Express* was an enthusiastic supporter of the proposal for a 75,000-capacity stadium with an indoor sports complex, citing this as the way forward for British football, but with hooliganism a growing social phenomenon, politicians and local residents were less keen.

'Ally Pally,' opened in 1873 as a counterpart to the Crystal Palace, had a racecourse until 1970 but difficulty dealing with crowds of even 10,000 in an area not particularly well served by public transport was one of the reasons why the proposal came to nothing. So darts rather than professional football is the principal sporting activity there today, the two clubs having been left to solve their respective stadium problems much later in the day – and much more expensively.

Like Arsenal, the Seventies had begun well enough for **Tottenham,** the pain of seeing their neighbours claim the league title at White Hart Lane and then emulate the 1961 Double soon diluted by winning a cup in three successive seasons as well as the start of regular European competition.

The 1971 Football League Cup was won following plenty of luck in the draw and a Wembley final against Aston Villa of the Third Division. Spurs took it with two late goals by Martin Chivers, who had taken over as principal goalscorer once a fading Jimmy Greaves departed for West Ham in an advantageous part-exchange for Martin Peters.

Chivers ended the 1970/71 full campaign ever-present in 58 games, with 34 goals, and the following two seasons his returns were 42 and 33. Long striding and powerful, he gave due credit to Alan Gilzean, especially for the latter's deft headwork, although Chivers found it harder pleasing Bill Nicholson and coach Eddie Baily, whose first scouting report after an England Under-23 international called him 'a big lazy sod'.

The reward for the League Cup winners was a return to Europe for the UEFA Cup, which brought two outstanding performances to oust AC Milan in the semi-final (2-1, 1-1) and an all-English final in which Wolves were beaten 2-1 at Molineux (both goals by Chivers) before a draw in London.

An eventful League Cup semi-final was lost 5-4 on aggregate to Chelsea but the following season Spurs took the trophy back, knocking out Liverpool and Wolves on the way to a deadly dull final against Norwich, won with a goal by Ralph Coates. Europe brought two more long runs but first frustration, losing a semi-final to Liverpool on away goals and then disgrace when supporters rioted during the 2-0 defeat in the second leg of the final against Feyenoord.

Tottenham were fined but the longer-term repercussions were worse. Nicholson had been horrified by the events in Rotterdam, as he was by many of the trends in modern football, and resigned when the first four league games of the 1974/75 season were all lost.

His proposal to appoint a dream-team of Danny Blanchflower and Johnny Giles – still a top player – was ignored by chairman Sidney Wale, who stunned supporters by turning to a former Arsenal captain in Terry Neill, who had been managing Hull City. In an interview with *The Times* a good while later, Nicholson could not even bear to mention his successor's name, referring only to 'the Arsenal man'.

When Neill left two years later for Highbury, there was further surprise that the next man in should be his assistant Keith Burkinshaw, with Peter Shreeve later becoming coach. Both were low profile, so much so that the latter was universally and incorrectly known as 'Shreeves', even by the club.

If the board had acted perversely in appointing Neill, they deserved credit for sticking with Burkinshaw after his first season, 1976/77, ended bottom of the table.

They returned to the top division immediately, although it was tighter than seemed likely early in the season when scoring 14 goals in two successive home games against Oldham (5-1) and Bristol Rovers (9-0). In the end, a tense goalless draw at Southampton on the last day ensured promotion in third place, ahead of Alan Mullery's Brighton only on goal difference.

The summer of 1978 brought one of the most dramatic transfers in London football history after the phone rang in Burkinshaw's office and Sheffield United's manager Harry Haslam, who had good contacts in Argentina through his coach Oscar Arce, asked if Tottenham would like to buy Ossie Ardiles, the little midfield star of the country's recent World Cup triumph.

Reckoning that two members of the squad would settle in more easily than one, Burkinshaw flew to Buenos Aires and suggested to Ardiles that Ricky Villa, taller and stronger, although he had made only two substitute appearances, should also join. Villa scored in their joint debut, a 1-1 draw away to reigning champions Nottingham Forest on the opening day, which promised more than was delivered in their first two seasons. For all the pair's talents, Tottenham's greatest needs were for a goalscorer, a dominant centre-half and a top goalkeeper. The Argentinians' first home game was a 4-1 defeat by Aston Villa and, in the fourth league match, Spurs were routed 7-0 at Liverpool to leave them bottom but one, without a win.

Only after signing two new strikers, Steve Archibald and Garth Crooks, for substantial sums in the summer of 1980 did they look capable of winning anything. To supporters' delight, they then replaced Neill's Arsenal as the country's top cup team.

Quarter-finalists in 1978 and '79, they went all the way in 1981, Villa cementing his popularity with one of the great Wembley goals to beat Manchester City 3-2 in a replayed final. Twelve months later, after an extra-time defeat by Liverpool in the League Cup Final, the FA Cup was retained in the club's centenary year, 1-0 against Terry Venables's QPR after a 1-1 draw. Glenn Hoddle, never quite trusted by England managers although otherwise recognised as one of the most gifted midfielders of his generation, scored both the goals but Ardiles and Villa both missed the final while the Falklands War raged.

Significantly, Spurs had knocked out Arsenal in one or other of the cups for two successive seasons, and in 1982 finished above them (in fourth place) for the first time in half a dozen years. There was the excitement and prestige as well of two good runs in the Cup-Winners' Cup before defeats against Barcelona (in the semi-final) and Bayern Munich.

A European trophy, the UEFA Cup, followed in 1984 when Anderlecht were beaten on penalties at White Hart Lane after two 1-1 draws, future goalkeeping coach Tony Parks making the crucial save. It was an emotional night for Burkinshaw had decided to resign at the end of the season, citing disenchantment with the expansionist regime of Irving Scholar and Paul Bobroff and leaving with the line 'there used to be a football club over there'.

Scholar shook hands on a deal to secure Alex Ferguson from Aberdeen, who then changed his mind, so after also considering Sven-Goran Eriksson, Spurs settled for continuity by appointing Shreeve(s). Third behind Everton and Liverpool in an excellent first season, he was replaced after dropping to tenth in his second by David Pleat, who repeated the pattern.

In 1986/87, Pleat employed a five-man midfield behind the prolific Clive Allen, son of Double hero Les, who scored a remarkable 49 goals as the team once more finished third behind the Merseyside pair. They also reached the League Cup semi-final, losing after three epic games with Arsenal, and the FA Cup Final, suffering an agonising defeat through an own goal by Gary Mabbutt, the hugely popular Bristolian who suffered throughout his career from diabetes.

Forced to resign after tabloid revelations about his private life, Pleat was succeeded by Terry Venables, who brought off two transfer coups in successive summers by signing Paul Gascoigne from Newcastle and his former Barcelona striker Gary Lineker. Twenty four league goals in Lineker's first season helped Spurs back up to third place, but the sale of Chris Waddle to Marseille hinted at financial troubles ahead.

* * * * *

From being winners of the FA Cup and a major European competition, through near-bankruptcy, three relegations and the lowest position in the club's history, the Seventies and Eighties were a mainly sorry tale for **Chelsea**. Only right at the end did they threaten something better again.

Just under two weeks after Arsenal completed their league and cup Double at Wembley in May 1971, Chelsea became the fourth London club to win a European trophy.

Their opponents in the Cup-Winners' Cup Final, Real Madrid, had lost their Sixties lustre and their Spanish League title, meaning they were absent from the European Cup for the first time since it began. They had even been beaten away to Cardiff City before winning the second leg, but still presented quite a challenge after Dave Sexton's side had eliminated Manchester City (1-0, 1-1) in the semi-final.

> **Chelsea** (4-3-3): Bonetti; Boyle, Dempsey, Webb, Harris; Hollins (Mulligan), Hudson, Cooke; Weller, Osgood (Baldwin), Houseman.
>
> **Real Madrid** (4-4-2): Borja; Jose Luis, Zunzunegui, Zoco, Benito; Pirri, Grosso, Velazquez, Perez (Fleitas); Amancio, Gento (Grande).

The Karaiskaki Stadium in Athens was full to its 45,000 capacity, although none of the spectators realised they would not see the trophy won. Officials had already put blue and white ribbons on it ready for the presentation as Chelsea led going into the last minute with Osgood's goal, only for defender Ignacio Zoco to capitalise on John Dempsey's error. Madrid were on top in extra time without scoring again.

For the replay two days later, thousands of fans had naturally returned home, reducing the attendance to under 20,000. Those who went back to London were able to watch live on television, with John Hollins, injured in the first game, as summariser. Tommy Baldwin replaced him in an attacking formation that took the game to the Spaniards and won it with goals by Dempsey and Osgood before late retaliation by Sebastian Fleitas.

If it was the end of an era for Madrid, the great Francisco Gento making his last appearance in the replay, Chelsea could not have believed it was the beginning of the end for the King's Road swingers. Indeed, Osgood, full of pride and champagne, predicted 'we are going to become the greatest team London has seen'.

Not quite. Financial problems caused by building a new East Stand and deteriorating relations between Sexton and several star players meant that within two years they were in mid-table and, by the end of 1973/74, were avoiding relegation by one point, with Hudson sold to Stoke and Osgood to Southampton after both had been dropped and refused to train.

The board backed the manager, only to sack him the following October after a poor start. 'We can't go on scrambling to avoid relegation season after season,' said chairman Brian Mears. After a crucial 2-0 defeat at Tottenham in April, they went down anyway. Former full-back Eddie McCreadie took over and promised promotion within two years, which he achieved with a young side, including starlet Ray Wilkins, despite the club almost being wound up in May 1976.

McCreadie then shot himself in the foot by resigning over a contractual issue and by the time he begged to be re-instated, youth team coach Ken Shellito had been appointed as a calming influence. As he struggled, chairman Brian Mears tried to bring in the famed Yugoslav coach Miljan Miljanic, who watched Chelsea come from 3-0 down at home to Bolton in October 1978 to win 4-3 with a Sam Allardyce own goal, and declared that they did not need anyone.

Alas, they did, but could not find the right man. Danny Blanchflower, a contented *Sunday Express* columnist out of love with the modern game, was a hopelessly romantic appointment, the season ending bottom of the table with five wins in 42 games.

He gave up early the following season and was followed by his assistant Geoff Hurst, whose reign, assisted by Bobby Gould, consisted of longish runs of good results and then bad, none of which anyone could ever explain. Hurst's successful spell as caretaker got him the job permanently while Mears tried in vain to secure the proven talents of John Bond and Terry Venables. At the end of the 1979/80 season, Hurst was left needing a favour from his old club West Ham to secure promotion, but having won the FA Cup two days earlier they were hardly in the mood for an away game with Sunderland, who won it and went up instead, Chelsea losing out on goal difference.

Despite missing out on signing Hamburg's Kevin Keegan, who Mears claimed had shaken hands on signing before joining

Southampton instead, promotion hopes abounded the following season. Eight wins in nine games before Christmas, however, were followed by an awful finish of nine matches without a single goal and 12th place.

Hurst was sacked and Mears, who had replaced his father as chairman in 1969, brought in John Neal then stood down too, making way for the vice-chairman of Wigan Athletic. 'What Chelsea need…under the leadership of the new owner Kenneth Bates, is a period out of the limelight,' he wrote.

That was never going to happen. In a testing first season, the abrasive Bates, who had bought the club for £1 and inherited £2m of debt, found himself thrust into a long-running conflict with property developers Marler Estates, who were able to buy the freehold to Stamford Bridge and wanted to develop it. Not until the end of the decade was the threat finally lifted and, in 1992, the Chelsea Pitch Owners bought it.

On the field, finishing 18th in the Second Division in 1982/83, two points from relegation, was the worst position in Chelsea's history. That made winning the title the following season all the more impressive on the back of some outstanding Neal signings. Kerry Dixon, bought from Reading, was teamed up with the volatile David Speedie, the pair of them served from the wing by Pat Nevin from Clyde.

That trio scored 55 out of 90 league goals, 28 of them by Dixon, who added 24 more back in the First Division, with Chelsea sixth for two seasons in succession.

The transition from Neal to John Hollins worked well initially but in his third season, 1987/88, they suffered a dreadful run of 21 games without a win and were eventually relegated under the new play-off system.

Second Division Middlesbrough's victory in the second leg of the play-off final at Stamford Bridge led to some of the worst crowd trouble that even Chelsea's most notorious fans had been involved in.

Bates at one point not only put up a fence with barbed wire on top but wanted to add one strand of 12-volt electric wire similar to those on his farms. Scotland Yard had no objection to 'this relatively harmless device' but the Greater London Council dissuaded him by saying they would close the ground.

With non-seating areas closed as an FA punishment, the 1988/89 season started badly and against Walsall in October the crowd was 6,747. Results, however, picked up spectacularly under Liverpudlian Bobby Campbell, and with Dixon back on form (25 goals) even without the departed Nevin and Speedie, the title was won with 96 goals and 99 points, 17 ahead of runners-up Manchester City.

Chelsea were back and ready for the dramatic changes the Nineties would bring to English football.

* * * * *

The personnel changes natural to any club over the course of a decade seemed more dramatic than most at **West Ham** in the 1970s, in that Ron Greenwood and the sainted trio of Moore, Hurst and Peters all departed. Results remained stubbornly similar: good cup runs, while relegation concerns abounded.

Peters was first to leave in March 1970, joining Tottenham in part-exchange for a fading Jimmy Greaves. His final total at White Hart Lane, including the FA Charity Shield, was 267 goals but he would add only 13 more in east London and, after only nine in 32 appearances during 1970/71, he retired.

It was almost with a relegation to his name, the Hammers having scraped 20th place thanks to a strong finish to the season. Geoff Hurst was past his best too and after only eight league goals the following campaign he left for Stoke City, with Bryan 'Pop' Robson taking over the main striking responsibilities.

Sixth place in 1972/73 on the back of the dynamic little Robson's 28 goals proved a false omen and dropping to 18th in another flirtation with the bottom of the table persuaded Greenwood that it was time to move upstairs and let John Lyall take charge of the team. The former full-back, forced to retire aged 23, did so three games into the 1974/75 season as the cull of

London managers continued, before going on to make his mark by winning the FA Cup.

In 1972, the Hammers had been denied a return to Wembley when Stoke City beat them in an epic three-game League Cup semi-final, ending in the mud of neutral Old Trafford with Bobby Moore in goal for the injured Bobby Ferguson (and saving a penalty, though he could not keep out the rebound). Three years later, they beat Arsenal at Highbury in the sixth round and Ipswich in a replayed semi-final, with two goals each time from Alan Taylor, a slight, blond-haired trier signed from Rochdale for £40,000 with only a modest scoring record.

Moore, who at various times had been desperate to join Arsenal, Tottenham or Derby County, finally left early in 1974 for Second Division Fulham, who would now be West Ham's cup final opponents.

> **West Ham** (4-3-3): Day; McDowell, T Taylor, Lock, Lampard; Bonds, Brooking, Paddon; A Taylor, Jennings, Holland.
>
> **Fulham** (4-4-2): Mellor; Cutbush, Lacy, Moore, Fraser; Conway, Mullery, Slough, Barrett; Mitchell, Busby.

With Alan Mullery also in a Fulham side managed by Alec Stock, the build-up was vast and colourful, at least in London. For the rest of the nation, the game hardly lived up to the billing but Lancashire had the hero in Taylor, who remarkably scored another two goals to give him almost as many in three successive cup ties as the seven he had managed at Rochdale in 55 games.

'Bargain of all time!' the *Sunday Express* headline said of him. 'It was a team thing and that is what it has got to be at Wembley,' was Lyall's characteristic response.

After an equally bright start the following season, going top of the table in November, Taylor and the team faded so badly in the league that they finished no higher than 18th while concentrating on the European Cup-Winners' Cup. Great Upton Park comebacks against Den Haag and Eintracht Frankfurt got them to the final, where Anderlecht made the most of home advantage in Brussels to win 4-2.

For the next two seasons, avoiding relegation depended on the final home game. In 1977, a Manchester United side with their minds on the FA Cup final were beaten 4-2, but 12 months later defeat by runners-up Liverpool sent Lyall's team down instead of QPR.

A supportive board of directors stuck with him, even though it took three seasons to return, the second of them bringing another FA Cup Final. From losing to Newport County in the previous year's third round, the unpredictable Hammers beat West Bromwich, Orient, Swansea, Villa and, in an eventful replayed semi-final, Everton, with Frank Lampard Sr becoming the unlikely hero with the winner at Elland Road.

With Arsenal having knocked out Liverpool after four games, it was another Cockney cup final instead of a Merseyside one.

> **Arsenal** (4-4-2): Jennings; Rice, O'Leary, Young, Devine (Nelson); Price, Talbot, Brady, Rix; Stapleton, Sunderland.
>
> **West Ham** (4-4-1-1): Parkes; Stewart, Bonds, Martin, Lampard; Pike, Allen, Brooking, Devonshire; Pearson; Cross.

As heavy underdogs, West Ham felt entitled to play a little more defensively, Lyall and his assistant Eddie Baily withdrawing Stuart Pearson behind David Cross. In the 13th minute, Pearson crossed and a stooping Trevor Brooking, now in his 13th year at the club, headed the most famous goal of his career.

It was the only one of the game, although there should have been another for 17-year-old Paul Allen, the youngest FA Cup finalist, who was cynically cut down by Willie Young as he broke clear.

The following October, Upton Park experienced one of its most surreal occasions when West Ham were ordered to play Castilla, the B team of Real Madrid, behind closed doors in the Cup-Winners' Cup after their supporters caused trouble in the first leg. They went through comfortably but were well beaten in the third round by a superb Dynamo Tblisi team.

The priority was the Second Division and with nippy striker Paul Goddard from QPR an excellent foil for the taller, stronger Cross, the title was won by 13 points and the League Cup Final only lost to Liverpool in a replay at Villa Park.

In eight more seasons during the Eighties, they finished in the top half four times and during 1985/86 were closer than ever before to the league championship. Phil Parkes, also from QPR, was an excellent goalkeeper who had cost a record £525,000, Tony Gale and Alvin Martin formed a reliable central defensive partnership, Alan Devonshire matured into the midfield successor to Brooking, who retired in 1984, and Tony Cottee had emerged from the youth team as a prolific scorer, grabbing four in the 10-0 League Cup win over Bury in 1983.

A lack of height in attack when he played alongside Goddard was resolved by signing the colourful Frank McAvennie from St Mirren who, when he could be kept on the straight and narrow, was formidable. His first half-season brought 18 goals in 21 games, with West Ham third behind Manchester United and Liverpool. Ron Atkinson's United fell away to finish fourth but Liverpool produced one of their storming finishes and, in the end, had 88 points to Everton's 86 and West Ham's 84.

Not untypically, the Hammers were back in danger of relegation by the following spring and in 1989 the late-season revival was left too late. With Cottee having been sold to Everton, top scorer was Leroy Rosenior with just seven goals.

Lyall, who had been refused permission to join QPR in 1984, appeared to think his job was safe and had the shock of his life when told his contract would not be renewed. His thirty-four years at Upton Park were over.

* * * * *

QPR' extraordinary double-your-money offer to Lyall after Terry Venables was lured to Barcelona in the summer of 1984 included a house with a lake to indulge his fish-keeping hobby, and showed the continuing ambition of chairman Jim Gregory.

In charge from March 1965, Gregory had overseen the rise from the Third Division to the First and a failed attempt to create a new west London force by merging with Brentford (see Chapter 5). In the Eighties, the merger talk would be with Fulham after Rangers had first come close to becoming champions of England and twice played in European competition.

At the start of the Seventies, the task for Gordon Jago, an eloquent former Charlton defender who had briefly managed the United States national team, was to achieve promotion back to the top division. He did it in some style in 1973, having replaced Rodney Marsh with the equally flamboyant Stan Bowles.

With Irishman Don Givens (23 goals) and England's Dave Thomas on the wings, and Gerry Francis and Terry Venables in midfield, it was a team as exciting as the 1967 Wembley winners that followed up by finishing eighth in the First Division ahead of Arsenal, Tottenham, Chelsea and West Ham, all of whom they beat that season. In April, Loftus Road's record attendance of 35,353 was set for the visit of champions Leeds United.

Behind the scenes, however, there were problems, with three different assistant managers leaving during the season and Jago resigning 'in a fit of temper' then staying on. He remained for only a few months, departing at the end of September amid reported player unrest. But despite a poor start, with only one win in ten games, the team recovered so well under replacement Dave Sexton that 11th place was still the best in London again. The following season, they came closer than ever to the First Division title.

Sexton was reunited with John Hollins and David Webb from Chelsea and made a shrewd signing in Arsenal's Frank McLintock, while Scottish international Don Masson replaced Venables in midfield. By winning eight of their last nine games in 1975/76 Rangers were top of the table, but Liverpool had a game in hand away to struggling Wolves, from which they needed a win or low-scoring draw. The home side were leading with quarter of an hour to play, before Liverpool scored three times to take the title.

Decline followed and, in 1977, Sexton left for Manchester United, to be followed by a succession of short-lived managers and relegation under Steve Burtenshaw. Tommy Docherty, whose first spell under Gregory lasted 28 days, survived for 17 months.

Players like goalkeeper Parkes and former manager Les Allen's son Clive were sold to other London clubs for big money and it took the return of Venables from Crystal Palace as manager in October 1980 to bring about a transformation in prospects.

It was not a universally popular one as Rangers clearly gained an advantage from their newly installed artificial pitch, manufactured in Canada and costing £350,000. Passing was smoother and suited the Venables style (ten years after he had co-authored the novel *They Used To Play On Grass*, which also predicted all-seater grounds), but the high bounce took much getting used to for visiting players. Losing 2-1 to Luton Town, the eventual champions, in the first game on it in September 1981 did not disprove that notion. Rangers lost only one more home game all season, to Chelsea on Boxing Day, in finishing fifth, two points from promotion.

In the FA Cup Blackpool, Grimsby and Venables's former club Palace were all beaten on the plastic, setting up a semi-final at Highbury against First Division West Bromwich Albion that was won by a goal from Allen, now back at the club via Palace.

Holders Spurs having seen off Leicester, there was to be another all-London final, which went to a replay thanks to Terry Fenwick heading an equaliser. For the second game, captain Glenn Roeder was suspended and Allen was out injured but Rangers gave a good account of themselves without being able to come back from Glenn Hoddle's early penalty, Simon Stainrod having a goal controversially disallowed.

> **Tottenham** (4-4-2): Clemence; Perryman, Miller, Price, Hughton; Hazard (Brooke), Roberts, Hoddle, Galvin; Crooks, Archibald.
>
> Replay: unchanged, same substitution.

QPR (4-4-2): Hucker; Fenwick, Hazell, Roeder, Gillard; Flanagan, Waddock, Gregory, Currie; Stainrod, Allen (Micklewhite).

Replay: Neill for Roeder, Micklewhite for Allen. Burke substitute for Micklewhite.

Those exploits established Rangers as promotion favourites for 1982/83 and they won the title by a full ten points from Wolves, again losing only two home games (including another Christmas ambush by struggling Chelsea). After an excellent first season back, finishing as the top London club in fifth place, Venables – who by then had already been made managing director and second largest shareholder – was offered the chance to buy the club before Gregory changed his mind.

A lucrative offer to join Barcelona in the summer of 1984 proved timely for Venables but bad news for Rangers. They were almost relegated the following season after Alan Mullery was sacked and only revived towards the end of the Eighties under Jim Smith (despite a feeble 3-0 League Cup Final loss to his previous club Oxford United), then Trevor Francis and Don Howe.

By that time, there was greater drama off the pitch than on it.

* * * * *

On 24 February 1987, a new London newspaper, the *London Daily News*, published by Robert Maxwell, had a sensational sports story for its first-ever edition. 'London soccer clubs to merge' ran the front page. The back page headlines were 'Sold down the river', 'Fulham RIP' and 'Goodbye to the Cottage'.

QPR and **Fulham** had agreed a merger that looked more like a takeover. QPR would have the manager in Jim Smith and the ground at Loftus Road. Fulham, struggling near the foot of the Third Division on tiny gates, would supply the chairman in the controversial figure of David Bulstrode, who said: 'It's become the survival of the fittest in west and south London. One club on its own in London can't survive on gates of 2,500.'

After a week of protests, the Football League management committee decided to block the move. Bulstrode, chairman of property developers Marler Estates, who also owned Stamford Bridge, still took over at QPR after buying out Gregory, but Jimmy Hill managed to put together a consortium to save Fulham and became their chairman.

Although the outcome was a welcome development, the whole episode showed how low Fulham had sunk. Bulstrode was barely exaggerating about the gates: the previous week's midweek game against Rotherham had been watched by 2,352 and, although almost 6,000 turned up for the next match once the merger news broke, a season that included heavy home defeats by Port Vale (6-0) and Chester (5-0) needed a late revival to avoid relegation to Division Four.

How had it come to this? The Seventies had in the main been great fun, beginning with promotion back to the Second Division in 1971 and continuing under Alec Stock with an FA Cup Final after Alan Mullery, back from Spurs, persuaded Bobby Moore to join up for their joint swansong in a couple of mid-table seasons.

Mullery left in 1976, upset that Alec Stock had reneged on a promise that he would succeed him as manager. Moore hung on until playing his final game at Blackburn in May 1977, by which time not only had the prodigal son Rodney Marsh returned but none other than George Best had joined him.

On 4 September, all three turned out in the fourth game of the season against Bristol Rovers, whereupon Best scored the only goal of his debut after just 71 seconds. Their first two home games averaged crowds of 23,000, more than double the previous season's norm, and the talk was of promotion, but after all the early entertainment the season fell apart. It would not have been untypical if Fulham had been relegated, and it took a 6-1 win over Orient in Moore's last London match (with the crowd down to 7,656) to ensure that did not happen.

Ernie Clay, the bluff Yorkshireman who had supported George Eastham during his dispute with Newcastle United (Chapter 5), was an increasingly influential boardroom figure and Stock resigned after Bobby Campbell was made team manager. Best played a few games the following season then departed for Los Angeles Aztecs, and by 1980 relegation had indeed materialised.

Another famous old boy, Malcolm Macdonald, who had been chief marketing executive, unexpectedly took over from Campbell and with Ray Harford as his talented coach enjoyed a successful four-year spell that almost included two successive promotions. In 1981/82, drawing 1-1 at home to Lincoln on the final day ensured a return to the Second Division at the visitors' expense and a year later there was an even more dramatic finish.

In third place for most of the season, with Gordon Davies scoring prolifically, and Ray Houghton joining Ray Lewington in a cultured footballing midfield, Fulham flagged near the end and needed to win their final game away to Derby, who had to win to guarantee staying up.

As home supporters crowded the touchlines long before the end to celebrate what would be a 1-0 win and safety, Fulham's Robert Wilson was actually tackled by one fan. With almost a minute and a half to play, the crowd rushed on, wrongly assuming the game was over and the players fled to the dressing-room. Fulham, who would have needed two goals in the chaotic last few minutes, demanded the game should be replayed but the Football League disagreed and so Leicester were promoted instead.

It was the beginning of a long decline, continuing with relegation under Harford in 1986 and Clay selling up – selling out, supporters would say – to Marler Estates the same year, which also featured a 10-0 League Cup defeat at Liverpool.

Jimmy Hill may have been a popular choice as chairman but after one brighter season in 1989, finishing fourth with Lewington as manager, the decade ended with Fulham as close as they had ever been to the Fourth Division.

* * * * *

Amid football's serious financial problems in the Eighties, when attendances fell after the Heysel disaster of 1985 to a record low of 16.5 million from the post-war high of 41.3 million in 1948/49, there could have been two separate mergers in the London turf wars. Even before the QPR-Fulham proposal, a businessman from a poor Kilburn family had long had his eye on bringing together Crystal Palace and **Wimbledon** as a new force in the South West.

Ron Noades was a straight-talking property developer, a kindred spirit to Ken Bates, and something of a football visionary. Unfortunately, many of his visions were disliked.

Growing up as a Derby County supporter after sticking a pin into a list of First Division clubs, he became chairman of Southall in the Isthmian League, moving on two years later in the summer of 1976 to non-league Wimbledon, which he bought for less than £3,000.

Keen as the club became to disassociate themselves from the Wombles, the furry recycling enthusiasts of Elisabeth Beresford's books who spawned a children's television programme and the most successful pop group of 1974, Wimbledon FC did also emanate from the local Common.

There, in 1889, 12 years after the nearby All England Club started its tennis championships, old boys from Central School formed a team called, logically enough, Wimbledon Old Centrals.

Within half a dozen years, they had won the Clapham League and after a couple of name changes and briefly disbanding and reforming, they settled in on disused swampland at Plough Lane in 1912. Progressing as many clubs did via the Athenian League to the stronger Isthmian League, they were exceptionally successful in the 1930s, winning the league title four times from 1931–36 and reaching the Amateur Cup Final for the first time.

A hat-trick of titles from 1962–64 then prompted a move to the Southern League, where they became semi-professional and finished runners-up to Hereford United in their first season at the new level.

The outstanding player of the time was Eddie Reynolds, a big, fearless Belfast centre-forward signed from local rivals Tooting & Mitcham, whose scoring record for the Dons in successive seasons from 1959 was extraordinary: 40, 47, 55, 55, 53, 33, 57.

Not surprisingly Reynolds was star man when they finally won the Amateur Cup in 1963, heading all four goals in the 4-2 win over Sutton United at Wembley, after which they survived the demands of 10 games in 21 days to win the league as well.

The Football League at the time was effectively a closed shop, impoverished clubs being re-elected year after year by their friends in the top two divisions (who had most of the votes).

In the 1970s that slowly began to change, although when Wimbledon applied in 1976 on the back of two successive Southern League titles and one stunning FA Cup run, they received just three votes.

Manager Allen Batsford, appointed from Walton & Hersham in 1974 and taking several players with him, had transformed the team from a mid-table outfit to one that in his first season produced a sensation by winning 1-0 away to First Division Burnley, the first such result by a non-league team for more than 50 years. The fourth-round draw brought a visit to league champions Leeds United, who on 25 January fielded their full first team in front of 46,230 at Elland Road but were held 0-0 in a defiant defensive display typified by bearded goalkeeper Dickie Guy saving Peter Lorimer's penalty eight minutes from time.

Disappointment when Plough Lane was waterlogged, causing the replay to be postponed, was mitigated by the financial benefit of helping the club's debts by moving it to Selhurst Park, where more than 45,000 paid and saw midfielder Dave Bassett, one of the players brought by Batsford from Walton, deflect a shot by Johnny Giles past Guy for the only goal.

So the ambitious Ron Noades initially saw potential at the club. Helped by a third successive Southern League title in 1977 and another brave FA Cup performance in holding Jack Charlton's Middlesbrough, he was able to campaign vigorously for Football League membership under the slogan 'Dons 4 Div 4'. Workington, geographically isolated and applying for re-election for the fourth successive season, were the obvious target and Wimbledon received 27 votes to their 21, giving London its first new league club since the ill-fated Thames in 1930.

Like Thames, however, the newcomers found it a crowded field. The club secretary had once complained: 'It says little for the sporting people of Wimbledon that they do not turn out in greater numbers.' That was in 1907, and 70 years on it was questionable whether much had changed.

The crowd for the opening league game, a 3-3 draw against Halifax Town, was respectable enough at 4,616 but fixtures often clashed with either Chelsea or Fulham just up the District Line, and the northern clubs who dominated the Fourth Division proved no sort of attraction. For Hartlepool's first visit in February, only 1,440 turned up.

On the field it was eventful. After finishing 13th in that inaugural campaign the Dons were promoted, relegated, promoted and relegated in four successive seasons. But crowds were down to an average 2,500 and Noades had begun to seek radical solutions. In 1979, he bought the little-known Milton Keynes City FC (formerly Bletchley Town) for £1, putting three Wimbledon directors on the board with a view to the same highly controversial relocation that eventually took place 24 years later. The plan was dropped within a year as Noades looked nearer to home.

* * * * *

Crystal Palace had also been up and down in the Seventies. Having reached the top division for the first time in their history in 1969, they never managed to establish themselves and in two disastrous seasons went from the First to the Third divisions.

The flamboyant Malcolm Allison, one of those better suited to coaching than management, achieved no more than a run to the 1976 FA Cup semi-final, losing to Southampton at Stamford Bridge, and only when Terry Venables moved up from midfield general to manager the following year did Palace return to the Second Division.

Venables was sufficiently well thought of to have been offered the Arsenal job ahead of Terry Neill in the summer of 1976. At

Palace, he brought on many of the club's promising youngsters, like Kenny Sansom and Vince Hilaire, and in his second season, 1978/79, led them back to the First Division by beating Burnley in front of a new record crowd for Selhurst of 51,801.

Jimmy Greaves, as his ghostwriter has confirmed, may well have been responsible for suggesting they would be the 'Team of the Eighties'. It was not his greatest prediction: by May 1981, Palace were relegated again after a demoralising season on and off the pitch.

After losing nine of the first ten league games, Venables left for QPR, having learnt that his job had been offered to Blackburn's Howard Kendall. With the club stuck firmly at the bottom of the table, takeover rumours abounded and in December Fulham's Ernie Clay announced he had made a bid to chairman Raymond Bloye.

Noades denied any interest, then in January bought a 75 per cent share of the club for £600,000 and sold Wimbledon to Lebanese director Sam Hammam for £40,000. Ernie Walley and then Allison (in his second spell) had been holding the fort as managers but Noades brought Dario Gradi with him from Wimbledon, Palace finishing the season of four managers bottom of the table by 13 points.

Although crowds had dipped alarmingly, there was obviously greater potential than at Wimbledon. Noades finally discovered a more successful manager in Steve Coppell, appointed in 1984, but his thoughts turned to a merger after Wimbledon astonishingly beat Palace to both the First Division and then the FA Cup Final.

When Gradi left for Selhurst the Dons turned to Dave Bassett, who decided the way forward for a club with such limited finance was direct football. Like Watford under Graham Taylor they made it work spectacularly, winning the Fourth Division in 1983 and then promotion from the Third 12 months later.

In each of those seasons, they won Capital Radio's £25,000 as London's top scorers, reaching almost 100 league goals by emulating Watford in using big strikers like Stewart Evans and Alan Cork to feed on long balls and crosses. Those associated with the club in those days insist that this was the time of the real 'Crazy Gang', fostering unique team spirit amid the atmosphere of a ramshackle Plough Lane ground where even in the Fourth Division championship season the average gate was 2,347.

It was still barely 4,500 for the 1985/86 season, when Wimbledon improbably won promotion to English football's top division, and only that high because of local derbies with Charlton, Fulham, Millwall and Palace – not one of whom managed to beat them either home or away.

It was something of a gamble to pay a club-record fee of £125,000 for striker John Fashanu from Millwall in the run-in, but it paid off handsomely, leaving Wimbledon unbeaten in the final 16 games and promoted to the First Division nine years after leaving the Southern League.

'Deep down the future of Wimbledon Football Club worries me,' Bassett had said a couple of years earlier. Noades was still thinking the same sort of thing and even as the upstarts took the First Division by storm – top of the table after five games – he began negotiations for either a ground-share or merger at Selhurst Park, with Plough Lane being sold for development. News came out in February 1987 at a time when Wimbledon were actually attracting slightly larger crowds than their neighbours, but apart from the resignation of Wimbledon chief executive Colin Hutchinson there were no further developments.

By winning their last four games, completing a double over both Chelsea and Manchester United, the Dons finished an incredible sixth and would have qualified for Europe but for the ban imposed on English clubs after Liverpool fans' appalling behaviour at the Heysel European Cup Final.

Bassett's departure to succeed Taylor at Watford might have been expected to herald an end to Cinderella's partying, but under Bobby Gould and Don Howe they not only finished seventh the following season but celebrated the greatest day in the club's 99-year history.

An FA Cup run brought wins over West Bromwich Albion and Mansfield Town, then a 3-1 success away to Newcastle and a 2-1 home win with ten men over Watford, who had sacked the unsuccessful Bassett only five months into the season. For the semi-final against Luton at White Hart Lane, Gould played up to the image of unfashionable underdogs by driving most of the team in a VW mini-bus, struggling to convince both the police escort and the gateman who they were.

In front of the smallest FA Cup semi-final crowd in memory – 25,963 – the abrasive Mick Harford put Luton in front before Fashanu equalised from a debatable penalty and little Dennis Wise popped up with a winner.

Since the Wembley opposition would be Liverpool, champions by nine points and aiming for the Double, Wimbledon were given virtually no chance of repeating their Amateur Cup Final success of 25 years earlier.

In retrospect, they should have been. Only narrowly beaten at Anfield six weeks earlier, they had won there the previous season, spitting at the 'This Is Anfield' sign on the way down the tunnel. Gould was one of the few who believed they would win, and he and Howe used all their wiles to ensure it: a kickabout on the Wembley pitch two days beforehand in front of an enraged groundsman, sending the players out for a drink the night before the game, moving Wise to the right to help combat John Barnes and putting the dressing-room clock back in order to keep Liverpool waiting in the tunnel.

> **Liverpool** (4-4-2): Grobbelaar; Nicol, Gillespie, Hansen, Ablett; Houghton, McMahon, Spackman (Molby), Barnes; Aldridge (Johnston), Beardsley.
>
> **Wimbledon** (4-4-2): Beasant; Goodyear, Young, Thorn, Phelan; Wise, Jones, Sanchez, Gibson (Scales); Cork (Cunningham), Fashanu.

Vinny Jones's first tackle on Steve McMahon, too early for the deserved punishment and still frightening all these years later, set the tone. The two key moments thereafter are engraved in Wimbledon history. In the 37th minute, Lawrie Sanchez, whose brother had £100 on him at 33-1 to score the first goal, did just that by heading in Wise's free-kick. Then, in the 60th minute, Dave 'Lurch' Beasant produced the first penalty save in an FA Cup Final.

Hammam, the extrovert Lebanese who had been managing director and was now owner, told Gould after the game that now was the time to sell the best players while their value was at its highest. He was true to his word, and that summer Beasant and defender Andy Thorn left for Newcastle, where they finished bottom of the table, with Wimbledon 12th.

Howe also moved on, to QPR, and so did Gould in December 1990 to join him, but only after making the inspired recommendation of Joe Kinnear as successor.

* * * * *

Palace, meanwhile, stabilised in the first and by far the longest of Steve Coppell's numerous periods at the club. Unusually for a modern manager it lasted nine years, from being given a first chance in 1984 at the age of 28 after his premature retirement as a Manchester United and England winger with a serious knee injury – 'the blind leading the blind', he candidly admitted of his early steps in management.

He established them as a top-six club in the Second Division for three successive seasons from 1986–88 before achieving promotion in 1989 behind Chelsea and Manchester City via the play-offs, when Blackburn were overcome despite a 3-1 defeat in the first leg. The key had been bringing together as a striking partnership Ian Wright, a late starter, from Greenwich Borough and Mark Bright from Leicester City. From a quiet start in 1986/87, the pair flourished with 45 goals between them the following year and 48 in the promotion season.

To their undoubted annoyance, however, Palace had to watch not only Wimbledon, but south London's other two teams as well shoot past them into the First Division.

Charlton's was a remarkable tale, starting from the lower half of the Third Division after three struggles against relegation from 1970–72, the last of them ending in failure. Theo Foley was sacked after bringing in three forwards who would help transform fortunes in Derek Hales, Mike Flanagan and Colin Powell.

Their goals, and those of Arthur Horsfield, helped earn promotion to the Second Division and kept them there, although Hales and Flanagan became most famous for fighting each other in a 1979 FA Cup tie at home to non-League Maidstone. Both were sent off but when Hales was re-instated after initially being sacked, Flanagan walked out and eventually joined Palace.

Another relegation and promotion in successive seasons was followed by a deepening financial crisis, caused partly by the Safety of Sports Grounds Act imposing a limit of only 13,000 on The Valley. But Mark Hulyer ended the Gliksten dynasty by taking over as the Football League's youngest chairman at 32 and, in October 1982, stunned football by somehow persuading Allan Simonsen, twice European Footballer of the Year, to join from Barcelona for a fee of £300,000 payable over three years.

After various contractual problems he made a belated debut against Middlesbrough the following month, scoring as Charlton were beaten 3-2 in front of twice the 5,000 crowd who had watched their previous home game.

It was an unlikely marriage that ended after 16 games, in which the little Dane scored nine times, including two in a 5-2 home win over Chelsea. He returned to his home-town club Vejle in March when it became clear Charlton could no longer afford to keep him.

They finished the season in the bottom six of the Second Division, the main encouragement being that former schoolteacher Robin 'Lennie' Lawrence was nevertheless impressing as a down-to-earth manager in comparison to his pie-in-the-sky chairman.

He did so in spite of an increasingly perilous financial position. The club had to survive numerous winding-up orders during 1983/84, including one from Leeds United over an unpaid transfer fee for Welsh forward Carl Harris and another from the Inland Revenue. Meanwhile, Gliksten was claiming the club owed his company more than £500,000.

After a High Court judge declared the club 'hopelessly insolvent' at the end of February, the official receiver padlocked the Valley gates and a league game at Blackburn had to be postponed. Sunley's had emerged as potential saviours and early in March, with deadlines running out, their rescue package was finally accepted by the High Court and the Football League.

Gliksten cannily retained control of The Valley, which caused the next crisis 18 months later. He wanted to reclaim two acres of land behind the main (west) stand at the same time as the GLC, reacting to the Bradford fire, ordered the huge east terrace to be closed.

Supporters turning up for a home game against Crystal Palace on 7 September 1985 were therefore horrified to receive a leaflet announcing that after the next home game against Stoke a fortnight later, the club would be sharing Selhurst Park on a seven-year lease. Ron Noades had his ground-sharing agreement at last, though not with the club he expected.

On 21 September, 8,858 were at The Valley's final game, in which Robert Lee, once a turnstile operator there, scored the last goal in a 2-0 win. The next 'home' game was against Sunderland at Selhurst, where 5,552 (a larger crowd than Palace's a week later) saw another win.

Many supporters nevertheless boycotted the move and casual support had clearly been lost. For the game after that, the gate was down to 3,141. What was extraordinary, however, was the team's form. Flanagan had unexpectedly returned, via QPR, and was scoring regularly, backed up by Lee and John Pearson, while former West Ham midfielder Alan Curbishley added valuable experience.

Second in the table at Christmas, like Wimbledon they found the money for a new striker in the promotion push, paying Manchester City £45,000 for Jim Melrose, and after two exciting draws with Millwall and a double over Fulham, they went to Carlisle for the penultimate game. True to the spirit of the whole season, Lawrence's team came from 2-0 down against the relegation strugglers to win 3-2 and secure promotion. A goalless draw with Wimbledon watched by more than 13,000 then ensured they finished runners-up to Norwich, with the equally indomitable Dons third.

Staying up for even four seasons was just as much of a triumph. Bottom on Boxing Day in the first one, they survived by way of the play-offs introduced to help reduce the top division from 22 clubs to 20. The final against Leeds went to a third game at Birmingham, in which centre-half and captain Peter Shirtliff became the unlikely hero with both goals in extra time for a 2-1 win.

The second season came down to avoiding defeat away to Chelsea in the final game, which was achieved in a 1-1 draw by Paul Miller's deflected shot, sending the Stamford Bridge side into the play-offs instead (which they lost). In 1988/89, there was a three-point safety margin, but relegation in a poor 1989/90 campaign had an air of inevitability.

More importantly came confirmation of the new owners' intention to return to The Valley, following a long campaign by supporters, spearheaded by the *Voice of the Valley* fanzine. There was still much frustration ahead and it would be another three and a half years from the announcement at Woolwich Town Hall in March 1989 before it happened.

* * * * *

Not only Charlton and Wimbledon, but **Millwall** too were in the top division by the end of the Eighties. They thought they had made it much earlier, on what turned into a traumatic day in April 1972.

While they were beating Preston at The Den, rumour spread that promotion rivals Birmingham City were losing at Sheffield Wednesday. If results stayed the same, Millwall would be up for the first time in their history. At the final whistle there was an ecstatic pitch invasion, suddenly halted by an announcement over the tannoy: Birmingham had won and would go up unless they lost their final game away to Orient three days later.

Thousands of Millwall fans crossed the Thames to cheer on Orient, swelling the gate to a near full house of 33,363. London United fought in vain as Birmingham won by the only goal and Millwall had many more days in the doldrums to endure before finally achieving their dream in 1988.

After Benny Fenton joined the managerial cull of autumn 1974, they went down to the Third Division in 1975 and 1979. The second time it took six years to return, attendances having declined to little more than 4,000 and, in 1982 for Chesterfield's visit, to 2,265.

George Graham took them back up in 1985 before leaving for Arsenal with his assistant Theo Foley a year later. The new partnership comprised two Scots who knew their way round London and had worked together at Brentford. This time, John Docherty was the manager and Frank McLintock his assistant, which meant Millwall employed the direct play Docherty loved, as opposed to what he called 'fanny football'.

The ball was knocked up to Tony Cascarino and Teddy Sheringham, served excellently by wingers Jimmy Carter and Kevin O'Callaghan, while in midfield one of the great Millwall legends, Terry Hurlock, knocked over anyone in his way.

Only three points above relegation in 1987, before Cascarino joined from Gillingham, they increased the number of goals scored from 39 to 72 – 42 of them from the twin strikers – in storming to the Second Division title, which was clinched away to Hull City in a seventh successive victory.

Gloriously, on 1 October 1988, the Lions even stood looking down on the rest of English football following a 3-2 home win over QPR, Cascarino having scored eight goals in the first six games.

They were still third in mid-March before dropping to finish tenth, a home defeat by Wimbledon beginning a slump in which Spurs won 5-0 at The Den and no more games were won. Five matches into the following season they were top again, but injuries hampered a thin squad and in February Docherty and McLintock were sacked after winning one game in 18. Avuncular chief scout Bob Pearson was surprisingly appointed but replaced within two months by Bruce Rioch before the team finished bottom of the table and went down with neighbouring Charlton.

* * * * *

The 1970s were one of the better decades in the history of **Orient,** featuring not only an FA Cup semi-final and a famous giant-killing but a night when one extra goal would have meant ascending to the top division for only the second time.

That frustrating evening was on 3 May 1974, when victory at home to middle-of-the-table Aston Villa would mean promotion at the end of a campaign notable for some excellent push-and-run football under manager George Petchey. Like the 1961/62 season, it stalled towards the end, but this time had an unhappy ending, a 1-1 draw with Villa in front of almost 30,000 meaning that equally unpretentious Carlisle United went up instead.

Petchey was a lifelong London football man. Born up the road at Whitechapel, he had been a wing-half with West Ham, QPR and Crystal Palace, and was coach at Selhurst Park before moving to Leyton in 1971 when Jimmy Bloomfield was lured away by Leicester City. Reinforcing Bloomfield's Third Division champions with a number of Palace players, he enjoyed a spectacular cup run in his first season when Chelsea, the 1970 winners, were downed 3-2 in the Brisbane Road mud after leading 2-0. Arsenal were fortunate to win the subsequent quarter-final 1-0.

A brilliant prospect in Archway-born winger Laurie Cunningham had emerged and moved on (to West Bromwich Albion) by the time Chelsea and Arsenal featured again in Orient's next FA Cup run in 1978.

Signing Peter Kitchen from Doncaster Rovers for £25,000 to remedy the chronic shortage of goals that had almost resulted in relegation proved masterly, although Petchey did not survive to reap the benefit. He was sacked only two games into the 1977/78 season to facilitate the return of Bloomfield.

It took the last of Kitchen's 21 league goals, away to Cardiff, to ensure Second Division safety in a desperate finish, after his scoring exploits brought FA Cup wins away to First Division Norwich, at home to Blackburn and then at Stamford Bridge. Away to another First Division side, Middlesbrough, in the quarter-finals, Orient were given little chance but they held out for a goalless draw and won the replay with Kitchen's seventh cup goal and one for his striking partner, the taller Joe Mayo. The semi-final back at Stamford Bridge was an anti-climax, with Arsenal winning 3-0 after two deflected goals and a third from Graham Rix.

Even though Kitchen was sold to Fulham the following year, Orient appeared to be showing genuine ambition when former England forwards Peter Taylor and Stan Bowles were signed. For whatever reason, neither was a success and once young winger John Chiedozie was sold, Bloomfield resigned.

By the summer of 1985 Orient were in the Fourth Division for the first time. The board commendably kept faith with manager Frank Clark, who after three near-misses and a name-change back to Leyton Orient returned them to the Third. There was at least one serious financial crisis along the way, in 1986, and in the early Nineties there would be another, amid the unlikely and tragic circumstances of the Rwandan civil war.

* * * * *

For **Brentford**, life went on in much the same sort of way, which was something in itself after QPR's predatory ambitions of 1967. They also made an eventual step-up, after one false start, from the Fourth Division to the Third.

Division Four in the Seventies was a lonely place for a London team, and when Brentford escaped in 1972 on the back of big striker John O'Mara's 25 goals, it was only for one season. Mick Everitt and John Docherty failed to get them out again after that but Bill Dodgin Jr did so in 1977/78, the season that Wimbledon arrived in the Football League, to produce a couple of genuine London derbies. Graham Taylor's Watford were champions but the Bees, finishing fourth, scored more goals, Steve Phillips getting 32 and Andy McCulloch 22.

They stayed in Division Three for the whole of the Eighties, mostly in mid-table, although close to relegation in 1984 and never threatening at the other end of the table. That would come soon enough in the new decade.

Chapter 7

Greed is good (1991-2000)

The Premier League, pay-per-view television and all-seater eras begin, dominated just like the original Football League by the North and Midlands; five seasons until a London side even makes the top three, then Arsene Wenger, one of the first foreign managers, makes Arsenal a force again; Chelsea, under the controversial Ken Bates, rebuild Stamford Bridge and their fortunes; after Crystal Palace's greatest season, Barnet, founded 1888, reach the league 103 years later; Wimbledon finish in the top six then begin a long slide; new ground for Millwall but Charlton get back to The Valley and reach the Premier League; Fulham flourish under colourful foreign ownership, overtaking QPR.

T HE 1980s marked a low point for attendances and crowd behaviour, related issues in which the main London clubs and their supporters' 'firms' played a significant part. The 1990s changed everything.

Time and circumstances were right as pressure for reform grew out of tragedy.

In a horrific few weeks in May 1985, the Bradford fire and Heysel deaths showed up the shocking state of grounds at home and abroad. After Hillsborough four years later, the *Sunday Times* famously declared football to be 'a slum sport played in slum stadiums'. Once Lord Justice Taylor's report into Hillsborough appeared in January 1990, advocating all-seater stadiums and warning 'the scale of the changes I recommend will necessarily require heavy expenditure', minds had to be concentrated on improving the game's parlous finances.

The process had begun much earlier, with talk of a 'Super League', a British League, even a European League. (The continent's biggest clubs, concerned about losing revenue because of early elimination from the European Cup, secured a new system and new name in 1992, the Champions League, guaranteeing them more games).

In England, the First Division clubs had begun to demand a greater share of what spoils there were, although it was Brentford's chairman, Martin Lange, who proposed the introduction of play-offs as part of a ten-point plan thrashed out at Heathrow Airport in December 1985 and accepted at a Football League EGM four months later. The top division was also to be cut to 20 clubs by 1989 and for the first time there would be automatic promotion for the top non-league club to Division Four.

A self-elected 'big five' clubs – Arsenal, Tottenham, Everton, Liverpool and Manchester United – were the most vocal proponents of change, although Spurs chairman Irving Scholar won over a majority with his view that television must be made to pay much higher sums for coverage.

In the stand-off, the 1985/86 season had no televised football at all for several months, the negotiators having turned down £17m over four years and then been forced to accept just £1.3m when it returned to the screens for half a season with the Charlton-West Ham FA Cup tie in January '86.

Football had always been afraid of live coverage. An early attempt, in 1960/61, foundered after just one game (between Blackpool and Bolton), when Arsenal and Spurs refused ITV permission to cover their matches. *Match of the Day* highlights, introduced in August 1964 with Liverpool's exciting 3-2 win over Arsenal, proved a popular compromise, although the 92 clubs shared just £5,000 – a paltry £54 each.

By 1983/84, the clubs felt ready to try a limited number of live games and when Spurs played Nottingham Forest in the first of them in October, backed by paid-for TV adverts to 'be one of the team', the crowd of 30,596 was higher than for the previous game at White Hart Lane against Everton.

Significantly, that season's deal was shared by ITV and BBC, alternating games. The breakthrough came when ITV's Greg Dyke admitted that the two companies had been operating a cartel to keep the price down and negotiators realised the key was to have an exclusive contract on offer to the highest bidder. They were helped in that by the arrival of satellite television.

In January 1988, the nascent British Satellite Broadcasting approached the big five, who had morphed into the big ten with the support of West Ham and four others, but Arsenal's chairman Peter Hill-Wood did not trust their financial projections and ITV became the preferred option.

They were eventually persuaded to cough up £11m over four years from 1988, which was how Brian Moore came to be the commentator describing Michael Thomas's goal – 'it's up for grabs now' – in the epic climax to the 1988/89 season at Anfield.

Football politics now shifted from television to the composition and power of the top division, with the London clubs again playing a leading role. Ken Bates of Chelsea, a vocal and influential member of the Football League management committee, and kindred spirit Ron Noades of Palace infuriated Arsenal and Spurs by having a motion passed to return the division to 22 clubs.

Crucially, however, that also alienated the Football Association, who knew it would hinder the England team. Building on new public support for the national side after the 1990 World Cup, and egged on by Arsenal's David Dein and Liverpool's Noel White, they seized their chance to come up with 'The Blueprint for the Future of Football'.

Published in June 1991, it proposed establishing The Football Association Premier League from 1992/93, reducing to 18 clubs within four years. The Football League were outflanked and the damage to them could have been even worse. Noades subsequently claimed he was only one club short of recruiting 18 who would form a Second Division of the new league.

Television interest was evident from the start and at an extraordinary meeting of the 22 clubs (extraordinary in every way), ITV lost out to Rupert Murdoch's BSkyB, desperate to use sport as what he called the 'battering ram' to revive the ailing company, backed up by highlights on the BBC.

A key figure, and hardly a disinterested one, was the new Spurs chairman Alan Sugar, whose Amstrad company made satellite dishes. In a classic Arsenal-Spurs confrontation, Dein tried to have the Tottenham chairman banned from voting for that reason but received no support and Spurs' vote proved decisive in securing the necessary two-thirds majority.

The new five-year deal was purportedly worth £304 million which, although never actually achieved, still meant a whole new world for the lucky 22 who would begin the 1992/93 season. In addition, ITV paid more than £25m for Football League and League Cup matches, plus Leeds United and Manchester United in Europe.

* * * * *

Of London's record eight representatives in the top division of 1989/90, six –Tottenham, Arsenal, Chelsea, Wimbledon, QPR and Crystal Palace – were still there for the inaugural Premier League season, but rather like the original Football League a century earlier, it was the North and Midlands who initially dominated. Not for five years did a club from the capital even make the top three as Manchester United won four of the first five titles and Blackburn Rovers just pipped them to the other one.

Arsenal, who had repeated their 1989 success much more easily in 1991, seven points ahead of Liverpool this time, again emerged as the London club most likely to challenge. They were able to build on a double triumph in the domestic cups in 1993, both against Trevor Francis's Sheffield Wednesday, who were overcome 2-1 in the League Cup and by the same score in a replayed FA Cup Final the following month.

That paved the way for triumph in the European Cup-Winners' Cup, a characteristic 1-0 win thanks to Alan Smith's goal against Gianfranco Zola's Parma in the final after capable Torino and Paris St Germain sides had been beaten by that same familiar scoreline at Highbury. Ian Wright, signed from Crystal Palace for £2.5m in 1991, missed the final but had his best return for the club that season, scoring 34 of his eventual 185 goals.

A return to the European Cup in 1991 had been less successful, bringing a home defeat in extra time by Benfica, followed by a catastrophic loss at Wrexham in the FA Cup. The live commentary on Radio 5 confidently switched away from the Racecourse Ground after Smith put Arsenal ahead, only to return in haste when the Fourth Division team scored, twice, for a stunning victory.

In the league, there were fourth places in 1992 and 1994 before a drop to mid-table during the dramatic 1994/95 season in which George Graham controversially departed. A Premier League tribunal found him guilty of accepting more than £400,000 from the Norwegian agent Rune Hauge in connection with Arsenal's acquisition of John Jensen, the midfielder who was part of Denmark's unexpected European Championship success of 1992, and the Norwegian full-back Pal Lydersen.

Graham insisted these were unsolicited gifts from a grateful agent and that he had returned the money to Arsenal, who nevertheless dismissed him three months from the end of an unsuccessful season.

New signings John Hartson and Chris Kiwomya had not had the desired effect in supporting Wright after Alan Smith was injured, and Arsenal finished 12th, below Spurs, QPR, Wimbledon and Chelsea, as well as suffering the ignominy of a home defeat by Millwall in the FA Cup.

They were better in the Cup-Winners' Cup, Wright's goals earning another appearance in the final but this time Real Zaragoza beat them 2-1 with a freak goal which, to the delight of Tottenham fans, was scored from the halfway line by former Spurs midfielder Nayim.

For all the sad circumstances of his demise, Graham's record was formidable. He left his successors plenty to build on, above all a relentlessly drilled defence which, in what proved to be Bruce Rioch's only season as manager, conceded just 32 goals – the best in the league. They finished fifth and only lost the League Cup semi-final to fourth-placed Aston Villa on away goals.

Rioch had impressed as Bolton Wanderers won an FA Cup tie at Highbury and then achieved promotion from the newly titled First Division. It was an irony that his legacy would be signing the great Dennis Bergkamp from Internazionale, but that a lack of enthusiasm for other potential foreign recruits caused him to fall out with the board and leave shortly before the start of the following season.

'He didn't share our vision for the future of the club' chairman Peter Hill-Wood told the annual general meeting in August 1996, adding that Arsenal had secured 'a replacement of considerable international reputation,' who could not yet be named. Then, with a slip of the tongue he named him anyway, a manager with such an international reputation that the *Evening Standard* bill poster asked: 'Arsene Who?'

The world soon learnt the answer to that. Joining from Grampus 8 in Japan, where he had learnt the importance for foot-ballers of good diet, Arsene Wenger's first gift to the club had been made before his arrival with the signing of the little-known Patrick Vieira. Despite having to cope with a string of personal problems and addictions among the squad that had caused Rioch to compare himself to the agony aunt Marje Proops, Wenger had them briefly top of the table and finishing third, with 23 goals from Wright while the 20-year-old Vieira established himself in midfield.

Recruitment in 1997 showed how internationalist Arsenal had become with Marc Overmars, the speedy Dutch winger, joined by three players from Wenger's former club Monaco, including Emmanuel Petit, Vieira's new partner and a replacement for the departed Paul Merson.

The team suddenly gelled from Christmas, rising from fifth place to overhaul Manchester United after being 11 points behind them at the start of March with two away games in hand.

From the days of 'one-nil to the Arsenal', London's first Premier League title was secured on the back of wins in quick succession over Blackburn by 4-1, Wimbledon 5-0 and Everton 4-0. A goal by the newly fit and sober Tony Adams in the latter game, surging forward from defence to crash in a half-volley, summed up the new regime perfectly.

Bergkamp was named Footballer of the Year, with Adams receiving the second highest number of votes. Ian Wright was injured in January but Nicolas Anelka took over his shirt and scoring mantle in both the league and a strange FA Cup run.

Held at home by Port Vale, Crystal Palace and West Ham before winning the replays (on a penalty shoot-out at Vale Park and Upton Park), Wenger's team beat Wolves 1-0 in the semi-final with Christopher Wreh's goal and suddenly realised the club's second Double was in sight, 27 years after the first.

> **Arsenal**: Seaman; Dixon, Keown, Adams, Winterburn; Parlour, Vieira, Petit, Overmars; Anelka, Wreh (Platt).
>
> **Newcastle**: Given; Pistone, Dabizas, Howey, Pearce (Anderson); Barton, Lee, Batty, Speed; Ketsbaia (Barnes); Shearer.

A year on from their Premier League collapse, which saw them lose the title to Manchester United, Newcastle were a more prosaic side under Kenny Dalglish than Kevin Keegan, reflected in a fall from runners-up to 13th place, scoring only 35 goals.

With an extra man in midfield, they had their moments, notably when Alan Shearer hit a post, but that was after Overmars had scored from Petit's pass. In the 69th minute Ray Parlour, named man of the match, sent Anelka through to complete his outstanding half-season with the second goal.

The one disappointed Arsenal player was Ian Wright, who was passed over for Wreh when Bergkamp declared himself unfit and sat forlornly on the substitutes' bench. Wright joined West Ham that summer while Vieira and Petit went off to win the World Cup for France.

Easily forgotten is that, in his first full season, Wenger could even have achieved a unique domestic Treble but for a narrow 4-3 aggregate defeat in the League Cup semi-final by Chelsea, who then beat Second Division Middlesbrough at Wembley. His 'considerable international reputation' was now assured and was hardly marred when Alex Ferguson's United had the better of them the following season in the league (despite Arsenal conceding only 17 goals) and also in a memorable FA Cup semi-final replay, after Bergkamp's penalty was saved by Peter Schmeichel and Ryan Giggs raced away to score the winning goal and bare his hirsuite chest to the world.

* * * * *

From the mid-Nineties, **Chelsea** became London's second club. In between his campaign to make sure the big five clubs did not enjoy all the financial spoils, the abrasive Ken Bates slowly won the new battle of Stamford Bridge, seeing off the property developers drooling over such prime west London land, as well as shaming many of the racists who sold the National Front newspaper outside the ground and had made life hell for emerging black players like winger Paul Canoville.

The Second Division championship team of 1989 was clearly strong enough to make a decent fist of things back at the higher level. Briefly top in November, they finished fifth behind Spurs and Arsenal and even won a Wembley trophy, the Full Members Cup, in front of more than 76,000.

From that starting point, the next few seasons were disappointing. Manager Bobby Campbell did not enjoy moving upstairs, planning new hotels and car parks, and under Ian Porterfield and caretaker David Webb Chelsea were 14th and 11th.

Glenn Hoddle did three seasons before leaving to manage England, yet never once finished in the top half of the table either. What Hoddle did was reach a cup final, take the club back into Europe and attract the first of the stellar foreign names now taken for granted by supporters.

The cup final came in 1994 after a run beginning about as inauspiciously as was possible for a Premier League club: a goalless draw at Stamford Bridge against Barnet, who had voluntarily surrendered home advantage. Chelsea, who had been bottom but one in the league over Christmas, were found out in the final, even if 4-0, including two penalties, was a flattering victory margin for a Manchester United side completing the Double.

For Hoddle's third and final season, one of the great names of European football, Ruud Gullit, was on board, signed with the help of investment by new director Matthew Harding. Sadly, the gregarious Harding, highly popular with supporters, soon made a bitter enemy of Bates and then tragically died in 1996 in a helicopter crash returning from a League Cup tie at Bolton.

Gullit was a natural choice to take over as manager the following summer, when recruitment continued at impressive levels: Gianluca Vialli, who had just won the Champions League with Juventus, French defender Franck Leboeuf, Lazio's Roberto di Matteo and, in November, Gianfranco Zola from Parma.

With Gullit sensibly restricting his own appearances, the new boys flourished. Zola was named Footballer of the Year after only half a season. Chelsea ended up sixth in the Premier League and goals were shared so widely that despite nobody hitting more than Vialli's nine, only four teams scored more.

Di Matteo contributed seven from midfield and a famous one in the FA Cup Final, smacked past Middlesbrough's Ben Roberts from 25 yards after a record-breaking 43 seconds. Eddie Newton added the second in a 2-0 win.

Fourth, third and fifth in the next three seasons (albeit behind Arsenal each time), Chelsea enjoyed two further Wembley wins, over Middlesbrough again in the 1998 League Cup Final, when Frank Sinclair and Di Matteo scored in another 2-0 success, and

1-0 over Aston Villa in the 2000 FA Cup Final with yet another Di Matteo goal.

The 1997/98 total of 71 league goals was the club's best in the top division for almost 30 years, a tribute to what Gullit chose to call 'sexy football'. Yet by the time they won the Cup Winners-Cup in Stockholm, beating Stuttgart with Zola's goal, the Dutchman had been sacked.

He fell foul of Bates – not a wise move by anyone – for stalling on a new contract, then demanding it should be as a player-manager (despite waning form and fitness) and eventually insisting on far more than Chelsea could afford 'netto' – tax-paid.

It was with Vialli as player-manager that the club proceeded and in his first full season, 1998/99, they could have won the league. Beaten only three times, but stymied by three successive draws in April, they finished third, four points off the top and three behind runners-up Arsenal, who took a crucial four points off them.

Marcel Desailly, Gus Poyet and the less successful Brian Laudrup were the latest distinguished recruits, followed by Didier Deschamps in the following season, when on Boxing Day 1999 at Southampton Chelsea sparked much anguished debate by fielding the first all-foreign XI in British football history:

> De Goey; Ferrer, Thome, Leboeuf, Babayaro; Petrescu, Deschamps, Di Matteo, Ambrosetti; Poyet, Flo.

* * * * *

If it was galling for **Tottenham** to watch Arsenal raking in the trophies, seeing Chelsea achieve so much was doubly so. One FA Cup and one League Cup at either end of the decade were poor compensation, especially given the off-field convulsions that began early on with revelations of unsustainable debt caused by two factors: the diversification into a 'leisure group' that Keith Burkinshaw had complained about, and (echoing Chelsea's problems under Brian Mears) an overrun on the East Stand development.

Third place in 1990 under Terry Venables, ahead of the seven other London clubs in the top division, and an excellent start to the following season with Gary Lineker and BBC Sports Personality of the Year Paul Gascoigne starring, hinted at a promise that was only fulfilled in the FA Cup. That pair scored all three goals in a rare triumph over Arsenal in the Wembley semi-final, Gascoigne hammering a stunning free-kick past David Seaman, but his behaviour in the final threatened to undermine Spurs' very existence as much as the result.

In debt to the tune of £22m, the Spurs board had reluctantly agreed to sell the man-child of a midfielder to Lazio for around £8m. Hyped up for his last game with the club, Gascoigne flew into one wild tackle on Garry Parker worth a booking, then another on Gary Charles that should probably have had him sent off. Instead he was carried off with knee ligament damage. It was a costly challenge in every sense for the club and player.

After Stuart Pearce scored from the resulting free-kick, Spurs rallied with spirit to equalise through Paul Stewart and then win the cup just as they had lost it four years earlier – to an own goal. Winning captain Gary Mabbutt, the victim against Coventry in 1987, will have sympathised with Des Walker, whose header beat his own goalkeeper in extra time. The follow-up to the final was all about the threat to Gascoigne's impending move, which the Italian club agreed could go ahead at a later date, while reducing the fee to £4.8m subject to his full recovery. Spurs eventually pushed them up to £5.5m, despite a further knee injury he suffered at a night-club.

Meanwhile, Scholar was talking about investment in the club to Robert Maxwell who, despite already being involved at Oxford and Derby, had loaned Spurs £1m to prevent Barcelona recalling Lineker because of overdue payment.

Venables, horrified by the thought of working for Maxwell and always up for a new challenge, spent his summer putting together a consortium to take over the club. He ended up as co-owner and chief executive, with East End entrepreneur Alan Sugar as chairman in a partnership doomed to die a painful death.

It also seemed a waste of Venables' coaching ability. Without it and even with 28 goals from Lineker before leaving for Japan in an £850,000 deal, Spurs were no higher than 15th. When Venables returned to the playing side, it was with Ray Clemence and Doug Livermore as fellow coaches but Arsenal achieved revenge by winning the FA Cup semi-final against a weaker Spurs and so did Forest for the second year running in the League Cup.

Sugar and Venables had grown apart from their earliest days and, in May 1993, a row at a board meeting about – of all things – the White Hart Lane computer system ended with Sugar throwing a letter at him that effectively said, in the catchphrase made famous by his later television programme *The Apprentice*: 'You're fired'.

In June they met in the High Court, with Spurs fans outside chanting their support for Venables. Much mud was thrown and he failed to extend an injunction that would have kept him in the job. Within a year he had a rather better one, as manager of England in the run-up to Euro '96, demonstrating the coaching ability that might have improved Tottenham had he concentrated on that.

'We were on the verge of great things,' Venables believed, although the defeats in 1992/93 at Sheffield United (6-0), lowly Leeds (5-0) and Liverpool (6-2) suggested greatness might have taken a while longer.

An old Tottenham hero in Ossie Ardiles arrived as manager, but lasted only one full season, the team dropping from eighth to 15th and starting the following campaign badly. Spurs had fallen foul of a draconian punishment for illegal payments to players by the Scholar regime, which was initially 12 league points, a £600,000 fine and ban from the FA Cup. Sugar won back a little support from fans by fighting all this at his outraged best, and the eventual damage was reduced to a fine of £1.5m instead.

The brightest spot as Gerry Francis replaced Ardiles for three years was the form of Jurgen Klinsmann, one of the Premier League's first genuine overseas superstars, who scored 29 goals before leaving when Spurs just missed out on European football, finishing seventh after a bad run-in, and losing an FA Cup semi-final heavily to Everton.

Further signings of the quality of David Ginola and Les Ferdinand pushed them no higher over the next couple of seasons and not until George Graham, so heavily associated with Arsenal, took over from the hapless Christian Gross in 1998 was there a trophy, the League Cup of 1999, won after a dour pair of semi-finals against Wimbledon and a 1-0 victory over Leicester at Wembley, where Justin Edinburgh was sent off.

It was a poor return for Sugar's eight years as chairman and he had almost had enough.

* * * * *

For three successive seasons at the end of the Nineties, Spurs finished below not only Arsenal and Chelsea but **West Ham** too. Having sacked John Lyall in 1989, they had found the right replacement at last in Harry Redknapp, one of London football's most colourful figures.

His contemporary in a West Ham shirt, the swashbuckling Billy Bonds, was the more popular player, rapturously welcomed as successor to the ill-starred Lou Macari in 1990 but never likely to be comfortable as a manager. As team-mates avowed, Bonds, like Paul Scholes years later, was the first player out of the dressing room and off home to his family, south of the river, where he had been brought up and always lived.

Despite that, he led West Ham to the 1991 FA Cup semi-final, lost 4-0 to Forest (thereby missing out on a final against Spurs) after Tony Gale was harshly sent off, and also the first of two promotions on either side of an immediate relegation. Redknapp, having made an excellent start in management with Bournemouth, came in as assistant for the second promotion season of 1992/93.

The following campaign, the club's first in the Premier League, involved a recovery from a bad start to finish 13th, but the eventful four and a half years had worn down Bonds. In the summer of

1994, Redknapp was tempted by a return back to Bournemouth as managing director so the board offered him the West Ham job with Bonds moving upstairs, recreating the Greenwood-Lyall relationship of 20 years earlier.

Bonds decided to leave altogether and fell out with his former team-mate, who had to contend with suggestions that he had stabbed his friend in the back. Be that as it may, Redknapp established the club as a solid Premier League team and with the benefit of some outstanding young academy products like Rio Ferdinand, Frank Lampard and Joe Cole, plus the mercurial talents of Paolo di Canio, had them finishing as high as fifth in 1999 and back in European football for the first time in 18 years.

* * * * *

Unable to capitalise on the best season in their history, 1990/91, **Crystal Palace** became the Premier League's first yo-yo team, forever dropping out, fighting their way back but lasting no more than a season. Keeping up with whether or not Steve Coppell was manager was equally tricky.

Coppell was very much in charge when his team followed Wimbledon in inflicting one of the great FA Cup shocks on an otherwise dominant Liverpool in 1990. Two seasons after the Dons' Wembley victory, Palace went into the Sunday semi-final at Villa Park almost equally long outsiders. They were missing injured striker Ian Wright, in the bottom six and beaten twice that season by Kenny Dalglish's league leaders – 9-0 and 2-0.

At half-time, Coppell was less concerned than his players about a 1-0 deficit, telling them to keep things tight, not concede again and then play on any nervousness that Liverpool might suffer. In fact, the second half could hardly have been more chaotic. Mark Bright equalised almost immediately, former Spurs defender Gary O'Reilly had them in front but, in the 81st and 83rd minutes, goals by Steve McMahon and John Barnes (a penalty) seemed to have ended hopes of a first Palace final.

The Londoners were not done, however, and Andy Gray, one of their non-league recruits, secured a dramatic equaliser before another one, Alan Pardew, headed the most famous goal of his career in extra time.

'The Eagles dared, the Liver birds drooped, and after one of the most amazing turnarounds seen in an FA Cup semi-final, Crystal Palace are at Wembley, legends in their own Sunday lunchtime,' reported the *Guardian*.

Manchester United eventually won another extraordinary semi-final, 2-1 against neighbours Oldham in extra time after a 3-3 draw, and the competition had more excitement in store at Wembley.

> **Crystal Palace**: Martyn; Pemberton, O'Reilly, Thorn, Shaw; Barber (Wright), Gray (Madden), Thomas, Pardew, Salako; Bright.

> **Manchester Utd**: Leighton; Phelan, Bruce, Pallister (Robins), Martin (Blackmore); Webb, Ince, Robson, Wallace; McClair, Hughes.

> Replay: **Palace** subs Madden for Salako, Wright for Barber; **United** Sealey in goal, no subs.

In contrast to their Anfield debacle, Palace had won at Old Trafford that season and United, in the lower half of the table again, were under considerable pressure to win a first trophy for Alex Ferguson after three and a half seasons. They came back well after O'Reilly headed an early goal, taking a 2-1 lead through old warriors Bryan Robson and Mark Hughes.

Wright, not considered fit to start but summoned from the bench, equalised straightaway in the 72nd minute and had Palace in front with his volley in extra time before Hughes also scored his second goal of the match.

For the replay five days later, Ferguson reluctantly dropped his goalkeeper Jim Leighton, bringing in the more outgoing Londoner Les Sealey, and left-back Lee Martin's goal won a game in which Ferguson later accused Palace of 'one bad tackle after another'.

The following season United inflicted a first defeat of the campaign on them, but not until November. By that time, Palace were in the top four and from Christmas onwards stayed in third place, which was already assured before United were beaten 3-0 in the return game at Selhurst on the final day. They missed out on European football because England had only one UEFA Cup place post-Heysel, which went (ironically) to runners-up Liverpool, and had to settle for winning the Full Members Cup at Wembley, 4-1 against Everton.

The Wright-Bright combination produced 24 league goals that season, plus 16 more in the cups, and became coveted. Arsenal's David Dein recalls catching Ron Noades a little off guard in September by asking how much he wanted for either, and on being told £2.5m for Wright, who had won his first England cap in February, he quickly clinched the deal.

Bright departed for Sheffield Wednesday a year later and, on the last day of that 1992/93 season, Wright scored for Arsenal in the 3-0 defeat that sent Palace down on goal difference.

Coppell resigned and the yo-yoing began, initially under his former assistant Alan Smith. Straight back up in 1994 as champions on the back of Chris Armstrong's 23 goals; down again after Palace fan Matthew Simmons was kung-fu kicked by Eric Cantona in the season when they reached both domestic cup semi-finals and four teams were relegated to trim the size of the Premier League; back two years later via the play-offs, with technical director Coppell now in charge of the team again and drily predicting 'ten months of misery'.

He was right. The team finished bottom and the balding Italian midfielder Attilio Lombardo was briefly installed as manager as new owner Mark Goldberg bought out Noades, who charged him £22m (having paid £600,000 in 1981), still kept the freehold to the stadium and even had three games as caretaker manager after Lombardo.

Terry Venables, having been manager of England, then Australia and chairman of Portsmouth, returned to Selhurst for only a few months, leaving in January 1999 as the club entered administration. After all the excitement, Palace were now just another struggling club with financial worries.

* * * * *

Still crazy after all those years, **Wimbledon** finally came up against hard reality in the Nineties, but went down fighting (literally, some would say) only after confounding expectations for a good while longer than anyone could have expected.

Resisting all Ron Noades's attempts at a merger with Crystal Palace, they felt obliged after the publication of the Taylor Report to agree to a ground-share at Selhurst, replacing Charlton as tenants in 1991.

Plough Lane, used for reserve games for a few seasons, was eventually built on from 2005–08 as Reynolds Gate, with other heroes like Batsford, Bassett, Cork and Sanchez commemorated in the names of the blocks of flats.

The last first-team match there in May 1991 was, coincidentally, against Palace, for whom Ian Wright scored a hat-trick in a 3-0 win that did not prevent Ray Harford's side finishing seventh. The average crowd was 7,631 and although that dropped by a few hundred in the first Selhurst season, the greater capacity for London derbies and visits by teams with large away support meant it rose to a peak of 18,707 in 1998/99.

Contrasts could be vivid. In January 1993, a crowd of 3,039 (the top division's lowest since the Second World War) turned up to see Everton, but four months later Manchester United's visit as the first Premier League champions attracted 30,115.

One of the few blips on the field was after promoting Peter Withe from reserve team manager to succeed the Blackburn-bound Harford in autumn 1991. The former Aston Villa striker attempted to impose new discipline on the remnants of the crazy gang but after one win in 13 games another internal promotion, of the popular Joe Kinnear, proved far more successful.

From a late run to make the top six in 1993/94, however, with Dean Holdsworth backing up John Fashanu in physical power and goals, plus an occasional run to domestic cup semi-finals, the struggle to stay in the new league became more difficult and was finally lost in 1999/2000.

Owner Sam Hammam, like Noades, could see no long-term future for the club in London and after a doomed proposal to relocate to Dublin, he decided in 1997 to cash in, selling 80 per cent of his shares to Norwegians Bjorn Rune Gjelsten and Kjell Inge Rokke for £25m.

The rest followed when the relegation writing was on the wall, the Norwegians having unsuccessfully installed their countryman, the Anglophile and direct football proponent Egil Olsen as manager.

Hammam, whose own writing on the wall included scrawling obscene graffiti in the visitors' dressing room at Upton Park, supposed to outrage and fire up the team, was also reported to have made £8m from the sale of Plough Lane to Safeway. He was ensconced at Cardiff City by the time the dream move to Dublin's fair city became a less romantic one to Milton Keynes.

* * * * *

Charlton and their supporters, though they had had enough of Selhurst Park, were forced to endure another 17 frustrating months in exile before the longed-for return to The Valley. During that time, they formed their own single-issue political party on the back of a brilliant advertising campaign, attracting almost 15,000 votes in local elections and prompting Greenwich Council to agree planning permission for their old home.

Meanwhile, the team played on the other side of the Blackwall Tunnel at Upton Park, at the beginning of a unique four-year period under joint managers. When Lennie Lawrence unexpectedly decided to join Middlesbrough in the summer of 1991, the club decided that Alan Curbishley and Steve Gritt could do the job jointly.

They did exceptionally well, despite regularly having to sell players like future international Robert Lee to maintain any chance of returning home – and in one case to pay the month's wages – and yet mostly remaining in the top half of the Second Division.

On 5 December 1992, the players of Charlton and Portsmouth emerged from The Valley's Portakabin changing rooms to a tear-jerking reception and 13 minutes after the start of the first match there for seven years, Scottish midfielder Colin Walsh drove in the only goal of the game.

In the summer of 1995, the difficult decision was taken to dispense with joint managers, leaving Curbishley in charge and Gritt out in the cold. Although he went on to save Brighton from dropping out of the Football League, subsequent events proved Charlton had chosen the right man. Immediately taking them into the 1996 play-offs (and a painful defeat by Palace), Curbishley went a step further two years later.

The board's support allowed the purchase of key men like striker Clive Mendonca from Grimsby for a club-record £700,000 and midfielder Mark Kinsella from Colchester, a steal at £150,000. In the run-in towards the end of the season, defenders Danny Mills and Eddie Youds were added at bargain prices and, together with Sasa Ilic, an Australian who had walked into a bar asking if anyone knew of a club in need of a goalkeeper, Charlton kept seven successive clean sheets to confirm a place in the play-offs.

Ipswich were twice beaten 1-0, so Ilic went to Wembley for the final against favourites Sunderland having not conceded a goal for 13 and a half hours. On an astonishing May bank holiday afternoon, he then picked the ball out of his net ten times but still emerged on the winning side after saving the 14th kick in the penalty shoot-out that followed a thrilling 4-4 draw. Mendonca, a boyhood Sunderland fan, scored the first hat-trick in a play-off final and centre-half Richard Rufus, one of many talented products of the Charlton youth system, headed a rare goal. The London side had trailed 2-1, 3-2 and 4-3 and their triumph against the odds seemed to sum up the club's resilience over the previous dozen years.

Relegation the following year, despite finishing above Nottingham Forest and Blackburn, was not entirely unexpected but they would return stronger.

* * * * *

While their three south London rivals all had a share of the new Premier League riches, **Millwall**, relegated in 1990, missed their chance. The best opportunity was for an immediate return when four teams were promoted in 1991 to push the top division back to an unwieldy 22 clubs.

Unable to capitalise on a fine start and Teddy Sheringham's 33 goals, they made the play-offs but a 4-1 defeat away to Brighton in the first leg left them too much to do. Three years later, under Mick McCarthy, there was a similar heavy semi-final defeat to Derby County.

The home leg at the New Den was marred by crowd violence, proving that moving home did not mean an entirely new leaf had been turned over.

Millwall were the first in the capital to respond to the Taylor Report by building a brand-new stadium, less than a mile from the old one, where an anti-climatic last game after 83 years in May 1993 was lost 3-0 to bottom club Bristol Rovers in front of the season's biggest crowd of 15,821.

The first league game at the far less intimidating new venue, rather bland in appearance with its four identical stands, was equally underwhelming, with Southend United inflicting a 4-1 home defeat, watched by little more than 10,000. Later that season, however, the inaugural FA Cup tie set an attendance record that has stood ever since, 20,093 seeing Arsenal win with a last-minute goal by Tony Adams.

The 1995/96 season brought a dreadful slump from being top in December to relegation on goal difference after McCarthy left in February to become Republic of Ireland manager. Jimmy Nicholl, Billy Bonds and Keith 'Rhino' Stevens all failed to come close to a return from the third tier.

Not until 2000 did they even make the play-offs, copying the Charlton model of joint managers as the more cerebral Alan McLeary joined Stevens. But Wigan Athletic won the semi-final by the odd goal. It was hardly the brave new Bermondsey world that had been envisaged.

* * * * *

Never have **QPR** looked down on **Fulham** from a greater height than in the mid-Nineties, although the positions were soon reversed.

In 1992/93, for instance, Rangers finished as the top London club, fifth in the Premier League and ahead of Liverpool, while the club they almost took over a few years earlier languished in the third tier on gates of below 5,000.

The following season, Gerry Francis again proved his worth as manager, earning a big move to Tottenham by taking QPR to ninth place, as Fulham dropped into the bottom division for the first time in their history.

Francis, an England captain at the age of 23, first impressed in management under difficult circumstances at Bristol Rovers from 1987–91, when he left them in the middle of the Second Division to return to Shepherd's Bush. Three years there, with Les Ferdinand leading the attack as a 20-goal-a-season man, attracted Tottenham's attention but led to relegation for Rangers in Ray Wilkins's second season as his successor.

When Francis returned in 1998, they had not only failed to mount a promotion challenge but in two successive years were a single point off going down again. The first time they won only two games from Boxing Day onwards, forcing a 2-2 draw in the penultimate game away to Manchester City, which sent City down instead. The very next season was even tighter, only goal difference and a remarkable 6-0 win over Crystal Palace saving Francis's team on the final day.

Had they gone down, they would have passed a buoyant Fulham on the way up, in every sense, under new owner Mohamed

GREED IS GOOD (1991-2000)

al-Fayed, the owner of Harrods. The flamboyant Egyptian bought the club in 1997, taking over as chairman from Jimmy Hill, who was drained by ten years of problems on and off the pitch in what he summarised as a miserable experience.

Craven Cottage badly needed redeveloping and Fulham were losing £500,000 a year. In another twist to London's ancient turf wars, moving to Stamford Bridge, which might have happened in 1905, was now proposed for 1990. With Cabra Estates, the successors to Marler, desperate to develop the lucrative riverside ground after Ernie Clay sold out to them, and offering Fulham millions to move, 'it made economic sense,' Hill said.

He was nevertheless not upset when Chelsea failed to offer acceptable terms and Fulham were able to agree a new lease with the Royal Bank of Scotland and the right to buy the freehold for £7.5m, which would eventually be done when Al-Fayed took over, promising Premier League football in five years. Investing heavily in players and management, they did it in four.

In February 1996, Fulham were 23rd in the bottom division, having just been watched at Craven Cottage by the lowest crowd in their history: 2,176. The first managerial saviour turned out to be Micky Adams, promoted from player-coach, who steered them away from the threat of the Conference and to immediate promotion the following season with 21 goals from Scotsman Mike Conroy.

'A director at the club told me I was going to be the Alex Ferguson of Fulham,' Adams once said. 'I signed a five-year contract... and four months later I was sacked.'

He was not a sufficiently high-profile name for Fayed, who in September 1997 pulled off a coup by attracting none other than Kevin Keegan as chief operating officer, with Ray Wilkins as his team manager. Towards the end of a promising season, Fulham lost their last three league games and Keegan fired his friend Wilkins before the play-offs, taking charge himself but losing the semi-final to Grimsby Town.

The following year, however, they romped to the title with 101 points, losing only narrowly in the domestic cups to Liverpool and Manchester United. When Keegan left to manage England, Paul Bracewell was given only one season as a replacement with a team lacking goals, before Al-Fayed hired Jean Tigana for the next stage of development. QPR, finishing one place below them, could only look on enviously.

* * * * *

Brentford, managing for once to steer clear of all the ground-sharing and merger proposals, ascended to the Second Division in 1992 for the first time since 1954. Six successive wins to end the season sent them up as champions ahead of Birmingham.

Immediately losing top scorer Dean Holdsworth to Wimbledon for £720,000 was not a good sign and despite Mancunian Gary Blissett's 21 goals at the higher level, they fell away badly in the second half of the season, with defeats at Millwall (6-1), West Ham and Charlton contributing to a drop from tenth at Christmas into the bottom three.

The ebullient David Webb replaced Phil Holder and with a prolific pair of strikers in Nicky Forster (24 goals) and Robert Taylor (23), the Bees were unlucky not to go back up in 1995. Top with three games to play, they lost a crucial one 2-0 away to Birmingham, who took the only automatic promotion place that season. Brentford lost the play-off semi-final on penalties to Huddersfield, who went up instead.

Two years later, they were again top for long spells before falling away after Forster was sold to Birmingham, this time losing the play-off final to Crewe, who reached the second tier for the first time in more than 100 years. Once again the leading scorer, Carl Asaba, was sold, to Reading, and a heavy price paid. Under Micky Adams, no longer wanted by Fulham, the team plunged to relegation, going down on the final day at Bristol Rovers as Burnley saved themselves.

Enter the familiar figure of Ron Noades, unexpectedly taking charge of the team itself. An earlier Brentford manager, the former Spurs captain Steve Perryman, once said of modern football: 'All the managers want to be chairmen and all the chairmen want to be managers.' If Venables proved the first part, Noades proved the second with rather more success.

In his first season, 1998/99, working with Ray Lewington as coach, he oversaw a storming finish of 16 games without defeat to clinch the Third Division title, Lloyd Owusu from Slough Town emerging as a new goalscorer. Noades was duly named divisional Manager of the Year. With the club re-established in the third tier, he stood down in 2000 after an embarrassing FA Cup defeat at home to Kingstonian and recalled his trusted former protege Steve Coppell to take over.

* * * * *

It was an eventful decade for **Leyton Orient**, although many of their hardships had to be seen in the context of the genuine disaster that caused them. Tony Wood, a coffee merchant, had taken over in 1986, only for his business to be ruined amid the appalling Rwandan civil war and genocide of the early Nineties.

Orient, after four comfortable seasons in the middle of the Third Division, began to sink in 1993/94 and the following season finished bottom under Chris Turner and John Sitton, the latter becoming famous for his obscenity-laden 'bring your dinner' dressing-room rant caught in the documentary 'Orient: Club For a Fiver'.

Wood announced he would sell the club for five pounds and found a buyer by telephoning the snooker and darts impresario and boyhood Orient fan Barry Hearn. 'The whole thing is alien to my regular financial dealings,' said Hearn, who nevertheless could not resist, and spoke of creating a community club and a team full of local players.

He brought in a local boy from better times, Tommy Taylor, as manager, and stayed loyal to him for five years of mixed success, from a low point in the bottom four of the whole Football League. Taylor slowly lifted Orient to the play-offs in 1999.

Hearn, never averse to a publicity stunt, also signed 47-year-old Peter Shilton as goalkeeper, enabling him to play his 1,000th game live on Sky Sports in the 2-0 win at home to Brighton in December 1996, with a rare attendance of almost 8,000.

* * * * *

It took **Barnet,** technically founded in 1888, 103 years to reach the Football League, but once they did few clubs can have had a more eventful beginning.

On 17 August 1991, in front of 5,090 people, Barry Fry's team were beaten 7-4 at home by Crewe Alexandra. Three days later they hosted Brentford in the League Cup, changed the goalkeeper and drew 5-5. By the end of their first month, they had also won 6-0 away to Lincoln City.

As Fry, an extrovert with heart problems who tended to race down the touchline every time his team scored, said when he heard of Graeme Souness's health suffering: 'If you think Liverpool is a danger to your health, try managing Barnet.'

The additional hazard for Fry, a former Busby Babe who played briefly for Orient, was having as a chairman Stan Flashman, the country's best known ticket tout. ('They can call me what they like if the colour of their money's right'). But Fry had been warned. This was his second spell at the club either side of 18 months with Maidstone United.

Following his return in the summer of 1986, Barnet were Conference runners-up three times in four years before finally winning the title and with it automatic promotion in 1991.

The original Barnet club, formed in 1888, was disbanded 14 years later, returning in a merger between Avenue FC and Barnet Alston. From 1907, they played at Underhill in the familiar black and amber.

The 1930s, the era of local winger and war-time England international Lester Finch, brought two Athenian League titles followed by the 1946 FA Amateur Cup with a 3-2 win against Bishop Auckland at Stamford Bridge.

Turning professional a year after Wimbledon in 1965, they also joined the Southern League, winning their first game 10-1 against Hinckley. Founder members with Wealdstone of the Alliance Premier League in 1979, they struggled in Fry's first spell as manager and were in the hands of the official receiver at one stage.

But at the end of that first Football League season, they were in the play-offs, losing a little unluckily to Blackpool. Gary Bull, cousin of England international Steve Bull of Wolves, was the principal and prolific striker.

Barnet, like other newcomers, found the South East overcrowded with league clubs. The gate for the first game was not matched again that season or even the following one, when automatic promotion was achieved by finishing third in a chaotic campaign when they might have shared Maidstone's a fate of being forced out of the league bankrupt.

The season had begun with a mass transfer request over a pay dispute and then a transfer embargo, and continued with a £50,000 fine for irregular payments and not keeping proper accounts. Before the end of it, Fry had moved to Southend United, sacked for the umpteenth but final time by Flashman, who left as well because of ill health.

In June, a new five-man consortium had to reassure the Football League the club could fulfil its fixtures the following season, which with assistant manager Ed Stein and several players following Fry to Southend was doomed from the start. Barnet lost their first ten games, won only five out of 46 and stayed bottom all season with crowds ending up below 2,000. In those circumstances, the goalless draw at Chelsea in the FA Cup third round, having given up ground advantage to make some money, was one of the most remarkable in the club's history.

Some stability was badly needed and was gradually achieved after telecommunications entrepreneur Tony Kleanthous bought the club in 1994. 'I took over a club nearly £2m in debt, with a dilapidated stadium, no assets, no facilities and average support of 1,500,' he said. Mere survival was the first aim. Moving from

Underhill, with its sloping pitch and stands hemmed in by housing, became a longer-term objective.

In the meantime, under old hand John Still, London's other Bees even reached the play-offs in 1998 and 2000, which was something to be proud of.

Barnet's struggles might have acted as a warning to any other London wannabes, yet in the following decade the same John Still would bring a different one into the league.

Chapter 8

Plus ca change (2001-16)

Arsenal's record-breaking run as top London club for nine seasons in a row is ended as Abramovich buys Chelsea and hires Mourinho; but it is under Roberto di Matteo that they become London's first European Cup winners after 56 years; Wenger's Arsenal move grounds but struggle to win trophies; London stages the Olympics again and Spurs and West Ham vie for the stadium; Barnet and Brentford plan new homes too; Dagenham & Redbridge rise and fall; Wimbledon disappear to Milton Keynes and are then reborn in Kingston; Arsenal, Chelsea and Tottenham the biggest three in the capital – just like 100 years ago.

O N 23 April 2003, a Russian oligarch with a shy smile called Roman Arkadyevich Abramovich watched Manchester United beat Real Madrid 4-3 on a thrilling Champions League night and decided he must buy an English football club.

At that point, some 115 years after the start of league football, London had won the title 15 times (12 of them by Arsenal) but never had the top two clubs in the same season. Once Abramovich, who had made his fortune in the sell-off of Russian state industries at bargain prices, bought **Chelsea** it happened immediately – for two seasons running. Within three years, they had become English champions more times than in their previous century of football.

What Chelsea in the 1990s most lacked was a 20-goal striker. Jimmy Floyd Hasselbaink, a powerful Dutchman born in Surinam and previously with Leeds United, arrived in the summer of 2000 via Atletico Madrid to remedy that by scoring 26 and 29 goals in successive seasons.

Unexpectedly, he found himself playing for a familiar new manager barely a month into his first campaign when the popular Gianluca Vialli was sacked after only five league games. There was inevitable talk of dressing-room rifts, which Vialli added to by claiming an unnamed 'Mr Nice Guy' was responsible for his demise.

Chelsea stuck to their continental pattern by appointing Hasselbaink's former Atletico coach Claudio Ranieri, the charming Roman who would lead Leicester City to the most improbable of Premier League successes 16 years later.

Helped by record signing Hasselbaink's goals, and with William Gallas and Frank Lampard on board, Ranieri was able to finish in the top six two seasons running.

Then, in 2002/03, came a dramatic last game, winning what was effectively a play-off for the final Champions League place at home to Liverpool.

Had Chelsea missed out, Abramovich would probably still have bought them in preference to the other candidates Tottenham, situated in a less glamorous part of town and having just finished in mid-table for the eighth successive season. But the promise of additional prestige and income from Europe's premier club competition did no harm. Nor was he deterred by the scale of debt that was worrying the chief executive at Stamford Bridge, Trevor Birch, an unflappable insolvency expert whose experience looked as if it might be needed at Chelsea. A £75m Eurobond was due for repayment and Birch was working hard on 'restructuring' – i.e. delaying – it.

Barely concerned with such trivial sums, Abramovich and his inner circle agreed an outline deal in a matter of minutes and, in early July, bought control for an estimated £60m, plus the £80m debt threatening to cripple the club.

There would be casualties. Ken Bates, hoping for a significant role as well as his eight-figure profit, left the following March, later referring to the new owners a little ungraciously as 'a bunch of shysters from Siberia'.

Birch also left, 'disappointed' to make way for Peter Kenyon from Manchester United. It was the policy now to acquire the best in every field, which Kenyon was deemed to be. So too with the manager. Ranieri may have delivered the runners-up position in May 2004, plus a Champions League semi-final (in which his tactics were widely criticised), but Jose Mourinho, whose Porto team were about to beat Chelsea's conquerors AS Monaco in the final, was the chosen man. 'I have top players and, I'm sorry, we have a top manager,' he told the first of countless entertaining news conferences. 'Please do not call me arrogant because what I say is true. I'm European champion, I'm not one out of the bottle. I think I'm a special one.'

In the summer of 2002, the financially stricken club's only signing for Ranieri had been midfielder Quique de Lucas on a free transfer. Immediately after his takeover a year later, Abramovich authorised expenditure of £110m in barely six weeks on players like Juan Sebastian Veron, Claude Makelele, Hernan Crespo, Joe Cole, Damien Duff, Glen Johnson and Wayne Bridge. Another year on, almost £90m bought Didier Drogba, Petr Cech, Arjen Robben, Ricardo Carvalho and others for Mourinho.

English football had never seen anything like it, and resentment was widespread. Mourinho, quickly welding together a team of real substance, won his first match – almost symbolically against Manchester United – and for the next two seasons left Sir Alex Ferguson, Arsene Wenger and everyone else eating his dirt. Chelsea won the title by 12 points from Arsenal, losing one game and conceding 15 goals, and then by eight points from United.

What they could not do was win the Champions League. In his first season, they knocked out Barcelona but lost controversially in the semi-final to Liverpool, whom they had beaten twice in the league and also in the League Cup Final. Three days after clinching the league title at Bolton with two Lampard goals, Mourinho's team lost at Anfield to what he famously called a 'ghost goal' by Luis Garcia, which Chelsea claimed had not crossed the line.

The rivalry with Liverpool became as acute as any in London. The following season, there were another five meetings, including two dull Champions League group games, before Barcelona took their revenge in the round of 16 and Liverpool won the FA Cup semi-final 2-1 to prevent a derby final with West Ham.

Mourinho's third year proved him to be mortal. Handicapped by injuries to Cech, who fractured his skull at Reading, and John Terry, Chelsea were top for only one week all season, in September. Signing Andriy Shevchenko for an exorbitant £29.5m did not work and Mourinho criticised the sale of central defenders Robert Huth and Gallas.

Liverpool – again – won the Champions League semi-final at Anfield, this time on penalties, and if beating champions Manchester United with Drogba's goal as the FA Cup Final returned to Wembley was welcome, a crack or two had appeared, along with a self-destructive streak in the manager.

His record going into the 2007/08 season was a remarkable 121 wins and 19 defeats. Losses off the field were rather more substantial than on it: £308m in three years. Abramovich did not care about that, but what did concern him was the style of football. Mourinho played the percentages, not the swashbuckling game that had entranced the owner watching United and Real Madrid.

Avram Grant, an Israeli coach of no great distinction, was brought in as Director of Football and Mourinho, from a position of what he assumed to be strength, again hinted at unsatisfactory transfer dealings. Florent Malouda for Arjen Robben was the only significant one in the summer of 2007.

Yet the end came shockingly soon, illustrating a lack of patience on all sides.

After a Champions League draw at home to Rosenborg on 18 September, when the crowd dropped below 25,000, Mourinho was suddenly gone. He had lost ten league games out of 120, none of them at Stamford Bridge (though the team scored five goals in a league game only once), and won six trophies.

Grant took over as manager with Steve Clarke as coach and, after a defeat at Old Trafford in their first game, results turned. A 1-0 loss to Arsenal in December was the only one in the league for the rest of the season, which finished with Chelsea in second place, only two points short of United. They lost the League Cup Final, painfully, to Tottenham, but laid the Liverpool bogey by winning the latest Champions League semi-final against them to qualify for a first final in the competition – against United in Moscow.

> **Chelsea**: Cech; Essien, Terry, Carvalho, A Cole; Makelele (Belletti); Ballack, Lampard, J Cole (Anelka), Malouda (Kalou); Drogba.
>
> **Manchester United**: Van der Sar; Brown (Anderson), Ferdinand, Vidic, Evra; Hargreaves, Carrick, Scholes (Giggs), Ronaldo; Rooney (Nani), Tevez.

It was a long, tense night, kick-off not taking place until 10.45pm because of the time difference, and pouring rain only adding to the drama. In the first half Cristiano Ronaldo, playing wide left to exploit Michael Essien at right-back, leapt above him to head in Wes Brown's precise cross, but right on half-time the ever-reliable Lampard, Chelsea's leading scorer for the third time in four years, equalised.

In extra time, Drogba was sent off for raising his arm to Nemanja Vidic, which crucially meant he would not take part in the penalty shoot-out. After Ronaldo's kick was saved by Cech, Chelsea would still have won it had Terry not slipped as he went to shoot. Instead, at just past 1.30am, Van der Sar saved from Nicolas Anelka, a January signing from Bolton, and United had their third European Cup.

There should have been a repeat of the final the following season after interim manager Guus Hiddink, replacing the unsuccessful Luiz Felipe Scolari in February, lost only one of his 22 games in charge. The crucial game, however, was a 1-1 draw with Barcelona in the Champions League semi-final second leg at Stamford Bridge, where Chelsea were denied three or four penalties and went out on the away goal scored by Andres Iniesta in the last minute. Hiddink's last game was the FA Cup Final, won 2-1 against Everton.

Carlo Ancelotti, calm and urbane, was next up, an experienced Italian who had won the European Cup twice as a player and twice as manager with Milan. He would not do so with Chelsea, but along with assistant Ray Wilkins did bring the club's first league and FA Cup Double in his first season, 2009/10.

His team appeared to have found the missing blend of success and showmanship, summed up by winning the last two home games 7-0 against Stoke and 8-0 against Wigan. Sunderland and Aston Villa also had seven goals put past them in a Premier League total of 103 –29 of them to Drogba and 22 to Lampard.

The cup was won with a Drogba goal against Portsmouth, the only disappointment having been a Champions League defeat by Mourinho's Internazionale, the eventual winners.

From two successive 6-0 wins to start the following campaign, however, Chelsea found Manchester United too good for them, Ferguson's team winning both legs of a Champions League quarter-final and recapturing the league title by nine points. Ancelotti was ungratefully shunted aside within half an hour of the last game, just like Wilkins earlier in the season.

He certainly felt no benefit from the purchase for an absurd £50m of Fernando Torres from Liverpool. Confidence shot and managing only five goals in his first 50 games, the Spaniard did well in the end to score as many as 45 in 172 appearances over three years.

After employing a mini Mourinho in Andre Villas-Boas, Chelsea eventually settled for bringing back the real thing in 2013, but only after astonishingly becoming European champions at the end of their worst league season for ten years.

Villas-Boas was sacked in March 2012 with the team fifth in the league and apparently doomed in Europe after losing the first leg of the knockout round 3-1 in Naples. Di Matteo immediately brought back some of the old guard and engineered a 4-1 win in the return, before reaching the finals of both the FA Cup (after demolishing Spurs 5-1 in the semi-final) and the Champions League in another unlikely comeback, away to Barcelona with ten men following Terry's first-half dismissal.

Winning the domestic cup for the fourth time in six years when Drogba scored (as he always did in finals) to beat Liverpool 3-2, Chelsea finished only sixth in the Premier League and went to Munich as heavy underdogs to meet Bayern in their own backyard.

> **Bayern Munich**: Neuer; Lahm, Boateng, Tymoshchuk, Contento; Schweinsteiger, Kroos; Robben, Muller (Van Buyten), Ribery (Olic); Gomez.
>
> **Chelsea**: Cech; Bosingwa, Cahill, Luiz, Cole; Mikel, Lampard; Kalou (Torres), Mata, Bertrand (Malouda); Drogba.

There was little doubt what the pattern would be in what was effectively an away game for Chelsea, who used the young Ryan Bertrand in midfield to help Ashley Cole deal with Robben, but still appeared on the verge of defeat three times. Thomas Muller put them behind in the 83rd minute, only for Drogba to equalise with a header. In extra time, Cech saved a penalty by Robben and, in the penalty shoot-out that Chelsea seemed to be hanging on for, they trailed 3-1. Cech saved two more penalties before Drogba, about to leave the club for China, struck home the decisive one and the suspended Terry, in full kit, rushed on to join the celebrations.

It was a dramatic year for the club captain, in which he was cleared in court of racially abusing Anton Ferdinand of QPR, but found guilty by the FA, who fined and banned him.

Bayern had had 20 corners to one and more than 30 attempts on goal in what the *Suddeutsche Zeitung* called 'the most one-sided final in Champions League history'. But Chelsea (and for the first time, London) had the cup with the big ears.

As *The Times* put it: 'What bloody-minded resilience and determination they have shown in the 12 weeks since they returned from Naples with their season, and seemingly their future, in disarray.'

Disarray has never been too far distant in the Abramovich era. Di Matteo lasted only three months of the following season, despite having been top of the table for much of it.

Rafa Benitez, veteran of the vintage Liverpool clashes with Mourinho, was booed by supporters in his first two home games after taking over, then won the third 8-0 against Villa and in a fine finish steered Chelsea to an FA Cup semi-final, third place in the Premier League and triumph in the Europa League by beating Benfica in Amsterdam. Appropriately Torres, much happier under his fellow countryman and former manager, scored in the final and finished the season as leading scorer with 22 goals in all competitions.

And so to Mourinho mark II, 'thinking of staying for a very long time'. Some hope. After a season of rebuilding, still reaching a Champions League semi-final against Atletico Madrid and finishing third despite only midfielder Eden Hazard scoring more than nine goals, he enjoyed one more triumphant campaign in 2014/15. The volatile Diego Costa arrived from Atletico to supply the goals, many of them laid on by Footballer of the Year Hazard, Drogba returned for a swansong and Terry enjoyed a fine season, passing the departed Lampard's 648 appearances (211 goals).

Top after three games, Chelsea stayed there and ended up eight points ahead of Manchester City, winning the League Cup against Spurs and losing four games out of 53 all season. Bizarrely, one of them was 4-2 at home to Bradford City in the FA Cup after leading 2-0, which still did not hurt as much as going out of the Champions League on away goals to Paris St Germain.

Mourinho had won the trophy with Porto and Inter, but would not do so with Chelsea. After sinking to 16th place the following October, he gave an uninterrupted seven-minute answer in a television interview inviting the board to back him or sack him, and in mid-December they reluctantly took the second option.

Hiddink arrived as fire-fighter again, this time less successfully, before handing over to Italian manager Antonio Conte, under whom a quiet life seemed unlikely.

* * * * *

For nine successive seasons between Arsene Wenger's arrival in 1996 and 2004, **Arsenal** were London's highest placed club, something not achieved by any team since their earliest days in Woolwich as the capital's only Football League side.

Supporters even instigated a St Totteringham's Day to mark the point in each season – often long before the end – when they were guaranteed to finish above their neighbours.

In 2016, that was celebrated for the 21st year in succession, but long beforehand Roman Abramovich's arrival in London ('parked his Russian tanks on our lawn… firing £50 notes at us', as Arsenal's vice-chairman David Dein put it) heralded a serious new local rival.

Runners-up to Manchester United for three years running from 1999–2001, Arsenal maintained their capital supremacy by winning the league in 2002 and 2004, and the FA Cup in 2002 (beating Chelsea in the final to complete Wenger's second Double), 2003 and 2005.

It hardly seemed feasible that the last of those triumphs – an undeserved one over United on penalties – would be the only trophy Wenger would achieve for another nine years, all the more so since his excuse for not winning more was the cost of a vastly complicated and expensive move from Highbury just up the road to the spanking new Emirates Stadium.

Ken Friar, the long-serving former chief executive in charge of the project, once said that if Arsenal had known what difficulty it would involve they might well have changed their mind and stayed put. The eventual cost was £390m, increasing the capacity from 38,500 to 60,000.

By the time they made the move in the summer of 2006, however, Chelsea had beaten them to two successive Premier League titles and even amid all the managerial upheavals at Stamford Bridge would continue to finish above them for seven of the next eight seasons, as well as winning the Champions League in the one when they failed to.

Wenger (and Mourinho) might have done better to have started slowly and built their club and their reputation from there. Working for far more patient employers, the Frenchman found himself hailed as a genius almost from the start and was therefore reluctant to change the methods on and off the pitch that had brought his early success.

'He spends Arsenal's money as if it's his own,' Dein would say, which in the first few years suited everyone. Not only that, he spent it on investments rather than luxury goods, improving cheap young foreign players to such an extent that they yielded a huge profit when sold on (Emmanuel Adebayor, Nicolas Anelka, Cesc Fabregas, Samir Nasri, Marc Overmars, Alex Song, Kolo Toure, Robin van Persie, Patrick Vieira etc). Allowing so many of them to join key rivals in Manchester did not go down well, however.

Until 2004, it had seemed like the best of both worlds. That year, the 'Invincibles' became the first team since Preston North End in the very first Football League season (of 22 matches) to remain unbeaten through a whole league campaign. But for a 1-0 FA Cup semi-final defeat by Manchester United, they would almost certainly have emulated proud Preston in an undefeated Double too.

There were naturally some close-run things among the 12 drawn games and, even in the final match, relegated Leicester City had the audacity to lead at half-time before two of Wenger's greatest recruits, Footballer of the Year Thierry Henry and Vieira, ensured history was made.

Henry scored 30 goals in the league and nine in other competitions, in which the one disappointment to add to the FA Cup defeat was losing a Champions League quarter-final at home to Ranieri's Chelsea.

Sixteen defeats in the next two league campaigns quickly dispelled any feeling of invincibility, and after saying farewell to Highbury with a 4-2 win over Wigan on 7 May 2006 (and a hat-trick by Henry), which lifted them to fourth place at a crucial moment, Arsenal began a long run at their new home in which the top two places were beyond them.

It was foolish to lose Dein, the friend and confidant who had been instrumental in bringing Wenger to the club (he wanted to do so even before Bruce Rioch took over from George Graham in 1995), and ridiculous to do so over his backing for the quiet American Stan Kroenke, who within a year of Dein's departure in 2007 had joined the board, later becoming the major shareholder.

Ensconced at the Emirates, where giant portraits of Arsenal greats, from founder David Danskin through Alex James and Liam Brady to Vieira and Henry, adorned the walls, Wenger regularly claimed that UEFA's proposed financial fair play regulations would enable Arsenal to compete better with *nouveaux riches* clubs like Chelsea and Manchester City on a playing field that was otherwise about as level as Barnet's Underhill ground, which hosted their reserve games. Once the European governing body backed off , however, under threat of legal action, he was left admitting that his club's self-financing model would remain a handicap.

The manager was courted by major overseas sides, turning down among others Bayern Munich and, in 2009, Real Madrid. In June 2008, the *Sunday Telegraph* confidently reported that when his contract expired three years later, he would become president of Paris St Germain.

Glenn Hoddle, an admirer from his days under Wenger at Monaco, said tartly of Arsenal: 'Every year, they've got a good team for the future.' Accused by Wenger early in 2014 of being afraid of failure, Chelsea's Mourinho produced one of the sharpest put-downs in their long-running squabble, calling his rival a 'specialist in failure'. 'The reality is he's a specialist because, eight years without a piece of silverware, that's failure.'

A few months later, after Wenger's 1,000th Arsenal match, the drought finally ended with victory in the FA Cup Final over lowly Hull City after being 2-0 down in ten minutes. Defeat and, as Wenger later admitted, he would have had to consider his position even if the supportive board did not. Instead he felt able to claim: 'I think it was a turning point in the lifetime of this team.'

In the side that day was Mesut Ozil, the gifted little German midfielder whose £42.5m fee suggested Arsenal were at last prepared to pay the going rate for proven quality. They followed by spending £46m that summer on forwards Alexis Sanchez and Danny Welbeck, retaining the FA Cup with a 4-0 demolition of feeble Aston Villa and despite failing to sign a single outfield player the following year were able to break into the Premier League's top two at a time when usual contenders like Chelsea and the Manchester clubs were all misfiring.

Greatly in Wenger's favour as he came under increasing criticism (once being booed by Arsenal fans at Stoke railway station and later facing a 'Time To Go' protest at a home game) was his record of qualifying every season for the Champions League, a necessity for the club's financial model and to attract the best players. That was extended to a remarkable 19 successive seasons, although critics pointed out that every chapter of the story had the same ending: defeat over two legs in the first knockout round.

The competition was always a source of much frustration, which unlike Chelsea's was never alleviated by claiming the big prize. The closest Arsenal came was in 2006, their last season at Highbury. After romping through the group, they knocked out Real Madrid, Juventus and Villareal without conceding a goal, although a new record of ten successive Champions League clean sheets was only achieved by Jens Lehmann's penalty save in the last minute of the Villareal semi-final.

Ten days after finishing the domestic season on a high by snatching fourth place from Tottenham in Highbury's last fixture, Arsenal travelled to Paris for the final against Barcelona.

> **Barcelona**: Valdes; Oleguer (Belletti), Marquez, Puyol, Van Bronckhorst; Deco, Edmilson (Iniesta), Van Bommel (Larsson); Giuly, Eto'o, Ronaldinho.
>
> **Arsenal** : Lehmann; Eboue, Toure, Campbell, Cole; Pires (Almunia), Gilberto Silva, Fabregas (Flamini), Hleb (Reyes); Ljungberg; Henry.

The game was billed as Ronaldinho, World Player of the Year, against Henry, named domestic Footballer of the Year for an unprecedented third time in four years.

In the event, neither shone in an exciting match shaped by a crucial incident in the 18th minute. Lehmann brought down Samuel Eto'o, conceding a free-kick, and was sent off even though he had not technically denied a goalscoring opportunity – the ball rolled to Ludovic Giuly, who put it in the net after the referee had blown.

Manuel Almunia took over in goal, with Robert Pires sacrificed in his last game for the club, and against the odds Arsenal's ten men went ahead in the 37th minute through Sol Campbell's header from a soft free-kick.

Henry and Ljungberg missed chances for a second goal and the defence held out for 40 minutes until Eto'o took Ronaldinho's pass to equalise. Then Juliano Belletti, who would join Chelsea a year later, squeezed in the winning goal.

Losing European ties decisively to Liverpool and Manchester United in successive seasons was followed by a depressing run in which a series of home defeats in the round of 16 undermined chances of progressing, and in the case of Bayern twice and unfancied Monaco brought further brickbats for the manager.

In the league, despite unexpectedly stealing the runners-up spot from Tottenham on the final day in 2015/16, the first ten years at the Emirates actually produced an average finishing position (3.4) worse than in the final decade at Highbury (2.0). The promised land had proved something of a mirage.

* * * * *

Tottenham in the early Noughties were being left behind, not only failing to challenge Arsenal and Chelsea but in 2003/04 finishing behind West Ham, Fulham and Charlton as well.

Alan Sugar finally grew tired of being a football club owner, trying to please supporters and players he characterised as 'Carlos Kickaball', and in February 2001 he sold up to ENIC, an investment company based in the Bahamas. They appointed the publicity-shy Daniel Levy as chairman and immediately courted popularity with supporters by sacking George Graham and installing Glenn Hoddle, who had been no more successful in his year at Southampton than at Chelsea.

Once again, the former midfield hero could do no better than mid-table positions. His team did reach the 2002 League Cup Final by beating Chelsea (5-1) for the first time in 28 meetings, only to lose to Blackburn Rovers, after which Chelsea took revenge by inflicting two of the three successive 4-0 defeats that an erratic Tottenham suffered.

With Robbie Keane the only notable signing the following year, there was no improvement and after six games of the 2003/04 season Hoddle, who had signed three more new strikers, was sacked. Losing later at home to Kevin Keegan's ten-man Manchester City in the FA Cup after leading 3-0 at half-time summed up another dismal campaign.

Dispensing with former playing icons as managers and coaches, Levy went for a director of football in Dutchman Frank Arnesen and a hapless head coach in Frenchman Jacques Santini, who resigned less than three months into the season.

Arnesen's fellow countryman Martin Jol, a big bear of a man who in slimmer and more hirsuite days was a physical West Bromwich Albion midfielder, proved more successful. With potent strikers in Keane, Jermain Defoe and Dimitar Berbatov, he achieved fifth position twice, and with it a UEFA Cup place, before learning during a tie at home to Getafe in October 2007 that he was being replaced by Spaniard Juande Ramos.

Jol deserved to take the team into the Champions League but on the eve of the final game in 2005/06, when they had to match Arsenal's result to pip them to fourth place, a bout of food poisoning laid several players low. West Ham, showing no sympathy for the sick, beat them 2-1 at Upton Park while Arsenal were winning their final Highbury match against Wigan.

Ramos lifted the team from 18th to 11th and won the League Cup after a first victory over Arsenal in 22 meetings (which, exactly like the long-delayed Chelsea win six years earlier, came by 5-1 in the semi-final). Chelsea it was who were then beaten in the

Wembley final, with an extra-time goal by centre-half Jonathan Woodgate.

Selling Keane to Liverpool and Berbatov to Manchester United swelled the coffers but hardly helped Ramos, who like Gross, Hoddle and Jol before him paid the penalty for bad results early in the season. In this case, two points from eight games was Tottenham's worst start since 1912. On the eve of a Sunday game at home to Bolton, Ramos was sacked and Portsmouth's Harry Redknapp appointed. They won, then fought back to draw 4-4 at Arsenal and finished the season a creditable eighth, as well as losing the League Cup Final only on penalties to Manchester United.

In his three full seasons, the colourful Redknapp finished fourth, fifth and fourth, succeeding where Jol had so narrowly failed by taking the club into the Champions League for the first time. Defoe and Keane had both been re-signed but the crucial goal that confirmed fourth place away to rivals Manchester City in May 2010 was scored by a very different sort of striker, the lanky Peter Crouch.

The European campaign had a chaotic start, with Spurs 3-0 down after half an hour on an artificial pitch in their qualifying round in Berne. They recovered to win 6-3 on aggregate and went on to top their group with 18 goals in six games, two of those matches particularly memorable ones against Internazionale. At the San Siro, Gareth Bale scored a hat-trick in a vain fightback from 4-0 down at half-time, unpredictable goalkeeper Heurelho Gomes having been sent off. At White Hart Lane, Bale was unplayable in a 3-1 win on an old-fashioned glory, glory night.

The capacity for a defensive collapse was also seen, however, in conceding four first-half goals at Fulham in the FA Cup and a 4-0 loss to Real Madrid that effectively ended an eventful European run after victory over Milan in the previous round.

There should have been another Champions League appearance in 2012/13 after Spurs again finished fourth. Chelsea were only sixth but pulling off their shock win in the Munich final earned them the right to defend the trophy by taking the fourth English place at Tottenham's expense.

Spurs went into the Europa League instead but it was under a new manager. Redknapp had been found not guilty of tax evasion in a harrowing court case in February that year, and then made hot favourite for the vacant England job, which went instead to Roy Hodgson.

As speculation raged about that appointment, Spurs dropped from third, ten points ahead of Arsenal at the start of February, to finish a point below them. Wanting a second year to be added to the remaining one on his contract, Redknapp was shocked to be sacked by Tottenham at the end of the season in circumstances not dissimilar to his dismissal by West Ham 11 years earlier. Levy's words to him – 'maybe we've just come to an end' – hardly provided either justification or explanation.

David Moyes was immediately made favourite for the job but three weeks later Andre Villas-Boas was appointed, four months after his sacking by Chelsea. Under him, fifth place, pipped yet again by Arsenal on the final day, plus a Europa League quarter-final, beating Inter again (3-0, 1-4), was not a bad season by any means after losing Luka Modric to Real Madrid and Rafael van der Vaart to Hamburg for a combined £37.5m.

Once Madrid set their sights on the ever-improving Bale that summer, it was only a matter of how much Tottenham could hold out for. Levy, one of the hardest of transfer negotiators, somehow pushed them to a world-record £85.2m. Franco Baldini, the latest technical director, spent almost all of it on seven foreign recruits with no Premier League experience, few of whom settled in particularly well. Christian Eriksen, the diminutive playmaker from Ajax, looked the best of the bunch, but by the time others like Erik Lamela and Nacer Chadli adapted to the physical challenges of English football, Villas-Boas was gone, sacked in December after a 6-0 defeat at Manchester City and a 5-0 loss at home to Liverpool.

Tim Sherwood, who had been working with the club's youngsters, was given an 18-month contract with a break clause, but after winning seven of his first ten league games either side of domestic cup defeats by West Ham and Arsenal, he found the ground shifting beneath his feet.

By the start of April, it was apparent that the talkative Sherwood would not be retained. Two days after finishing sixth, having lost only six league games out of 22, he was dismissed.

This time, the bookmakers had it right in tipping Southampton's Mauricio Pochettino, once a long-haired Argentine defender who played against England at the 2002 World Cup (tripping Michael Owen to concede the match-winning penalty). He proved one of Levy's better choices, eventually giving one of Sherwood's proteges, Harry Kane, a starting place and being rewarded with 59 goals in two seasons and third place in 2015/16, having challenged for the title until falling away at the finish.

The next task was to complete the transition to the new stadium next door without costs escalating way beyond the original £400m, or results suffering.

* * * * *

Once the Taylor Report insisted on all-seater grounds for the top two divisions, capacities were severely reduced. At the start of the 1992/93 season, examples, rounded up or down, were: Arsenal 28,000, Chelsea 37,000, Tottenham 33,000, West Ham 23,000.

Even with gradual increases and new stands, all four accepted over the next decade or two that major expansion was necessary and explored moving from homes established for the most part more than 100 years earlier. As already recounted (Chapter 6), visionary talks between Arsenal and Tottenham in 1974 about sharing a new stadium at Alexandra Palace came to nothing, but the former's bold move to a 60,000 stadium with extra executive, dining and conference facilities inspired their main London rivals. In 2016, Arsenal's annual matchday revenue of £101m – up from £37m at Highbury – was the highest in world football.

Chelsea explored several west London sites but found all of them impractical and made plans for another redevelopment of

Stamford Bridge. Tottenham and **West Ham** reluctantly decided they must move and thereby began the latest of the capital's turf wars, which would become one of the most bitter and drag in a third London club in Leyton Orient.

The battleground was the Olympic Stadium in Stratford, centrepiece of the 2012 summer Games, holding 80,000 spectators. Building it there fitted perfectly with government strategy for the regeneration of east London, but the more debatable question, as ever with major sporting events, was who would use it afterwards.

The original hope (and promise to the International Olympic Committee) of a 25,000-capacity national athletics stadium having proved unfeasible without an anchor tenant, West Ham, Tottenham and Orient were all suggested, along with a collection of London rugby union and rugby league clubs and even Essex County Cricket Club. Spurs already had their own Northumberland Development Project (NDP) going on and were seen in some quarters as using the Olympic bid to improve the terms of it.

In 2010, two bids were short-listed: from West Ham, backed by Newham Council, and Tottenham, backed by the Anschutz Entertainment Group. Geographically, West Ham were the more obvious choice, being about three miles distant as opposed to Tottenham's six.

More significant was that West Ham agreed to keep the athletics track, which could be covered over by retractable seating. Spurs proposed moving athletics out altogether to a redeveloped Crystal Palace stadium (not Selhurst Park). In February 2011, West Ham were selected, only for Spurs and Orient to win a judicial review, and later that year the process was abandoned, partly because of fears about illegal state aid.

Spurs eventually gave in to concentrate on the NDP project while Orient's populist chairman Barry Hearn, who claimed West Ham moving so close to Brisbane Road was against Football League regulations, remained keen to see what he could salvage. He therefore proposed either moving his club to a 25,000-capacity Olympic stadium or sharing it with West Ham, who rejected the idea.

They were named as the preferred bidder at the end of 2012 and after much further negotiation were given a 99-year lease, with UK Athletics allowed use of the stadium throughout July every year. Orient gave up in 2014, although two years later supporters' groups forced publication of the terms against West Ham's wishes, allowing Hearn to claim 'my dog could have negotiated a better deal for the taxpayer' than the club's £2.5m annual rent (halved if they were relegated).

There was widespread criticism that, just like Manchester City with the former Commonwealth Games stadium, the Hammers had been given a new home on the cheap, having paid only £15m towards the £272m renovation costs.

Delighted with the result, they staged an eventful farewell to Upton Park on 10 May 2016 by beating Manchester United 3-2 after the visitors' bus had been stoned outside the Boleyn Tavern. By achieving a best Premier League finish since 2002, manager Slaven Bilic fully justified his employment as the replacement for Sam Allardyce and ensured they went to the new ground on the sort of high required to fill it by attracting 25,000 extra fans.

Only five years earlier, they had been relegated for the second time since 2000. The first was in 2002/03 under the unfortunate Glenn Roeder. He had succeeded Harry Redknapp, who was sacked in 2001 after giving an interview to the Hammers fanzine *Over Land And Sea* in which he said of figures produced by the chairman Terry Brown about transfer deals: '[He] calls himself an accountant. He can't f------ add up'.

From talking about a long new contract, a disgruntled Brown foreshadowed Daniel Levy all those years later by suggesting the time had come to part company. Brown was known to be concerned about how the £18m received from Leeds that season for Rio Ferdinand had been spent, although there was never any great danger of going down despite a bad start and poor finish.

From 15th place, Roeder, the cultured former Orient and QPR defender, had them up to seventh but in a poor second season they were bottom at Christmas. After Roeder suffered a brain tumour, Trevor Brooking took over for the final three games, winning two and drawing the last, but Allardyce's Bolton saved themselves at the expense of his future club, who went down with 42 points, the highest total of any relegated team.

It was unlucky from that point of view, but careless in the extreme of a squad including David James, Nigel Winterburn, Trevor Sinclair, Joe Cole, Paolo di Canio, Michael Carrick, Jermain Defoe and Frederic Kanoute.

A good few jumped ship and Roeder was sacked early the following season. Promotion took two play-off finals in Cardiff under Alan Pardew, the first lost to Crystal Palace, the second won against Preston with a Bobby Zamora goal.

A year later, having finished ninth in the Premier League, they were back at the Millenium Stadium in the FA Cup Final and on the verge of winning it for the fourth time until Steven Gerrard thrashed in one of the best goals of his career. West Ham, having led 2-0 and 3-2, lost on penalties.

As the Premier League flourished, English football was becoming more and more attractive to overseas investors and the first Icelandic ones moved in at Upton Park in November 2006. Pardew's upwardly mobile career stalled in a shocking run of five goals in 16 games as he failed to integrate Argentine signings Carlos Tevez and Javier Mascherano into the side and new chairman Eggert Magnusson, described as a 'biscuit magnate', replaced him with Canning Town boy Alan Curbishley.

Having decided he could take Charlton no further, Curbishley took on the job he might have had when Redknapp left and, after dropping to a position nine points from safety, led his former club to a dramatic last-day reprieve by winning at Old Trafford. It was a seventh victory in the final nine games, but would still have counted for nothing had the Premier League imposed a points deduction after West Ham admitted third-party influence in the Argentine pair's transfer.

They were fined £5.5m but Tevez was allowed to continue playing and scored six goals in those last nine games. The club ended up paying Sheffield United, who were relegated instead of them, £18m in compensation.

In September 2008, Curbishley resigned after interference by the board in the transfer window, winning a claim for constructive dismissal and £2m compensation. Gianfranco Zola became not only the first foreign manager but one of only a few from outside London. He was followed by another, also more closely associated with Chelsea, in Avram Grant.

The result was two bad seasons, avoiding relegation by one place in Zola's second year and then suffering it under Grant in 2011. In the meantime, David Sullivan and former West Ham schoolboy player David Gold, whose fortunes were made in the sex industry, had bought their boyhood club after 16 years in charge of Birmingham City.

They were horrified by the level of debt, claimed at one point to be over £100m, so an immediate return after going down was essential. Sam Allardyce, who could not resist mocking notions of 'the West Ham way' of playing, was the pragmatic choice to do it and succeeded at the first attempt. One of his old Bolton players, the Portugese winger Ricardo Vaz Te, scored the crucial goal in the play-off final against Blackpool.

Allardyce lasted three more years, never winning the wholehearted support of the crowd and departing at the end of a season in which he had their team in fourth place at Christmas before ending up 12th.

His successor was a crucial appointment and the board got it right, ensuring they arrived at the Olympic Stadium in optimistic mood. Whether they could finally turn London's big three into four was an intriguing question.

* * * * *

A French manager and Egyptian owner – to say nothing of a Michael Jackson statue – at as down-to-earth a club as **Fulham** was yet another illustration of how cosmopolitan and exotic English football had become.

Mohamed Al-Fayed, continuing to pour money into the club, received his rewards by being serenaded before every home game as he walked across the pitch, waving a black-and-white scarf, and then seeing an imaginative appointment in Jean Tigana lead the team to the Premier League.

In his first season after replacing Paul Bracewell, Tigana won the Championship with 101 points and 90 goals and was then allowed to spend a startling £11.5m on another striker, compatriot Steve Marlet from Lyons. At the higher level, however, pleasant passing football was not matched by goals or results. Marlet flopped, nobody scored more than eight times and, in a bizarre interlude, the great Italian defender Franco Baresi was appointed director of football only to resign after less than three months. Tigana apparently found it difficult accepting diminished responsibilities, but towards the end of a second moderate season it was announced that the Frenchman would also leave, to be replaced by popular former defender Chris Coleman.

The club had at least played European football, winning the 2002 InterToto Cup when Junichi Inamoto's hat-trick beat Bologna in the second leg of the final. That meant entry into the UEFA Cup, eventually going out to Hertha Berlin in the 14th European tie of the season.

As Craven Cottage had to be vacated for two seasons for necessary upgrading, most of the games were played at Loftus Road, where David Bulstrode had planned to take the club on a permanent basis 15 years earlier. Fulham paid QPR £1m per year in rent and had gates as low as 14,000, even in the more successful 2003/04 season, when Coleman's management, Edwin van der Sar's goalkeeping and Steed Malbranque's midfield expertise lifted them into the top half of the highest division for the first time since 1960.

After declaring a loss of £33m, however, even Al-Fayed felt compelled to rein in the spending, as well as selling leading scorer Louis Saha to Manchester United and losing a costly High Court action against Tigana.

Not until Roy Hodgson took over towards the end of the decade would Fulham again make the top ten. Before that he had to engineer a great escape, Danny Murphy's late header at

Portsmouth in May 2008 saving them on goal difference after four months in the bottom three.

Finishing seventh the following season – the highest position in the club's history – meant another shot at Europe. The culmination of a stunning run was the Europa League Final against Atletico Madrid in Hamburg, a 63rd game of the season, in which Fulham were only beaten 2-1 in extra time. Along the way, Craven Cottage enjoyed one of the most memorable games in its long history when Juventus were knocked out after an early goal in the second leg had put them 4-1 ahead on aggregate.

Hodgson's achievements unquestionably helped towards landing him the England job later, and when they played Wales at Euro 2016 it was a meeting of two former Fulham managers, Coleman being in the other dug-out.

By then, alas, the club had sunk back into the second tier and were making a poor fist of even that. After good campaigns under Mark Hughes and Martin Jol, Al-Fayed finally sold in July 2013 to the Pakistani-American Shahid Khan, owner of the Jacksonville Jaguars NFL team, for a sum variously reported as between £150m and £200m.

Jol, under pressure from the start of the 2013/14 campaign, was sacked in December, as was the interim manager Rene Meulensteen three months later. German disciplinarian Felix Magath ('the ideal guy', said Khan) could not prevent relegation, and once he, Kit Symons and a couple of caretakers were moved on in late-2015, Fulham had had seven men in charge in three years and were back in the doldrums.

* * * * *

For half a dozen seasons in the Noughties, **Charlton** rivalled Fulham as over-achieving Londoners, but without a sugar daddy of anything like Al-Fayed's means. The supporter-inspired return to The Valley in 1992 and their subsequent performances made them much admired, as did the notion of being bankrolled by long-term fans like Richard Murray, whose comparatively modest fortune was made on the back of the television programme *Who Wants To Be a Millionaire?*

Luckily, manager Alan Curbishley's transfer dealings were excellent. Following relegation from the Premier League after one season in 1999, for instance, he was able to sell right-back Danny Mills for £4m, spend a quarter of it on a fine new goalkeeper in Dean Kiely and come back much stronger, winning the Championship ahead of Manchester City and finishing a remarkable ninth in the higher league in 2001, comfortably ahead of Tottenham and West Ham.

It was Charlton's highest placing for 47 years, followed three seasons later, with Paolo di Canio in the team, by seventh position, which should have been even better. At New Year they were fourth, having beaten Chelsea and Tottenham in successive games, but were forced to accept £10m from Chelsea for industrious midfielder Scott Parker, who believed he had a verbal agreement to join a top-three club. From the day he left, only four of the remaining 16 league games were won.

At one time or another, Charlton beat everyone except Manchester United, including winning at Highbury and Anfield for the first time in almost half a century. It was hard work, however, competing with the bigger boys on and off the pitch, and by 2005 Curbishley had decided it might be time to move on.

Although the news was kept quiet until the last home game, the 2005/06 season became an anti-climatic finale, in which from second place early on, with Darren Bent from Ipswich another inspired signing, Charlton sank to 13th. Six goalless draws in nine games had made some supporters restless, though due appreciation was belatedly given to Curbishley during his last Valley match, lost feebly to Blackburn, and the last league game at Manchester United, where long-time admirer Sir Alex Ferguson made a presentation to him before the Old Trafford side beat his team 4-0.

Supporters who had suggested it was time for a change became an oft-quoted example of taking care with what you wish for. Given the opportunity for a first new appointment since Curbishley was installed as sole manager 11 years earlier, the board made a bad choice in Iain Dowie from Crystal Palace – mainly, it seemed, to spite their neighbours, who duly took legal action – and then, after sacking him three months into the season, a worse one in Les Reed.

Former midfielder Alan Pardew inspired a brief revival, including beating Curbishley's West Ham 4-0, but could not do quite enough to keep them up.

It was the start of a sad decline, halted only briefly when Chris Powell led a return from the third tier in 2012. Two years later, and bottom of the Championship, he was sacked by the controversial new regime of Belgian politician and entrepreneur Roland Duchatelet, owner of a network of European clubs whose players and coaches were often moved around between them.

One of the managers, the Belgian Jose Riga, staved off relegation in 2014 but was then allowed to leave, and on his return two years later could not pull off the same trick and departed once more. Amid regular supporter protests, the club sank back into League One, memories of triumphs at Highbury, Stamford Bridge, White Hart Lane and elsewhere fading as fast as the club's reputation for doing the right thing.

* * * * *

Rather than anyone at Charlton, it was Simon Jordan, sometime owner of their neighbours **Crystal Palace,** who wrote a book entitled *Be Careful What You Wish For.* The story contained in it covered an eventful period from 2000, when he bought the club, to 2010, when he sold it, having lost, he claimed, some £45m through football along the way.

Unlike Ken Bates, Ron Noades, David Dein and other older and shrewder London football operators, the perma-tanned Jordan was an example of the maxim about how to make a small fortune from the sport: start with a large one.

His own large fortune came from selling his mobile phone company to One2One. It prompted him to buy Palace, the club he had supported, for £10m after the hapless Mark Goldberg had taken it into administration.

A 6-0 defeat by Millwall in a pre-season friendly did not augur particularly well and within a year Jordan had lost two managers, Steve Coppell and Alan Smith, and Palace needed to win their last game of the season, at Stockport, to avoid relegation to the third tier. They did so with Dougie Freedman's goal three minutes from the end.

Steve Bruce proved a better appointment, although he did not stay long and, in Jordan's fourth year, Dowie incredibly lifted Palace from 20th position on Boxing Day (beaten at home by Millwall) to victory in the play-off final over West Ham, Neil Shipperley scoring the only goal.

The pattern of lasting only one season in the top division continued, a little unluckily, when Charlton's undeserved late equaliser in a south London derby at The Valley sent Palace down by one point, enabling West Bromwich Albion to become the first team to survive in the Premier League after being bottom at Christmas.

Despite finishing sixth and fifth in the space of three seasons, Palace twice missed out in the play-offs, suffering home defeats in the semi-finals to Watford and Bristol City.

The economic meltdown of 2008 hit Jordan's businesses hard and, in January 2010, the club was placed into administration once more, which meant a deduction of ten points, pushing them from eighth in the Championship to 20th. Selling Victor Moses to Wigan on deadline day helped finances but not the chances of staying up, which was achieved with another crucial last-day result. Under Paul Hart, who had taken over from Neil Warnock, a 2-2 draw at Sheffield Wednesday sent the Yorkshire side down instead.

Steve Parish led a four-man consortium that took over in the summer of 2010, but there were five more managers in four years before Alan Pardew returned to his spiritual home and brought some success. After Tony Pulis had ensured they would have two consecutive Premier League seasons for the first time, Pardew led them to further mid-table comfort and reached the FA Cup Final, losing narrowly to Manchester United in a repeat of the 1990 final he had played in.

Additional investment from United States backers was expected to guarantee the sort of stability Palace ought to enjoy with their catchment area and potential, although supporters know better than to bank on it.

* * * * *

Palace's tenants **Wimbledon** continued to finish above them in the Championship for three seasons before their collapse in 2003/2004, having taken off to wage a controversial turf war elsewhere.

With gates at Selhurst falling as the probability of returning to the Premier League diminished, the Norwegian owners and their new chairman, Charles Koppel, were attracted by a come-on from the Buckinghamshire new town of Milton Keynes, whose development company had long been keen to take an established league team there rather than developing the Milton Keynes City club that Ron Noades briefly bought in 1979.

In August 2001, Dons supporters were devastated,to learn of the owners' intention to move some 70 miles north to a town better known for its roundabouts and concrete cows. Relief when the Football League rejected the plan only a fortnight later was tempered by Koppel's refusal to give in. After his appeal, claiming the club would go out of business if not allowed the move, the FA appointed an independent three-man commission, which approved it in May 2002 'based on exceptional circumstances, and not the beginning of a franchise system'.

From the start of the following season, protests and boycotts were stepped up. The game against Rotherham at Selhurst in October attracted an official crowd of 849, of whom 227 were visiting fans, and the average for the season was 2,786, a 60 per cent fall. Against this demoralising background, the team under Stuart Murdoch did well to finish as high as tenth, Irish international David Connolly and Neil Shipperley both topping 20 league goals.

Not surprisingly, the club went into administration a month after the season's end, giving music entrepreneur and property developer Pete Winkelman the opportunity to move in. With Connolly and Shipperley among 11 players sold, the denuded team were installed at the National Hockey Stadium in Milton Keynes, where the first crowd of the 2003/04 season was 1,145, who saw what turned out to be a rare win. There were only two more at home all season, the last of them in the final game as Wimbledon FC.

For the following campaign, the club was renamed Milton Keynes Dons. They moved to a smart new stadium in 2007, but gave up the rights to claim the heritage of Wimbledon FC and were forced to return some 500 items of memorabilia to the London Borough of Merton, including a replica of the FA Cup won in 1988.

In the meantime, refusenik supporters started their own club, **AFC Wimbledon,** which from a series of open trials on Wimbledon Common in June 2002 astonishingly reached the Football League within nine years. The new venture was a startling success from the day of the very first game, a pre-season friendly against Sutton for which a crowd of 4,657 turned up at the Kingsmeadow Stadium, shared with Kingstonian.

The club's first goal was scored against Bromley by Glenn Mulcaire, later a private investigator who was sentenced to six months in prison for his part in the News International phone-hacking scandal.

Managed by a former Dons player in Terry Eames, the team finished third in the Combined Counties League (the ninth tier of English football), then won it in an 'Invincibles' 2003/04 season of 46 league games (won 42, drew four, scoring 180 goals) and followed up with the Isthmian League Division One championship and Surrey Senior Cup.

They were able to claim a national record for senior football by remaining unbeaten in 78 league games from February 2003 to December 2004, when London's oldest surviving club, Cray Wanderers, finally ended the run.

By 2009, they had made the Conference under Terry Brown, who had narrowly failed to take Aldershot Town into the Football League. On 21 May 2011, he did so with AFC in a dramatic play-off final against Luton Town at the City of Manchester Stadium.

Having beaten Fleetwood 8-1 on aggregate in the semi-final, the Dons played out a goalless draw with Luton but won the penalty shoot-out 4-3. Captain and top scorer Danny Kedwell, who converted the decisive penalty, could not resist joining his hometown club Gillingham for the new season as the Dons, carrying an enormous amount of goodwill with them, brought League Two football to Kingsmeadow on 6 August 2011.

Live on television, they lost narrowly to Bristol Rovers in front of 4,629. After rising to third in the table, supporters had to grow used to unaccustomed struggles, dropping to finish 16th but with an impressive average crowd of 4,294 – less than 1,000 below capacity. Jack Midson, signed from Oxford United, was joint top scorer in the division with 18 goals.

It was a harsh as well as a brave new world, as Brown discovered when he was sacked early the following season after a fifth defeat in six games. Neal Ardley, who had played Premier League football for Wimbledon, proved a popular replacement as they clung on to Football League status by winning the final game of the season at home to Fleetwood, sending Barnet down instead.

Ardley rated that a better achievement than reaching the play-offs three years later, but was justly proud of beating Accrington, who had finished ten points above them, in the play-off semi-final and then triumphing over Plymouth at Wembley, where a crowd of almost 58,000 were present.

That meant further meetings, in League One this time, with MK Dons, the hated 'Franchise FC'. In December 2012, the clubs had been drawn together in the FA Cup second round at Milton Keynes, the home side winning 2-1 with a last-minute goal in front of their season's best crowd of almost 16,500. Two years later, AFC exacted revenge of sorts by winning 3-2 there in the rather less prestigious Johnstone's Paint Trophy.

Off the field, the club's next aim was to return to the borough of Merton (Kingsmeadow being in Kingston) with a 20,000-seater stadium (initially 11,000 capacity) on the site of the greyhound stadium on Plough Lane.

* * * * *

Of all the south London clubs this was the least eventful period for **Millwall** with the exception of one remarkable FA Cup season that ended in the club's only peace-time final. Champions of League One (the third tier) in 2001, with Mark McGhee as manager and 27 goals from Neil Harris, they reached the play-offs the very next season before losing the semi-final at home to Birmingham in the last minute amid sadly familiar crowd trouble.

The 2004 Cup run, begun with Dennis Wise as player-manager after replacing McGhee in December, featured a happy succession of matches against modest opposition – Walsall, Telford, Burnley and Tranmere – to earn a semi-final against Sunderland, a couple of places above them in the table and managed by one of Wise's predecessors, Mick McCarthy.

Having already beaten his team twice in the league, Millwall completed the hat-trick when Tim Cahill scored the only goal following a defensive error in the first half. Manchester United, who had beaten Arsenal the previous day, predictably proved more demanding opposition for a depleted side in the Cardiff final.

> **Manchester United**: Howard (Carroll); G Neville, Brown, Silvestre, O'Shea; Ronaldo (Solskjaer), Fletcher (Butt), Keane, Giggs; Scholes; Van Nistelrooy.
>
> **Millwall**: Marshall; Elliott, Lawrence, Ward, Ryan (Cogan); Ifill, Wise (Weston), Livermore, Sweeney; Cahill; Harris (McCammon).

The names alone in the respective teams suggested a one-sided contest, which is what materialised. It nevertheless took United until almost half-time to go ahead, when Cristiano Ronaldo got in front of Wise to score. Ruud van Nistelrooy added a penalty and scored the third and final goal, after which each side made an unusually sentimental substitution: Roy Carroll for Howard as United's goalkeeper and Millwall's 17-year-old Curtis Weston as the youngest ever cup finalist in one of only six games he ever played for the club.

Reaching the final did bring European football to the new Den, Hungary's champions Ferencvaros beating Wise's side (1-1, 3-1) in the final qualifying round of the UEFA Cup.

After a third successive mid-table season Millwall were relegated in 2006, only returning four years later with American John Berylson as chairman and main investor, and the impressive former Watford midfielder Kenny Jackett as manager.

In his first full year, they lost the Wembley play-off final to Scunthorpe after holding a half-time lead, but 12 months later were back again to beat Charlton's conquerors Swindon in front of more than 73,000 courtesy of Paul Robinson's goal.

Following one comfortable season in the Championship, four difficult ones were lightened only by reaching the 2013 FA Cup semi-final against eventual winners Wigan and culminated in relegation again in 2015.

Neil Harris, who had become the club's record goalscorer after surviving testicular cancer, was manager by then and took them to the 2016 play-offs and defeat at Wembley by Barnsley.

As with most of the club's history, the top echelon was still looking a long way away.

* * * * *

The start of the new millennium was a bad time for **QPR**, dropping to the third tier for the first time since 1967 amid serious financial problems and suffering one of their most humiliating FA Cup defeats.

Having been mid-table in 1999/2000, sitting bottom of the pile the following Christmas was an unexpected as well as unwelcome development. Gerry Francis resigned in February and the livewire Ian Holloway failed to prevent relegation despite (or because of) 43 players being used.

A low point of the club's modern history was then reached in November 2002 with a home defeat on penalties by Vauxhall Motors, the Ellesmere Port club from the Unibond League, watched by barely 5,000 people.

Holloway kept the faith and his job, leading Rangers to promotion in 2004 by winning on the final day at Sheffield Wednesday, a year after losing the play-off final in extra time to Cardiff (who had the advantage of playing in their home city).

The combustible combination of Holloway and new chairman Gianni Paladini, a former agent, caught fire early in 2006, when the manager was placed on gardening leave because of repeated speculation linking him with the vacant Leicester City job. He did not take it, but after winning none of their final 11 games the team only just avoided relegation. That summer, two men were found not guilty at Blackfriars Crown Court after Paladini claimed he had been intimidated, with a gun allegedly held to his head at the stadium, as part of a power struggle within the club.

As the team settled back into mid-table in the Championship, the equally colourful pair Flavio Briatore and Bernie Ecclestone took control. The Italian influence was increased when Luigi di Canio became one of nine managers in the four-year period from 2006–10.

The last of them, Neil Warnock, was one of the few to bring either stability or success. Having bailed out of Crystal Palace, he made use of additional financial investment provided by the steel magnate Lakshmi Mittal, described as Britain's richest man, to win the Championship in 2011 after mixing flair players like the Football League Player of the Year Adel Taarabt with the harder-working Shaun Derry and Clint Hill.

At the higher level, however, the mix was not right and even though new owner Tony Fernandes, used to the world of Formula

1 but not football, authorised an awful lot of expenditure, two poor Premier League seasons resulted. The first began with a 4-0 home defeat by Bolton and ended one place above relegation, Mark Hughes having replaced Warnock. The second, after 11 new players were signed, started in even worse fashion – 0-5 at home to Swansea – continued for 15 more games without a win and ended bottom of the table, with a despondent Harry Redknapp now in charge.

An era in which wages accounted for 91 per cent of the club's income was summed up when the highly paid full-back Jose Bosingwa, signed from Chelsea, refused to be a substitute for the derby against Fulham.

'You don't have to be a mind reader to see that we haven't had good value for money. It's pretty obvious,' said Redknapp of all the new blood. He managed to take Rangers straight back via the play-offs, thanks to leading scorer Charlie Austin recovering from injury just in time and Bobby Zamora driving in a last-minute goal at Wembley after Gary O'Neil had been sent off and Derby County were on top.

Once again, the glory was short-lived and, in 2014/15, they went down again, Redknapp making way for Chris Ramsey, who was sacked nine months later before returning as technical director.

Reckoned to have had more grounds than any other league club, Rangers continued to seek one larger than Loftus Road, where firmer foundations could be laid down than ever before.

* * * * *

In October 2002, **Brentford** announced their intention to move from Griffin Park to Lionel Road, only half a mile away. Twelve years later, plans for a new 20,000-capacity ground there were finally approved. Like the mills of God, the mills of stadium planners grind slowly. Ron Noades, the man behind the original proposal, lived just long enough to see the new site given outline planning permission in December 2013, but died the same month.

A regular proposer of mergers and ground-shares in 40 years of London turf wars, he had been prepared to take the Bees temporarily to non-league Woking as early as the 2002/03 season if a sale went through. The Football League rejected that plan and it was at Griffin Park, home since 1904, that the club continued with nine managers in as many years (of whom Steve Coppell and Martin Allen were the most successful), starting with Noades himself.

Three years later he gave up as chairman, and in 2006 sold his majority shareholding to the Bees United trust, which in 2012 handed over control to Matthew Benham, a long-time fan and betting odds specialist, who also became majority shareholder of FC Midtjylland, later Danish champions.

Slipping briefly to the bottom tier in 2007 at the start of Terry Butcher's ill-starred reign, Brentford quickly recovered and thrived under their former striker Andy Scott, who had been forced to retire while playing for Orient because of a heart defect. He had them promoted as champions in his first full season back, 2008/09, and then in the top half during a high-powered League One campaign featuring Norwich, Leeds, Millwall (the promoted trio), Charlton and Southampton.

Scott was sacked the following February after a 4-1 defeat by lowly Dagenham & Redbridge, but the next two permanent appointments were excellent ones. Uwe Rosler, the former Manchester City striker born in the old East Germany, became the club's first foreign manager, leading them to the brink of the Championship in a second season with a traumatic ending.

Needing to win at home to second-placed Doncaster in the final game, the Bees were awarded a penalty in the last minute with the score 0-0. Marcello Trotta, grabbing the ball from skipper Kevin O'Connor, hit the crossbar and with half the team motionless, Doncaster raced to the other end and scored.

Recovering sufficiently to beat Swindon in the play-off semi-final on penalties, Rosler's team lost the final at Wembley 2-1 to unfancied Yeovil.

In December the following season, he left them for Wigan Athletic but Mark Warburton, promoted from sporting director, continued the side's good run and after remaining unbeaten until the end of February had them promoted as runners-up to Wolves, eight points ahead of third-placed Orient.

The second season in 60 years back in the higher division was another outstanding one, in which Andre Gray from Luton proved a useful replacement for the departed Clayton Donaldson.

In fourth place towards the end of January, they suffered three defeats in four games, including the derby at The Valley, after which supporters were stunned by news that Warburton and his staff would leave at the end of the season.

The club's official statement was more informative about the reasons than is normally the case, explaining: 'There will be a new recruitment structure using a mixture of traditional scouting and other tools, including mathematical modelling. As part of the new recruitment structure, the Head Coach will have a strong input into the players brought in to the Club but not an absolute veto.'

Warburton was allowed to say in his next programme notes that the change 'does not sit comfortably alongside my own thoughts and ideas', but he was able to inspire the team to get back on track with good enough results (including a 4-1 success at Fulham) to make the play-offs again. Middlesbrough, helped by a last-minute goal at Griffin Park, proved too strong.

As Warburton took the high road to Glasgow and led Rangers back into the Scottish Premier League, Benham was forced to admit that 'mathematical modelling' let him down in appointing little-known Dutch coach Marinus Dijkhuizen, who departed after only eight league games with the team 19th.

Under Lee Carsley and then Dean Smith, both better grounded in English football, Brentford rallied to finish another season in the top half of the table.

Being forced to sell several players, including Gray to champions Burnley for a fee that could rise above £9m, emphasised that Brentford were still not at the same level as the Championship's big hitters, many of them boosted by huge parachute payments after dropping out of the Premier League.

But the sustained improvement and prospect of the new stadium contributed to a feelgood mood.

* * * * *

For all their problems down the years, **Leyton Orient** rarely suffered from unpopular owners. Controlling a small London club surrounded by bigger, richer ones was generally recognised as a thankless task. That all changed with Barry Hearn's unfortunate choice of successor when he finally bailed out in 2014 after 19 years.

Having followed the club for decades from the terraces and stands, Hearn was always realistic about how far he could take them without throwing away the fortune he had made transforming snooker and darts. His legacy was, he claimed, 'serious money in the bank' and a neat if odd-looking stadium holding no more than 9,271people with flats on all four corners.

Playing-wise, Hearn so nearly left on a high. When Peterborough were beaten at Brisbane Road to take the Os to a Wembley play-off final against Rotherham for Hearn's last match, there was every chance of following Brentford back into the top two divisions after an even longer wait (22 years). Two goals up at half-time, Russell Slade's team were brought back to earth with a double by their own former striker Alex Revell, and then lost the penalty shoot-out after leading 3-2.

Hearn must have assumed the club was on the up nevertheless. 'It's like looking at Barry Hearn 20 years ago but with more money,' he said of successor Franceso Becchetti. Nobody worried too much at the time about his line that the Italian was 'a hands-on type of operator', but successive managers would have cause to.

Slade, an excellent lower-division operator, left early the following season for Cardiff City claiming constructive dismissal and, by the end of it, Orient had had three more men in charge, two of them Italian. The last of them, Fabio Liverani, left after a team third the previous season finished bottom but one.

From promising beginnings in 2015/16 under Ian Hendon, with the Arsenal academy product Jay Simpson the country's leading scorer for some time, Orient dropped from the top of the table, then out of contention for the play-offs and finished with Kevin Nolan demoted from player-manager after 15 games in charge.

The mood was far worse than in the dismal days earlier in the millennium which saw three successive seasons from 2000–04 in the bottom seven of the lowest division. That followed the disappointment of the 2001 play-off final when Chris Tate scored the fastest goal on such an occasion, after only 27 seconds, against Blackpool, only to finish on the losing side.

East Ender Martin Ling, once a clever little midfielder with Orient and Swindon, led a revival that brought promotion in 2006 with another quick goal, scored in the crucial game at Oxford by Lee Steele after 12 seconds. Unable to make further progress, Ling was succeeded by Slade, who saved them from relegation, achieved two seventh places and then the unlucky third. There was also a famous FA Cup tie when Jonathan Tehoue equalised in the last minute at home to an Arsenal side who had just beaten Barcelona.

With a run of one defeat in 20 games at that stage of 2011, Hearn was apt to joke that for the first time in their history Orient could be bankrupted by win bonuses. For all his efforts over the Olympic Stadium, the far more serious worry five years later was that gates of 5,000 and the chances of flourishing under the new owner would fall even lower once West Ham settled in down the road.

* * * * *

A ground-share between Orient and **Barnet** was not the most obvious collaboration, but it was one suggested in 2001 as the club at the end of the Northern Line found themselves back in non-league football having had plans to move to the Copthall Stadium (later given to Saracens Rugby Club) overruled.

From the Division Three (fourth tier) play-offs in 2000, John Still's team suffered the agony of a 3-2 home defeat by Torquay on the final day 12 months later, which allowed the Devon club to survive at Barnet's expense.

With Underhill declared inadequate under new Football League stipulations, chairman Tony Kleanthous agreed to share Brisbane Road if they won promotion back, but the return did not materialise until 2005/06.

Under a bewildering variety of managers, Barnet this time stayed for eight seasons but never made the top ten, and in 2013 a fourth successive year in the bottom four led to relegation. It was the final season at Underhill after 106 years, ending dramatically when Graham Stack saved a Wycombe Wanderers penalty in added time to preserve a 1-0 victory for the capacity crowd of just over 6,000. (Wycombe, coincidentally, had been the visitors when the ground record of 11,026 was set for an FA Amateur Cup quarter-final tie in February 1952).

Kleanthous had continued to explore the possibilities for a new stadium. In 2007, work began on The Hive at Edgware in the borough of Harrow, initially conceived as a training venue but used from 2013/14 as Barnet's main ground, shared by the London Broncos rugby league team.

The new ground was christened with a friendly against Ipswich on 20 July 2013, with Edgar Davids, former Champions League and *Serie A* winner, as the slightly incongruous 40-year-old player-manager. A target for Conference opponents keen to have a notch on their gun, he was sent off three times in the first half of the season and eventually left the club in January.

Martin Allen, once christened 'Mad Dog' by West Ham team-mate Ian Bishop, then returned for a fourth spell in charge and oversaw a return to the Football League for the 2015/16 season, recovering from a slow start to finish 15th.

With their smart new stadium – chosen in 2015 to stage an England Under-20 international – the club seemed to be on a firmer footing at last, but their travails since their amateur days have shown how difficult it is to break into the London set.

* * * * *

The same applied to **Dagenham & Redbridge,** who followed Wimbledon and Barnet into the Football League in 2007, albeit by a different route. Dagenham FC, not founded until 1949, were very much the new boys in the club that finally emerged from the remnants of three distinguished former FA Amateur Cup winners all formed by 1900, who found their names obliterated in the final version (assuming, of course, that final it is).

With former leading amateur clubs from east London and Essex finding it hard in the semi-professional world of the 1970s, Leytonstone began the tortuous process by linking up with Ilford in 1979.

When their quaint little ground, overlooked by Leytonstone High Road railway station, was sold for development almost a decade later, they shared with old rivals Walthamstow Avenue at Green Pond Road and amalgamated with them in 1988 as Redbridge Forest (a name concocted from the boroughs of Redbridge and Waltham Forest).

Green Pond Road having also been sold, the new club then moved further east to share Victoria Road, the unpretentious home of Dagenham, and after a proposed new stadium nearer home fell through, merged with them too as Dagenham & Redbridge in 1992.

The one link through all of this was Dave Andrews, once a wing-half and England amateur international with Avenue and the Stones. He became chairman of the latter, then of Leytonstone-Ilford and Redbridge Forest, and finally Dagenham & Redbridge themselves.

The original Dagenham lost two successive Amateur Cup finals, in 1970 and the following season, but won the FA Trophy in 1980. The new club's first competitive match was far from home, won 2-0 away to Merthyr Tydfil on 22 August 1992 in the Vauxhall Conference, in which they finished third (and would have been runners-up but for being docked one point for fielding an ineligible substitute).

The highlight outside the league programme was an epic FA Cup first-round derby at home to Leyton Orient, lost 5-4 in front of a crowd of 5,300. Relegated to the Isthmian League in 1996 amid financial problems caused by a trustee stealing more than £500,000, they returned in 2000, holding Premier League Charlton to a 1-1 draw at The Valley in the FA Cup and only losing the replay in extra time.

In 2002, they reached the third round again, setting a new attendance record when 5,949 watched the defeat by Ipswich. There was much controversy that summer when Boston United, having pipped Dagenham to the Conference title and automatic promotion, were found guilty of financial irregularities, but the points deducted applied only to the following season.

In 2003, the Daggers made unwanted history as the first and only club beaten on a 'golden goal' in a major play-off final when Doncaster Rovers scored it in the 110th minute to earn the second promotion place. They therefore had to wait until 2007 to go up, appropriately replacing Boston, with Paul Benson (28 goals) as leading scorer.

The inaugural Football League game on 11 August was lost 1-0 at Stockport, and the first home game was a 2-2 draw against Wycombe. Significantly, the attendance was only 2,280, which for one later home game dipped to 1,328. That illustrated what the club were up against, but non-league stalwart John Still was back as manager and in the third season of league football led them to promotion via the play-offs. His team had taken only one point from two games against Morecambe, but in the semi-final first leg humbled them by a record 6-0 and went on to defeat Rotherham 3-2 in the Wembley final, Benson taking his total to 22 for the season.

A strong League One was harder work, although being relegated with as many as 47 points was tough to take. Orient, Brentford and Charlton were all beaten at Victoria Road, but losing eight of the last ten games was too much of a handicap.

It was the only season in which home gates averaged more than 2,100 and by the time of relegation from League Two in 2016, confirmed by defeat at Orient, the figure was 1,979.

* * * * *

And so it goes. There is the world of Arsenal, Chelsea, Tottenham and West Ham, and the lives of others – like Leyton Orient, Barnet, AFC Wimbledon and Dagenham & Redbridge. Half a dozen more from south-east and west London flit between the divisions, less sure of their place in the natural order of things.

Predictions tempt fate. What we know for sure is that following the example of Arsenal, Barnet, Millwall and West Ham, there will be new stadiums for Tottenham, Brentford and perhaps QPR and Wimbledon, all hoping to improve their status as a result of the extra finance.

As the influx of rich foreigners to the capital is reflected in football, new owners will doubtless emerge, convinced they have the nous and the money to win more followers and take new ground.

More than 100 years after Henry Norris decided Woolwich Arsenal had no future in south-east London, the turf wars show no sign of abating.

Appendix
Top London club season-by-season

(Division Two from 1893/94; Division One from 1904/05; Premier League from 1992/93)

*Denotes champions

1893/94 Woolwich Arsenal
1894/95 Woolwich Arsenal
1895/96 Woolwich Arsenal
1896/97 Woolwich Arsenal
1897/98 Woolwich Arsenal
1898/99 Woolwich Arsenal
1899/00 Woolwich Arsenal
1900/01 Woolwich Arsenal
1901/02 Woolwich Arsenal
1902/03 Woolwich Arsenal
1903/04 Woolwich Arsenal
1904/05 Woolwich Arsenal
1905/06 Woolwich Arsenal
1906/07 Woolwich Arsenal
1907/08 Chelsea
1908/09 Woolwich Arsenal
1909/10 Tottenham
1910/11 Woolwich Arsenal
1911/12 Woolwich Arsenal
1912/13 Tottenham

1913/14 Chelsea
1914/15 Chelsea

1919/20 Chelsea
1920/21 Tottenham
1921/22 Tottenham
1922/23 Arsenal
1923/24 West Ham
1924/25 Tottenham
1925/26 Arsenal
1926/27 West Ham
1927/28 Arsenal
1928/29 Arsenal
1929/30 West Ham
1930/31 Arsenal*
1931/32 Arsenal
1932/33 Arsenal*
1933/34 Arsenal*
1934/35 Arsenal*
1935/36 Brentford
1936/37 Charlton
1937/38 Arsenal*
1938/39 Charlton

1946/47 Arsenal
1947/48 Arsenal*
1948/49 Arsenal
1949/50 Arsenal
1950/51 Tottenham*
1951/52 Tottenham
1952/53 Arsenal*
1953/54 Chelsea
1954/55 Chelsea*
1955/56 Arsenal
1956/57 Tottenham
1957/58 Tottenham

1958/59 Arsenal
1959/60 Tottenham
1960/61 Tottenham*
1961/62 Tottenham
1962/63 Tottenham
1963/64 Tottenham
1964/65 Chelsea
1965/66 Chelsea
1966/67 Tottenham
1967/68 Chelsea
1968/69 Arsenal
1969/70 Chelsea
1970/71 Arsenal*
1971/72 Arsenal
1972/73 Arsenal
1973/74 QPR
1974/75 QPR
1975/76 QPR
1976/77 Arsenal
1977/78 Arsenal
1978/79 Arsenal
1979/80 Arsenal
1980/81 Arsenal
1981/82 Tottenham
1982/83 Tottenham
1983/84 QPR
1984/85 Tottenham
1985/86 West Ham
1986/87 Tottenham
1987/88 QPR
1988/89 Arsenal*
1989/90 Tottenham
1990/91 Arsenal*
1991/92 Arsenal
1992/93 QPR
1993/94 Arsenal

APPENDIX

1994/95 Tottenham
1995/96 Arsenal
1996/97 Arsenal
1997/98 Arsenal*
1998/99 Arsenal
1999/00 Arsenal
2000/01 Arsenal
2001/02 Arsenal*
2002/03 Arsenal
2003/04 Arsenal*
2004/05 Chelsea*
2005/06 Chelsea*
2006/07 Chelsea
2007/08 Chelsea
2008/09 Chelsea
2009/10 Chelsea*
2010/11 Chelsea
2011/12 Arsenal
2012/13 Chelsea
2013/14 Chelsea
2014/15 Chelsea*
2015/16 Arsenal

Total: Arsenal 58, Tottenham 21, Chelsea 20, QPR 6, West Ham 4, Charlton 2, Brentford 1.

League champions: Arsenal 13, Chelsea 5, Tottenham 2.

Select Bibliography

Barclay, Patrick *The Life And Times Of Herbert Chapman* (Weidenfeld & Nicolson, 2014)

Blake, Mike *Sam Bartram* (Tempus Publishing, 2006)

Blanchflower, Danny *The Double And Before* (Four Square, 1962)

Bose, Mihir *Game Changer* (Marshall Cavendish Business, 2012)

Butler, Bryon *The Official History of the Football Association* (Queen Anne Press, 1991)

Chapman, Herbert *Herbert Chapman on Football* (Garrick, 1934)

Cohen, George *My Autobiography* (Greenwater, 2003)

Curbishley, Alan *Valley of Dreams* (Harper Sport, 2006)

Dickinson, Matt *Bobby Moore, The Man In Full* (Random House, 2014)

Dutton, Paul and Glanvill, Rick *Chelsea, The Complete Record* (de Courbetin Books, 2015)

Giller, Norman *Denis Compton* (Andre Deutsch, 1987)

Glanvill, Rick *Chelsea FC The Official Biography* (Headline, 2005)

Glanville, Brian *Arsenal Stadium History* (Hamlyn, 2006)

Glanville, Brian *Football Memories* (Virgin, 1999)

Glanville, Brian *Soccer Nemesis* (Secker & Warburg, 1955)

Glinert, Ed *The London Football Companion* (Bloomsbury, 2009)

Goodwin, Bob *Tottenham Hotspur, A Complete Record* (Breedon Books, 1993)

Greaves, Jimmy *Greavsie, The Autobiography* (Time Warner, 2003)

Greenwood, Ron *Yours Sincerely* (Collins Willow, 1984)

Haynes, Graham and Twydell, Dave *Brentford FC – The Complete History 1889-2008* (Breedon Books, 2008)

Hill, Jimmy *The Jimmy Hill Story* (Coronet, 1998)

Holland, Julian *Spurs – 'The Double'* (Sportsmans Book Club, 1962)

Hugman, Barry *Football Players Records 1946–1984* (Rothmans, 1984)

Hurst, Geoff *1966 And All That* (Headline, 2005)

Inglis, Simon *The Football Grounds of Great Britain* (Collins Willow, 1987)

Jordan, Simon *Be Careful What You Wish For* (Yellow Jersey Press, 2012)

Kaufman, Neil and Ravenhill, Alan *Leyton Orient, A Complete Record 1881–1990* (Breedon Books, 1990)

King, Ian *Crystal Palace: A Complete Record 1905–2011.* (Derby Books, 2011)

Lidbury, Michael *Wimbledon FC, The First 100 Years* (Wimbledon FC, 1989)

Lovejoy, Joe *Glory, Goals & Greed* (Mainstream, 2011)

Lyall, John *Just Like My Dreams* (Viking, 1989)

McLintock, Frank *True Grit* (Headline, 2005)

Macey, Gordon *Queens Park Rangers, A Complete Record* (Breedon Books, 2009)

Mears, Brian *Chelsea, The Real Story* (Pelham Books, 1982)

Mullery, Alan *The Autobiography* (Headline, 2006)

Murray, James *Millwall, Lions of the South* (Indispensible Publications, 1988)

Northcutt, John and Shoesmith, Roy *West Ham United, A Complete Record* (Breedon Books, 1993)

Ollier, Fred Arsenal, *A Complete Record* (Breedon Books, 1992)

Powell, Jeff *Bobby Moore* (Robson Books, 1993)

Prole, David *Football In London* (Sportsmans Book Club, 1965)

Radford, Brian *Through Open Doors* (Harrap, 1984)

Redden, Richard *The Story of Charlton Athletic* (Breedon Books, 1990)

Redknapp, Harry *Always Managing* (Ebury Press, 2013)

Robinson, Michael (ed.) *English Football League and F.A. Premier League Tables 1888-2011* (Soccer Books, 2011)

Rollin, Jack *Soccer at War 1939-45* (Headline, 2005)

Roper, Alan *The Real Arsenal Story* (Wherry, 2004)

Rous, Stanley *Football Worlds* (Faber, 1978)

Scholar, Irving *Behind Closed Doors* (Andre Deutsch, 1992)

Seed, Jimmy *The Jimmy Seed Story* (Phoenix Sports Books, 1957)

Simpson, Matt *Leyton Orient Greats* (Breedon Books, 2008)

Stammers, Steve *Arsenal, The Official Biography* (Hamlyn, 2008)

Studd, Stephen *Herbert Chapman, Football Emperor* (Peter Owen, 1981)

Stock, Alec *A Little Thing Called Pride* (Pelham Books, 1982)

Turner, Dennis and White, Alex *Fulham, The Complete Record* (Breedon Books, 2007)

Tyler, Martin *The Story of Football* (Marshall Cavendish, 1976)

Tyler, Martin *Cup Final Extra!* (Hamlyn, 1981)

Venables, Terry *The Autobiography* (Penguin, 1995)

Walvin, James *The People's Game* (Allen Lane, 1975)

Wilson, Bob *Behind The Network* (Hodder & Stoughton, 2003)

Wilson, Jonathan *Inverting The Pyramid* (Orion, 2008)

Woolnough, Brian *Ken Bates, My Chelsea Dream* (Virgin, 1999)

Rothmans Football Yearbook, 1970–2003

Sky Sports Football Yearbook, 2003–2016

The list of players killed in World War I (Chapter 2) is drawn largely from the PFA booklet 'Footballing Heroes 1914–18'.

Select Webography
www.11v11.com
www.bbc.co.uk/sport/football
www.blog.woolwicharsenal.co.uk
www.european-football-statistics.co.uk
www.fchd.info
www.footballandthefirstworldwar.org
www.footballderbies.com
www.footballgroundguide.com
www.footipedia.com
www.historicalkits.co.uk
www.soccerbase.co.uk
www.soccer-history.co.uk
www.spartacus-educational.com
www.theyflysohigh.co.uk
www.worldfootball.net
www.youtube.com
London league club official websites and national newspaper
    websites.

Main Index to Clubs